Ghostly Communion

Reencounters with Colonialism: *New Perspectives on the Americas*

DARTMOUTH COLLEGE SERIES EDITORS
Agnes Lugo-Ortiz
Donald E. Pease
Ivy Schweitzer
Silvia Spitta

Frances R. Aparicio and Susana Chávez-Silverman, eds., *Tropicalizations: Transcultural Representations of Latinidad*

Michelle Burnham, *Captivity and Sentiment: Cultural Exchange in American Literature, 1682–1861*

Colin G. Calloway, ed., *After King Philip's War: Presence and Persistence in Indian New England*

Carla Gardina Pestana and Sharon V. Salinger, *Inequality in Early America*

Renée L. Bergland, *The National Uncanny: Indian Ghosts and American Subjects*

Stephen J. Hornsby, *British Atlantic, American Frontier: Spaces of Power in Early Modern North America*

Susana Rotker, *The American Chronicles of José Martí: Journalism and Modernity in Spanish America*

Carlton Smith, *Coyote Kills John Wayne: Postmodernism and Contemporary Fictions of the Transcultural Frontier*

C. L. R. James, *Mariners, Renegades and Castaways: The Story of Herman Melville and the World We Live In,* with an introduction by Donald E. Pease

Ruth Mayer, *Artificial Africas: Colonial Images in the Times of Globalization*

Irene Ramalho Santos, *Atlantic Poets: Fernando Pessoa's Turn in Anglo-American Modernism*

John R. Eperjesi, *The Imperialist Imaginary: Visions of Asia and the Pacific in American Culture*

John J. Kucich, *Ghostly Communion: Cross-Cultural Spiritualism in Nineteenth-Century American Literature*

Ghostly Communion

Cross-Cultural Spiritualism in Nineteenth-Century American Literature

John J. Kucich

Dartmouth College Press

Hanover, New Hampshire

Published by University Press of New England • Hanover and London

Dartmouth College Press
Published by University Press of New England,
One Court Street, Lebanon, NH 03766
www.upne.com
© 2004 by Dartmouth College Press
Printed in the United States of America
5   4   3   2   1

Library of Congress Cataloging-in-Publication Data
Kucich, John.
Ghostly communion: cross-cultural spiritualism in nineteenth-century American literature / John J. Kucich
     p.   cm.—(Reencounters with colonialism—new perspectives on the Americas)
Includes bibliographical references and index.
ISBN 1-58465-432-5 (cloth : alk. paper)—ISBN 1-58465-433-3 (pbk. : alk. paper)
1. American literature—19th century—History and criticism. 2. Spiritualism in literature. 3. Spiritualism—United States—History—19th century. 4. Literature and spiritualism—United States. 5. Intercultural communication in literature. 6. Occultism in literature. 7. Culture in literature. 8. Ghosts in literature. I. Title. II. Series.
PS217.S65 K83   2004
810.9'384—dc22   2004010718

For Christopher and Alexander,

and for Monica

Contents

Acknowledgments

For her wisdom and encouragement at the inception of this book and at every step of its writing, I wish to thank Elizabeth Ammons. Carol Flynn was also an invaluable resource and enthusiastic supporter from the beginning. Linda Bamber, John Brooke, Patricia Rodriguez, and Kathleen Brogan offered generous and insightful comments on parts or all of the manuscript. Lee Edelman, David Cavitch, Kevin Dunn, and many others made Tufts University a warm and exciting place in which to pursue scholarly work.

I wish to also thank the many people who've mixed the roles of friend and colleague along the way. Madhavi Menon and Christian Sheridan have been steadfast supporters and cheerful critics, as have, at different moments, Ted Munter, Kirk Wulf, Mark Santa Maria, Simon Holzapfel, Min Song, Robin DeRosa, Carmen Lowe, Melissa Baker, Sean Desilets, Ed Caldwell, Valerie Rohy, George Layng, Sophia Cantave, and Amelia Katanski.

Throughout this project, the staff of the Tisch library at Tufts were invariably patient and resourceful, and I am grateful to the American Antiquarian Society for guiding me through their collection. At University Press of New England, Phyllis Deutsch has been an immensely encouraging and efficient editor. I have benefited enormously from Jeffrey Weinstock's thoughtful criticism of the manuscript and from Leslie Cohen's meticulous reading of my prose.

My family and friends have followed this work with great patience and good humor; I owe them a deep debt. I owe the deepest to my wife, Monica, who has kept it in perspective and made it all possible.

Introduction

The Pueblo Revolt, the Salem Witchcraft Trials,
and Cross-Cultural Spiritualism

Spiritualism in America is generally said to begin in 1848 with the Rochester Rappings, when two teenaged farm girls claimed to have opened a channel of communication with the spirit world, and is usually regarded as a marginal religious movement created by and for a credulous fringe of European Americans.[1] I would like to begin by pushing the temporal boundary of spiritualism beyond the beginnings of European settlement in what would become the United States, and the cultural boundary beyond the narrow spectrum of European American religion. Spiritualism in America, I argue, long precedes the first European contact, and its provenance far exceeds the religious movement that briefly flourished in the Fox sisters' wake. Regular communication with a spirit world features prominently in Native American cultures, and Europeans and Africans brought spiritualism with them to America's shores. As important as it was to each cultural group, spiritualism also helped shape the terms by which these cultures interacted from the earliest days of contact to the present.

Spiritualism announced its presence in colonial times in spectacular fashion with two contemporaneous events almost a continent apart. One, the Salem Witchcraft Trials of 1692, occasionally finds its way into spiritualist histories as a prelude to nineteenth-century spiritual manifestations, but is rarely discussed as a political event and almost never as a cross-cultural one. The other, the Pueblo Revolt of 1680, is often treated in terms of cross-cultural politics, but rarely in terms of spiritualism. Though they occurred within twelve years of each other, the two have not been discussed together as examples of the range of spiritualist discourse present at least since the beginnings of European colonization in America. These events demonstrate that spiritualism and politics were from the beginning inextricably intertwined;

they are exemplars for how spiritualism crosses the cultural boundaries that define our nation.

I should say from the start that my definition of spiritualism is a broad one. Most literary and historical accounts examine "Spiritualism," treating it as a distinct religious movement that began in upstate New York and then spread throughout Western Europe and beyond, with a unified theology and an unbroken historical trajectory—hence the capital *S*. Yet "Spiritualism," with its core belief in communication with the dead through the agency of a medium, is but one example of spiritualism, a religious phenomenon predicated on regular contact with a spirit world; this phenomenon appears in cultures across the globe and throughout history. A broader perspective is more characteristic of anthropology, and it places the spiritualist movement that began in Rochester in 1848 in decidedly mixed company. Many such religions feature, like the Rochester Rappings, contact with the recently deceased, though many also involve communication with spirits that may or may not be human. All share a belief in an invisible world intimately engaged with the physical one. Studies confined to a more limited definition of spiritualism tend to read its most famous American manifestation within the narrower heritage of European occultism, Swedenborgianism, and evangelical Christianity.[2] With a broader definition, non-European spiritualist practices like conjure and the Ghost Dance provide an equally important context for the mediums and seánces that spread through European-American society in the mid-nineteenth century.

Such a shift in definition is decidedly political, but I believe the decision by most historians to study spiritualism without reference to non-European cultures and the decision of most anthropologists to study spiritualism without reference to European cultures also have a certain politics. The Rochester Rappings were, of course, shaped by a unique, and uniquely American, context, but they were not essentially different from other spiritualist practices around the world. A reading of spiritualism that fails to acknowledge this takes part in an ethic of American exceptionalism that at the least limits its resonance. More seriously, such a reading fails to notice that there is not one spiritualism in America, but many; that alongside the Rochester Rappings are spiritualist traditions, events, movements, and texts that spring from every corner of American cultural life.

The genealogy of American spiritualism includes, I will argue, not merely European occultism, but the myriad African and Native American religions that mingled on this continent; its manifestations include not just the Rochester Rappings, but a broad array of creole spiritualisms, from hoodoo to Santería, from the Virgin of Guadalupe to the Ghost Dance, and from faith healing to angelmania. Taking such a broad context into account is crucial in order to render American spiritualism in all its nuances and to shift spiritualism from a backwater of nineteenth-century popular culture to a site of rich, turbulent, and dynamic juncture among America's many cultures. This study seeks above all to explore how spiritualism mediated the power relations within and between cultures in the United States. Spiritualism offers a particularly useful example of how cross-cultural negotiations unfold, of how various peoples have, at various moments in our history, navigated the always tricky and often deadly currents between cultures.

Beginning with the Pueblo Revolt and the Salem Witchcraft Trials allows me to sketch some of the features of spiritualism as it emerged in the cultural interstices of colonial America and as it would unfold in later centuries. The questions I pose and begin to answer in my examination of colonial New Mexico and Massachusetts will then frame my analysis of spiritualism in nineteenth-century America. How did spiritualism mediate material conflicts within and between cultures? How did members of different cultures borrow and manipulate the spiritualist traditions of other cultures? What effect did such cross-cultural contact have on distinct spiritualist traditions? And, finally, how were such struggles imbricated within a wider field of literary and cultural production? The Pueblo Revolt and the Salem Witchcraft Trials stand in this study as preludes to a spiritualist synthesis that would emerge over centuries of intercultural politics. As preludes, too, they introduce us to the harmonies, themes, chords, and discords that resonate throughout the literature and history of spiritualism in American.

Discord of the Devil: Nuevo Mexico

By 1680, the Pueblo Indians and Spanish colonists had fought over control of the upper Rio Grande for generations. From their first contact, political conflict was mediated through religion. Estaban, an African who had survived Navarez's disastrous effort to conquer Florida, guided the first Spanish expedition to the "new" Mexico in 1539. He dressed himself as a holy man and demanded tribute of jewels, food, and women from each pueblo he entered, before being killed by the Zuni of Hawikuh (Knaut 22). Estaban's fortunes rested on a mixing of signs: he posed as neither Spanish priest nor Indian medicine man, but drew instead on the many spiritualities he had encountered in his years wandering among the native peoples of what would become the United States. His death signaled the dangers of trying to mediate two poles of identity, two categories of spirituality. Neither Christian nor Zuni, the African man wearing the trappings of Indian priesthood but bearing the threat of Spanish conquest could only figure as a devil from either perspective. Estaban prefigured the mestizo spirituality that would eventually take root in New Mexico, and marked its birth with his blood.

Pueblo culture survived the first century of Spanish conquest. The Franciscan friars never achieved a complete erasure of native religious and cultural practice. Yet by the middle of the century, the process begun by Estaban had taken root, and mestizos often formed a bridge between underground native ceremonies and official Catholic ones, participating in both and subtly transforming each (Knaut 83). Marginal from the perspective of Spanish and Pueblo culture, mestizos proved central in the emerging New Mexican spiritual synthesis. They would also play a central role in its unraveling. A mestizo culture might have emerged in New Mexico without widespread bloodshed. Yet by 1680 such a cultural and spiritual synthesis proved impossible: a Spanish crackdown on Pueblo medicine men a few years earlier showed that Spanish tolerance of Pueblo spirituality was waning, and served to unify the pueblos in resistance to Spanish cultural domination. Pueblo spiritualism sparked the rebellion. Having contacted Pueblo guardian spirits, a medicine man named Popé convinced most of the Rio Grande pueblos to join together in revolt, killing or driving out the missionaries living in the pueblos and, after several weeks of bloody fighting, forcing the entire Spanish colony out of New Mexico. A year and a half later, a Spanish force returned to the pueblos to assert Spanish might and, over the next dozen years, reconquer the area. One thing was especially clear to both the Spaniards and Pueblo Indians: spiritualism had proven one of the decisive battlegrounds for control of New Mexico.[3]

One of the first reports of incipient revolt to filter into Santa Fe in August 1680 illustrates how this material conflict was mediated through spiritual categories. A Spanish soldier, Pedro Hidalgo, described coming upon a party of Teguas Indians in war paint and carrying weapons. A friar, Juan Pío, approached a Spanish-speaking Indian named Nicolás to find out what was happening; they talked, and then Hidalgo watched as Nicolás accompanied the friar into a gully. Nicolás emerged alone a few minutes later "painted with clay and spattered with blood." The first blow of the Pueblo Revolt had been struck, and Hidalgo mediated his account of it through Catholic spirituality. Hidalgo's report of the friar's last words, "I will help you and die a thousand deaths for you," clearly mark Pío as a martyr. The words of the interpreter remain unrecorded, his body paint and the friar's blood enough, apparently, to mark him as a devil as surely as Pió is marked as Christ (Hackett 1:6–7). Hidalgo was less interested in what the paint worn by the Indians signified to themselves. It meant war, to be sure, but it also signaled the reabsorption of the Indians into a native spiritualism utterly at odds with Catholicism. Body paint was (and is) a means of communicating with and marshaling the power of a pueblo's guardian spirits (Parsons 379). Nicolás was not identified as a mestizo, but his name and his facility with Spanish may have made his allegiance suspect. His donning of body paint thus signaled before his fellow Teguas what the killing in the gully affirmed: by summoning the Teguas spirits, he affirmed his spiritual, cultural, and political identity as a Pueblo Indian. Popé's rebellion would take place on both military and spiritualist fronts, and, as the marked body of Nicolás indicates, the two proved inseparable. The phrase "discord of the devil," used by one of the friars to describe what Popé had unleashed, illustrates how, in the narrative battle of the Pueblo Revolt, a principal goal was to control the spiritualist terms of the conflict.

Yet even the ragged Spanish settlement at El Paso, where the refugees huddled for over a year gathering supplies and courage for the attempt at reconquest that would take place in 1681, was marked with Indian difference. The Señora de Guadalupe, whose name graced the modest presidio that the Spanish governor, Antonio de Otermín, built to protect the remnants of his colony, signifies both the Castillian shrine to the Virgin Mary and the mestizo icon of the Mexican church that shares its name. As the Pueblo Indians rebuilt their kivas and estufas from the remains of Catholic missions, Otermín's attempted reconquest, with all its Catholic rhetorical armaments, drew on the discourse of Pueblo spirituality as surely as his army drew on the manpower of Pueblo converts. Nothing illustrates this more clearly than the primary sources through which the Spanish piece together their narrative of the revolt, the native informants who appeared before the scribal arm of Otermín's small army.

Deciding what to call these members of various pueblos takes us to the core of their import. The various shades of meaning their names bear hint at the politically charged, subtly nuanced positions they claimed for themselves as they told their own stories. These Indians wove together bits of information about a popular movement involving dozens of pueblos, each of which was riven by conflicting claims of clan allegiance and varying levels of accommodation to Spanish culture, and each of which mirrored the linguistic and cultural divisions between the pueblos themselves. They then communicated across a cultural and linguistic chasm to a group of soldiers who had murdered or starved entire peoples, and who would clearly use these stories to shape their revenge. The position of the Indians whose stories appear

among the Spanish documents was delicate indeed. To call them "native informants," as I have done above, is to underscore their role in Spanish efforts
to fashion a Pueblo ethnography. It was not, of course, a name they used for
themselves. In fact, much of their testimony revolves around competing terms
(and competing inflections of Pueblo spiritualism) for the position they occupied between Spanish and Indian cultures: "mestizo" and "coyote." Moreover, their struggle over the terms of their identity prefigures the various
strategies that would be used to negotiate the cross-cultural terrain of spiritualism throughout American history.

Some members of the pueblos, no doubt aided by the Spanish scribe who
recorded their tale, carved out a mestizo position, fashioning a narrative of
the revolt that seamlessly marshals Catholic spiritual rhetoric to retell the
struggles of an Indian people in Old Testament terms. In this mestizo position, a colonized people accedes to the spiritualist rhetoric of a dominant culture in the interest of material survival. A Tegua named only as "Juan" gave
the first account of Popé, describing the medicine man to his Spanish inquisitors as one who "talks with the devil." Juan gave the first word, too, of
the cord made from sacred maguay fiber and knotted to signify the number of
days until the revolt. These two details indicate how much of Juan's testimony is shaped by Pueblo spirituality, an influence that distinguishes him
from more fully Christianized Indians. Yet Juan's testimony remains deeply
rooted in Christianity. According to Juan, Popé proclaimed "that the devil
was very strong and much better than God" (Hackett 2:235), and that the
Indians were to burn Catholic icons, to renounce their Christian names and
marriages, to forswear the Castillian language, and to plant only maize and
beans. For Popé, as for the Spanish, the crucible of revolt meant reorganizing
the most material elements of Pueblo society under spiritualist terms. Yet for
Juan, Popé can speak only with the devil, and native spirituality can be understood only in a "God-Satan" binary.

Other Indians forged a narrative position between these two extremes,
using spiritualism to create, in Richard White's term, a "middle ground," a
realm of "mutual invention" located at the juncture of multiple cultures (50).
Juan himself uses the term "coyote" to signify a Spanish-speaking Indian who
remains allied to Pueblo culture, and a declaration taken the next day demonstrates this different possibility. Pedro Naranjo, an eighty-year-old member of
the Queres nation and a baptized Christian, resists the totalizing rhetoric of
Catholic spiritualism. He, too, mentions that Popé "is said to have communication with the devil" while hiding in Taos, but Naranjo's devil won't remain
tied to the Spanish narrative. It fractures into "three figures of Indians who

never came out of the estufa," and who said "they were going underground to the lake of Copala." Popé then "saw these figures emit fire from all the extremities of their bodies, and that one of them was called Caudi, another Tilini, and the other Tleume" (2:246). These three are neither devils nor gods. They are figures poised between Pueblo and Spanish spiritualisms. For Naranjo, they figure a narrative of Indian spiritualism irreducible to Spanish rhetoric, but described nevertheless in terms accessible to his Spanish audience. Here, for the first time in documents of the Spanish reconquest, is an autoethnography, a record, to use Mary Louise Pratt's definition, "in which colonized subjects represent themselves in ways that engage with the colonizer's own terms" (7). Naranjo begins here to forge a narrative tradition located between the twin positions of mestizo and coyote. Unlike Juan, Naranjo opens a space for the articulation of a Pueblo culture not reduced to Spanish terms; instead, he seeks to lead a Spanish army bent on reconquest to a recognition of Pueblo difference. In Naranjo's account, Otermín can at least begin to understand that the Pueblo Revolt began because the Indians "had always desired to live as they had when they came out of the lake at Copala" (Hackett 2:247)—an expression of a physical culture inseparable from spirituality.

The wrestling of Juan and Naranjo over the terms of their identity and the nature of Popé's beliefs illustrate that spiritualism, especially in its cross-cultural manifestations, is a discourse of the borders. Victor Turner has theorized liminality in the context of puberty rites, a setting located between fixed social structures where the "amoral and nonlogical" rhythms of myth can flourish (577). The concept applies as well to the defamiliarizing effect of cross-cultural spiritualist discourse, in which the spaces on the edges of a familiar topography, such as the mountain caves of New Mexico, become suddenly privileged, where trickster figures like coyote and, indeed, the mestizo appear at the centers of power, wielding language full of parody and slippage. Such spiritualist crossings are full, too, of ciphers—objects like the maguay chord that communicate information to a select group, strengthen communal bonds among those in the know, and self-consciously exclude those who aren't. Yet such signs are anything but stable and fixed—like most communication in a liminal space, they are marked by excess signification; they figure wildly, unfixing ordered interpretive communities and destabilizing the political structures that surround them.

The liminal spirituality of people like Naranjo helped establish a position located between the spiritualist binary of Popé and Otermín. Juan reported that many Indians were ready to fight Otermín's forces to the death, but others were more ready to seek a middle ground. This latter group, according to

Juan, argued that the Spanish "must come and gain the kingdom because they were sons of the land and had grown up with the natives" (Hackett 2:238). They proved correct. While Otermín had neither the force nor the diplomatic skill to break the Pueblo coalition that Popé had fashioned, a Spanish army under a more moderate governor was able to reconquer the colony a decade later. After another revolt in 1696 failed to drive out the Spanish, both Spaniards and Indians settled into an uneasy harmony out of which emerged a hybrid spirituality unique in North America. The Pueblo Revolt was unique in its effectiveness. It was less singular in its marshaling of spiritualism. While few records of European conquest preserve so strong a record of Indian spirituality, contact between European and Indian peoples in North America would be marked by competing and hybrid spiritualities to the end of the Indian Wars at Wounded Knee and beyond.

Yet while the culture that emerged in New Mexico was remarkable for the durability of its spiritual synthesis, the Pueblo Revolt is merely one of the earliest episodes to bring into play elements of cross-cultural spiritualist negotiation that would recur throughout American history. Indeed, a dozen years later and almost a continent away, Massachusetts would be embroiled in a spiritualist upheaval following hard on the heels of an Indian revolt, King Philip's War, very nearly as successful as Popé's. Though markedly different in its spiritualist referents and less overtly shaped by all-out intercultural warfare, the Salem Witchcraft Trials nevertheless offer striking—indeed, at times uncanny—parallels to the discursive world of the Pueblo Revolt. These parallels point to the evolution, in the cultural borderlands of America, of a spiritualist hermeneutic whose features we can still trace.

The Devil's Book: Salem

Why are the Salem Witchcraft Trials so rarely thought of in terms of spiritualism?[4] Everything depends upon definitions, of course, and a few of the broader surveys of spiritualism in America begin with an account of witchcraft.[5] The trials, like the Pueblo Revolt and like nineteenth-century spiritualism, centered on the belief that an invisible, spiritual world could be contacted by the living and could manifest itself in the material world. Like nineteenth-century spiritualism, the witchcraft trials also are read only rarely as a cross-cultural phenomenon, despite the pivotal role played by an enslaved woman of West Indian origin, Tituba. It is upon Tituba I would like to focus.

Witchcraft in Salem Village began with girls in the household of the village minister. In the winter of 1692, Elizabeth Parris, the minister's nine-year-old daughter; Abigail Williams, the minister's eleven-year-old niece; and two neighbors a few years older began suffering from a mysterious ailment characterized by hallucinations, trancelike states, and pinching sensations. Samuel Parris soon exhausted nearby medical resources, and a neighbor, suspecting witchcraft, had Parris's slaves, John and Tituba, bake a witch cake using the afflicted girls' urine. According to English folklore, the cake, when fed to a dog, would reveal the name of whoever cast the spell. Though the mechanism remains unclear, the girls quickly accused three women of tormenting them in spectral form. Two, Sarah Good and Sarah Osborne, were middle-aged white women of low status, typical of the people who had been accused of witchcraft in New England. The third was Tituba.

Where exactly to place Tituba is one of the most enduring controversies surrounding events in Massachusetts in 1692, and the question highlights some of the difficulties faced by a critical methodology that foregrounds race and ethnicity. Elaine G. Breslaw's 1996 study attempts to set the record straight. Drawing on deeds from Barbados and Spanish etymology, she posits an Arawak origin for Tituba. The confidence of her claim is particularly striking when compared to an account offered by Peter Charles Hoffer in the same year: he presents an African etymology drawn from the Yoruba, "for Tituba is a Yoruba name" (2).

Breslaw and Hoffer are playing a scholarly identity politics when the dominant lesson of Tituba, it seems to me, is her ethnic ambiguity. Like the Indians who mingled Pueblo and Catholic elements into their testimony before Otermín's scribes, Tituba's intervention in the Salem Witchcraft Trials is not simply Yoruba or Arawak; it is at once both and more. As Breslaw argues, Tituba's background shows that she was probably familiar with both African and Native American folklore. Her testimony proves she was certainly familiar with English folklore as well. Why choose sides? "African" aptly represents the polyglot cultures that survived the Middle Passage to shape American culture from its beginnings; but "Indian," a European term that mixes the variety of Native American cultures into a rhetorical melting pot heated by the political and cultural fires of hegemony, is also not a bad term for a creole woman, either. Neither is the term "American," particularly if read with a multicultural inflection. If it has proven difficult to pin one distinct identity to Tituba, it is all the more important to keep several in mind when assessing her role in Salem. Like the "native informants" of the Pueblo Revolt, Tituba's liminal status is more signficant than the term we use to identify it. "American" highlights the intimate bonds Tituba shared with her accusers and her fellow confessors, reminding us that even Puritan New England was not entirely white and underscoring the distinctions between this manifestation of witch-hunting and its European cousins. "Indian" and "African" remind us of the cross-cultural context of the Salem witchcraft, the backdrop of colonization and slavery to the trials in Salem that made the divide between Massachusetts and England, like the divide between New Mexico and Spain, wider than a merely physical one.

The witch cake was baked on February 25, 1692. On February 29, warrants were issued for the arrest of Tituba, Sarah Osborne, and Sarah Good on charges of afflicting the four girls. The accused were examined the next day. Sarah Good at first denied the charge of witchcraft, but then abruptly accused Osborne of tormenting the children. Osborne also denied the charge, but accused no one in turn. At this point, there had been corroboration of the charge of witchcraft, but only from Good, who, though she acted the part of a cross and spiteful witch before the court, had neither confessed nor provided any convincing details; indeed, she impressed the court recorder with "the many lies she was taken in" (Boyer and Nissenbaum 1977, 6). Tituba was then called before the judges. Her examination is a remarkable example of a subaltern playing a very dangerous discursive game with her questioner—in her case, Judge John Hathorne:

(H)   Titibe what evil spirit have you familiarity with
(T)   none
(H)   why do you hurt these children
(T)   I do not hurt them
(H)   who is it then
(T)   the devil for ought I know
(H)   did you never see the devil.
(T)   the devil came to me and bid me serve him
(H)   who have you seen
(T)   4 women sometimes hurt the children
(H)   who were they?
(T)   goode Osburn and Sarah good and I doe not know who the other were Sarah Good and Osburne would have me hurt the children but I would not shee furder saith there was a tale man of Boston that shee did see
(Boyer and Nissenbaum 1977, 745–46)

And on it goes, with Tituba a half step (and only a half step) ahead of Hathorne's questions, giving short answers to his most probing questions, then elaborating in response to his follow-up questions. Like Naranjo's description of Popé, Tituba's is a classic narrative of the middle ground, taking suggestions from Hathorne and giving them back in a form familiar enough to be gratifying and unusual enough to highlight Tituba's cultural difference. Some of her responses put her in the best possible light; "last night there was an appearance that said Kill the children and if I would not go on hurting the children they would do worse to me" (748). Some elements of her testimony reinforce charges made by the children: "the man brought me to her and made me pinch her" (748); others make the witchcraft confession more believable. Some elements of Tituba's testimony, most notoriously the yellow bird, were picked up by accusers in good improvisational fashion; others were well within the discursive fabric of European witchcraft—witches riding sticks, secret meetings, names in a devil's book—and appeared throughout the testimony heard before the court. Significant parts of Tituba's testimony, however, stand apart.

An unusual number of animals appear in her testimony, from dogs to hogs to birds to rats to wolves, and a number of bizarre figures, like "a thing with a head like a woman with 2 leggs and wings" and "an other hairy thing it goes upright like a man" (748), that appear nowhere else. Breslaw argues convincingly that these signal a West Indian shift in the evolving narrative, an insertion of discursive elements drawn from the heterodox spiritualism of the Caribbean into the field of English witchcraft. Tituba claimed that her first meeting with other witches took place far from Salem, "at Boston," consonant with Arawak traditions that located evil forces outside the community; other accounts located meetings near the homes of accused witches. Tituba rode a stick to the meeting, but was "there presently" (749), a phrase more resonant with Indian trances than with other European accounts that trace a more conventional journey over trees and rooftops. Tituba never identifies the figure she meets, saying only "he goes in black clouthes a tal man with white hair" (749); others speak of a small black man identified specifically as the devil, a distinction that Breslaw traces to Arawak traditions of a kenaima, an evil spirit who, unlike the Judeo-Christian devil, assumed a physical body (126–30). Breslaw interprets other elements as veiled attacks on her master (a tall man dressed in black), the class of which he is a part (one witch is an unnamed well-dressed women from Boston), and the terms of her servitude (the devil's terms of service are limited to six years, unlike Tituba's lifetime slavery) (120–21).

Tituba's testimony, like the testimony of the Pueblo Indians before Otermín's inquest, is characteristic of the contact zone. Her testimony is not, strictly speaking, an autoethnography, since neither the Puritan authorities nor Tituba shows much interest in representing her cultural roots. Her testimony is instead an example of what T. H. Breen has termed "creative adaptation," in which a cultural outsider adopts elements of a dominant culture while infusing them with difference. Breen's term describes a process whereby Indian peoples transformed European culture by overdetermining many of its central elements. Thus Tituba offers an early example of how one of the most abject members of Massachusetts society transformed the terms of its existence. Her extension of the setting to include Boston, her hint of upper-class involvement, and her vivid descriptions of imps and animal familiars made her account of witchcraft at once more believable, more alien, and more terrifying than earlier accounts of witchcraft in New England. Tituba's blending of Puritan and creole beliefs linked usually disparate folk with elite English beliefs, adding fears of a pervasive satanic presence to an isolated episode of maleficium. Tituba's testimony is, like that of the Pueblo Indians Pedro Naranjo and Juan, a "middle ground"; like theirs, her testimony participates in the cultural rhetoric of the borderland. Her story, elicited in the give-and-take of a judicial inquiry, is rooted squarely in both cultures, and offered by someone who was fluent in each.[6]

Tituba's testimony, like Pedro Naranjo's, exemplifies a cross-cultural spiritualist practice. Borrowing from many cultures that Tituba inhabited, it signifies in each, and is charged by its remnant difference with a linguistic play that far exceeded the ability of the cultural elite to control it. The figurative excess characteristic of a liminal discourse brings us to another element of cross-cultural spiritualism. Spiritualism within a monocultural context is often striking in its ordinariness—the discourse of New England witchcraft, for example, was typically suffused with the petty details of domesticity in a manner not unlike the homely glow the Fox sisters wove around their séances. The creative adaptations of cross-cultural spiritualism, however, disrupt the familiar naturalizations of ideology. Such disruptions are, in a word, uncanny. Such critics as Priscilla Wald and Renée Bergland have convincingly argued that Freud's formulation of the uncanny applies equally to a subject's unsuccessful repression of childhood conflict as it does to a culture's unsuccessful repression of political conflict. In Bergland's terms, "[Q]uite literally, the uncanny is the unsettled, the not-yet-colonized, the unsuccessfully colonized, or the decolonized" (11). Such a reading of the uncanny suggests a communal, political understanding of ghost, spirits, and other hauntings that, Bergland argues, Freud himself repressed (11). This wider resonance of the uncanny is, however, a defining feature of what Kathleen Brogan terms "cultural haunting" (4). In cross-cultural settings like Salem and New Mexico, Tituba's and Naranjo's spiritualist testimonies can only be *unheimlich*, "unhomelike" or "unsettling," to their European listeners, recalling the material oppression they had attempted to forget in their effort to claim a colonized land as their own. Thus the spectacle of a mestizo returning from a gully painted in clay and covered with a friar's blood was uncanny to the watching Spanish soldier, and thus the West Indian elements Tituba inscribed within a European witchcraft were uncanny to the Puritan magistrates trying her case. What had appeared to be familiar and recognizable—Catholic spirituality or European witchcraft—to white observers was revealed, through this cross-cultural spiritualism, to be alien, hostile, and laced with the Other.

A cross-cultural spiritualist "outbreak" such as that spurred by Tituba need not take on such lethal overtones. Nevertheless, the free play that marks a moment of creative adaptation in the contact zone carries with it the possibility, at least, of severely disrupting the discursive mechanisms of cultural hegemony. Such a potent use of spiritualism, indeed, can be seen as an act of ghostly sabotage against the colonial subject. A woman as powerless as Tituba couldn't have sabotaged the system that enslaved her any more effectively. Her compelling account of occult activity unleashed the political unconscious of Puritan New England, fueling the judicial frenzy that left 156 people imprisoned, 4 of whom died in jail, 1 of whom was pressed to death, and 19 of whom were hanged. Few slave revolts in the mainland colonies resulted in as many deaths. Tituba herself proved too valuable to hang: she was rewarded for her cooperation with her life, and was eventually sold to pay her jail fees (Breslaw 174–75).

Witchcraft in Massachusetts had long been marked by the discourse of the contact zone. The devil himself was invariably invoked during the process of colonial dispossession—for the English colonists as for the Spanish, deviltry, especially in the wake of King Philip's War, was virtually synonymous with Indian culture. The testimony of Susanna Sheldon against Bridget Bishop is typical among the records of the trials in voicing what Puritan ideology tried to repress: she describes the devil as "a black man with a high crowned hat, with books in [his] hands" (Boyer and Nissenbaum 1977, 48). The worst Puritan nightmare is a black man with books, a figure of otherness representative of the Indians whose lands the Puritans occupied and of the enslaved Africans whose transport and labor had begun to enrich their theological utopia. The Puritans' dread of a black man's mastering the very medium through which the they had justified their own conquest speaks to how profoundly Puritan anxieties were rooted in hermeneutics, to how vulnerable they felt to subaltern manipulations of Puritan discourse.

It soon became clear that the discourse of witchcraft no longer effectively policed such anxieties: people lost their taste for hangings when respected citizens were led to the gallows. Moreover, the court so depended upon confessions to validate its witchcraft narrative that it spared the lives of confessors, beginning with Tituba. Soon so many of the accused confessed so quickly that the narrative collapsed under its own weight. A recoil against spiritualism in its witchly form followed, at least among the cultural elite of New England: no accused witch was executed in the colonies afterward, and the narrative of satanic discord that had fueled the trials was soon replaced by one of rationalist skepticism, accusations of fraud, and an occasional mea culpa of judicial misconduct. Cotton Mather's *Wonders of the Invisible World* (1692), published as the witchcraft trials drew to a close, is one of the last accounts to accept the accusations at face value, and one of the last as well to use the discourse of witchcraft in an effort to build a Puritan spiritualist teleology in which the forces of God and the devil played an active role in colonial politics. "The New-Englanders are a People of God in those, which were once the Devil's Territories" (1), he famously wrote. Yet even he, apparently, is unsure of where to fit Tituba into his narrative; her story doesn't appear. Richard Calef published *More Wonders of the Invisible World* (1700) shortly thereafter; he explicitly debunks Mather's spiritualist reading of the witchcraft trials, and his interpretation would remain the preferred narrative down to the present.[7]

Witchcraft didn't wholly disappear. People were accused well into the next century, but episodes remained local and were generally confined to the lower classes, where the lore of witchcraft mingled with other European folklore and fragments of more elite occultism that filtered down through the pages of almanacs and popular books of wonders (Hall). Much of the energy that fueled interest in witchcraft may have been channeled into the evangelism of the Great Awakening. Methodist revivals especially, with their lower-class milieu, their emphasis on direct spiritual contact, and their religious theater of trances and speaking in tongues, neatly filled the ideological shoes of witchcraft, and would lead, through a circuitous path, to the next setting of this study—the Burned-over District of upstate New York in the mid-nineteenth century. Before heading there, however, I would like to explore a bit more fully some of the critical and theoretical implications of beginning a study of American spiritualism so far from nineteenth-century Rochester and its environs.

Toward a Cross-Cultural Spiritualism

Connections between the Pueblo Revolt and the Salem Witchcraft Trials are not self-evident; nor are the two events self-evidently spiritualist in the terms used by most accounts of American spiritualism. Indeed, most elide the material and cross-cultural aspects of spiritualism. Early studies focused primarily on either proving or debunking claims of spirit communication. While the Spanish in New Mexico felt little need to verify Popé's contact with the spirits, Puritans from the beginning of colonization subjected evidence of witchcraft to the rigors of scholarship.[8] Scholars of later manifestations of spiritualism quickly followed suit, with early accounts weighing the merits of spiritualism's claim to scientific truth. Since Frank Podmore's *Modern Spiritualism: A History and Criticism* (1902) summarized the skeptical conclusions of the Society for Psychical Research, serious defenses of spiritualism have been few.[9] Academic histories have shifted from asking whether the physical phenomenon claimed by spiritualism actually occurred to why spiritualism as a cultural phenomenon occurred when and where it did. Such a shift offers the student of spiritualism a useful means of dodging questions about the veracity of séances and spirit manifestations by taking a somewhat elitist academic stance far above the fray. Yet reframing the question from "whether" to "why and how" remains useful. Such a reformulated inquiry allows us, first, to conceive of spiritualism more broadly, as a particular social discourse reappearing in a variety of contexts and forms rather than as a self-defined and cohesive pseudoreligion, and, second, to witness spiritualism within a broader context of discursive imbrication and political negotiation.

This historiographic shift in examining spiritualism is particularly visible in studies written in and about England. Logie Barrow's *Independent Spirits* (1986), Janet Oppenheim's *The Other World* (1985), Alex Owen's *The Darkened Room* (1990), and Helen Sword's *Ghostwriting Modernism* (2002) start with the arrival of spiritualism from America circa 1850 with the Fox sisters and their apostles, look backward at mesmerism, Swedenborgianism, and occult folk beliefs; and then weave spiritualism into the discourses of religion, reform, science, and psychology.[10] Yet these studies leave questions of a more material nature unexamined. Did women use spiritualism to gain a larger role in Victorian society? Did writers from marginalized social positions use spiritualism to challenge dominant political and sexual ideologies and shift the cultural landscape in significant ways? Did spiritualism somehow pave the way for people from different cultures to occupy more central cultural roles than they had before? Or did spiritualism serve to marginalize the women and men who advocated it? And how are we to read spiritualism's relation to other religious and social reform movements?

Recent studies of spiritualism in America have only begun to address such questions. Howard Kerr's *Mediums, and Spirit-Rappers, and Roaring Radicals* (1972) and *The Haunted Dusk* (1983), edited by Kerr, John Crowley, and Charles L. Crow, trace spiritualism's influence within a gradually expanding literary canon. These studies, however, offer little insight into the social meanings of a spiritualist discourse mediated through print. Michael Kenny, in *The Passion of Ansel Bourne* (1986), explains nineteenth-century spiritualism as a manifestation of multiple-personality disorder. Anne Braude is more effective in *Radical Spirits* (1989). She writes a history rooted squarely in the concerns of contemporary feminism but finely attuned to the very different cultural matrix of the nineteenth century. Still, Braude defines spiritualism narrowly, without reference to the cross-cultural imperatives that also shaped the era, and without a sense of how spiritualism fit into the broad cultural questions of slavery, immigration, and imperialism. Bret E. Carroll's *Spiritualism in Antebellum America* (1997) narrows spiritualism's scope even further, reading the movement solely in terms of its European, and especially Swedenborgian, roots. The most focused of recent accounts, *Cassadaga: The South's Oldest Spiritualist Community* (edited by John Guthrie et al.; 2000), offers a more tantalizing glimpse into a white middle-class movement that has regularly and blithely drawn on Indian cultures (Asian and American) for the past century and a half in a setting (central Florida) long rife with racial conflict. In Cassadaga, the cross-cultural politics of spiritualism are as striking as they are unexamined.

My own work is located within a critical terrain staked out by cultural studies and multiculturalism, as my examination of the Pueblo Revolt and the Salem Witchcraft Trials suggests. My use of the term "cross-cultural" in discussing these two events signifies, I hope, both an allegiance to and a distinction from the term "multicultural," and I would like to begin by locating my work in this particular critical borderland. Multicultural criticism has long insisted on recognizing distinct cultural identities; so, too, my reading of the Pueblo Revolt and the Salem Witchcraft Trials highlights the difference between the religions of Spain and England and the spiritual traditions of the people that those two nations colonized and enslaved. I try to avoid, however, some of the pitfalls of multicultural criticism.

In an effort to undercut the totalizing, exclusionary rhetoric of conservative ideology, some critics posit a counterhegemonic discourse that is equally totalizing. Thus some forms of multicultural criticism seek to banish any whisper of Western influence from texts that are all written and published within a Western literary culture. Why not stress instead the creative power of works that draw on both (or multiple) traditions present within a dominant culture? Western literary practice has been profoundly shaped by non-European (and, for that matter, multiple positions within European) traditions from its origins. People of color living in America, from Tituba to Toni Morrison, borrow freely from the various cultural traditions they inherit, from Native American to African to European. It is important to keep in mind, too, that these traditions are themselves hybrids, with firm roots dating back before the ages of European exploration, to be sure, but with myriad branches growing in response to centuries of contact between both European and non-European cultures. Much multicultural criticism has sought to locate an ethnically pure origin for contemporary multicultural writings, and such an imperative smacks ominously of the cultural nationalisms against which multiculturalist critics purport to write.[11] A cross-cultural methodology, by focusing on the intersections of various cultural traditions, can note distinct sensibilities without needing to totalize them.

A great many critics writing from within multiculturalism have recognized such problems, and most feel compelled to modify the term. David Palumbo-Liu uses "critical multiculturalism" to signify an approach that analyzes cultural tensions in addition to celebrating difference, while Wahmeena Lubiano invokes the terms "transformative multiculturalism" and "radical multiculturalism" to signify the oppositional force of her multicultural criticism in contrast to "noncritical pluralism." These critics' earnest modifications of "multiculturalism" bespeak a crisis in the term: it is vulnerable, on the one hand, to being coopted by a capitalist discourse anxious to maintain hegemony in an increasingly diverse United States and an increasingly global marketplace, and, on the other hand, to a devolution into identity politics. Multiculturalism has become for critics like Lubiano and Palumbo-Liu too vexed a term to stand alone. Each has added to it in order signify a critical practice distinguished from a problematic version of multiculturalism. And each critic's modifications share a number of imperatives for reading across cultural boundaries.

First, focus on cultural intersections rather than cultural essences. Palumbo-Liu especially defines his work against a merely celebratory criticism. A meaningful criticism located in a multicultural milieu, he argues, must begin by recognizing the value and integrity of the various cultures in a given historical context, but it must recognize next that cultural intersections are invariably marked by fissures and conflicts. It must recognize further that cultural identities are invariably shaped by these fissures and conflicts. Any attempt to articulate a coherent cultural essence eventually crosses cultural borders; every culture defines itself against its margins. Mary Louise Pratt is one among a great number of critics who have illustrated how European cultures have repressed the influence of non-European cultural contact in transforming their identity, and she is among the most vigorous in setting forth a "contact perspective," a critical methodology that treats cultural interaction not in terms of "apartheid," but in terms of "copresence, interaction, interlocking understandings and practices, often within radically asymmetrical relations of power" (7). My study thus centers on mestizo and creole figures located at the margins of their cultures. The Pueblo Revolt is obviously suited to a cross-cultural approach. Many studies of the Salem Witchcraft Trials, however, treat them as an extension of English and other European witchcraft episodes, ignoring the profound role non-European peoples and traditions played in texturing events around Salem, from Tituba's Caribbean modulations of witchcraft discourse to the undercurrents of Indian resistance that ran as a bass note underneath the proceedings.

Second, attend to the discursive nature of cultural conflict. The word "discursive," of course, stakes out a poststructuralist territory, signifying the nexus of power/knowledge formulated by Foucault to probe the mechanisms by which the processes of making meaning shape subjectivity along distinct and conflicted vectors of power. Of particular interest from a cross-cultural perspective is the process by which the stories, rituals, beliefs, and words that make up a distinct cultural discourse cross cultural frontiers to signify in very different contexts. Pratt draws special attention to such processes of transculturation in order to underscore that such cultural crossings occurred in multiple directions and had powerful effects, whether they were self-consciously colonial discourses (Spanish ethnographies of Pueblo religion), carefully calibrated autoethnographies (those given before Otermín's inquisitors by Pueblo captives), or improvisational creolizations (Tituba's testimony in Salem).

Indeed, the vastly different shapes these discursive border crossings took signal the importance of a third imperative: read such utterances in light of the material contexts that shaped them. Multiculturalism and Marxism have long been uneasy bedfellows. Materialist analyses of cultural conflict that grind their Marxist axes too fine run the risk of burying distinct cultural perspectives under a narrative of an incipient and rapacious capitalism. It is important, of course, to remember that cultural productions even by people facing colonization are not solely determined by their material context. Yet the material and political aspects of discourses like spiritualism become particularly highly charged when they cross cultural lines. Spiritualism, with its remarkable cultural ubiquity and concomitant knack for seeping through the walls that divide cultural traditions, offers a valuable opportunity to study how even an avowedly immaterial discourse must take a material manifestation. And indeed, a cross-cultural methodology highlights a materiality that a monocultural or essentialist multicultural approach would tend to elide. An examination of how Pueblo and Spanish spiritualisms collided during the Pueblo Revolt underscores the lethal politics that mediated the earliest written accounts of Pueblo spirituality, while a view of the Salem Witchcraft Trials from the vantage point of Tituba's creole modulations illustrates how profoundly Puritan spiritualist discourse was shaped by the pressures of colonization.

I have been speaking of spiritualism in the singular in order to stress its commonality across cultures, to give some traction to a cross-cultural analysis that, while aware of conflict, has room for cooperation as well. At other moments it is more useful to speak of *spiritualisms,* to emphasize the radical otherness of distinct spiritualist discourses—to follow, in short, a fourth critical imperative: preserve cultural difference. Sacvan Bercovitch, no multiculturalist, nevertheless offers a useful formulation of interpretation and otherness: "To interpret is not to make sense of a mystery 'out there.' It is to discover otherness as mystery (something 'overwhelming,' 'incomprehensible'), and then to explain the mystery as the wonders of an invisible world, a realm of meaningful 'silence,' resonant with universals. To investigate those wonders is not to come to terms with the new or unexpected" (4). Do not, in other words, overinterpret. Do not make the Other familiar; instead, respect difference. Draw connections, interpret by building resonance, but do not collapse cultural distinctions. If spiritualism has some universal appeal, it gains its resonance and its specific political valence in places like colonial New Mexico and Massachusetts through the interaction of autonomous spiritualist sensibilities.

A final imperative is powerfully articulated by Wai Chee Dimmock. Against a synchronic historicism that grounds a text's meanings in its contemporary context, she proposes reading a text across time, examining how it signifies differently in different contexts, a diachronic historicism, or resonance:

This approach tries to engage history beyond the simultaneous, aligning it instead with the dynamics of endurance and transformation that accompany the passage of time. This long view of history, restoring the temporal axis to literary studies, allows texts to be seen as objects that do a lot of traveling: across space and especially across time. And as they travel they run into new semantic networks, new ways of imputing meaning. (1061)

Dimmock's is a powerful plea against synchronic historicism as the answer to a literary text's meaning, a plea to read across time, to be aware of how a text's meaning is not rooted in context but in *contexts*. Hers is a methodology of "incipience," mining a text for extensive connections, reading for strange junctures, for intense interdisciplinarity (1065). Here, then, is my argument for juxtaposing Pueblos and Puritans: there is indeed a strange juncture between them, visible now thanks to a multicultural lens that finally allows both to resonate within an American tradition, though there was indeed precious little synchronic resonance between them. The events have begun, finally, to echo.

The Pueblo Revolt and the Salem Witchcraft Trials were fundamental in shaping multicultural syntheses in societies half a continent apart. By 1848, when spiritualism next rose to cultural prominence, New Mexico and New England were part of one nation, and my study will turn to exploring spiritualism's role in negotiating cultural conflict on this vastly larger stage. In individual chapters I frame my analysis of spiritualism around distinct, though interrelated, questions. How did writers from marginal social positions use spiritualism to tap into a wider audience while preserving their cultural difference? How did the conditions of local literary production shape spiritualism's transmutation into print discourse? As spiritualism entered into the national literary culture in the mid-nineteenth century, what role did it play in the struggle to forge and maintain a national consensus out of a diverse and far-flung populace? Within the larger struggle over the national consensus, how did spiritualism inflect the intense debate over the nature of gender and the role of women in society? How did spiritualism shape people's efforts to reimagine America by constructing utopian discourses of the afterlife? What were the politics and poetics of the shifting domain of spiritualist discourse from religion and reform to science and ethnography by the end of the nineteenth century? While these questions presuppose distinct mechanisms of inquiry, I will also approach each with two related critical imperatives: to focus on a few representative texts situated within the broader spectrum of American literary culture, and to examine each question cross-culturally.

Chapter 1, "Around Rochester," explores the social and literary milieu of

Rochester in the mid-nineteenth century. I will focus on a work that is not avowedly a spiritualist text, despite its origins in the very social circles that launched the Fox sisters to national prominence in 1849: Harriet Jacobs's *Incidents in the Life of a Slave Girl* (1861). This autobiographical account of slavery in North Carolina, published by an abolitionist press at the outbreak of the Civil War, is nevertheless deeply rooted in Jacobs's earliest immersion in the literary culture of Rochester in 1849; I'll argue that her work is artfully crafted to negotiate the cultural boundary that separated her own spiritual experience in the Deep South from the spiritualism that flooded the upstate New York abolitionist and feminist circles in which she found refuge.

Chapter 2, "Public Spirits," examines literary community on a national level through the lens of spiritualism. How do angels in Rochester differ, in other words, from angels in America? Specifically, the chapter will marshal spiritualist discourse to explore the evolution of the public sphere, as formulated by Jürgen Habermas and applied by Michael Warner to an earlier American cultural milieu, as mid-nineteenth-century America grappled with issues of national consensus—with decidedly mixed results. I will trace the trajectory of spiritualism as it moved beyond the horizons of Rochester to enter into a national literary culture, exemplified on the one hand by a relatively conservative and elitist national magazine press—a literary culture very much in line with the public sphere of an earlier generation—and on the other by a distinctly popular and heterogeneous press made possible by the creation of a mass reading public. A sampling of American print culture will illustrate how spiritualism served to help construct a unified national identity and, at the same moment, contest it.

Chapter 3, "The Politics of Heaven," explores spiritualism in conjunction with another avowedly political discourse mediated in the national print culture: utopianism. Elizabeth Stuart Phelps, in the tremendously popular *The Gates Ajar* (1870) and its numerous sequels, marshaled a spiritualist discourse of heaven in order to reshape social reform movements that appeared on the brink of failure. Her effort bears striking affinities to the Ghost Dance movement, a utopian spiritualist phenomenon that swept across Native American communities in the West at the end of the nineteenth century. These texts were the result of vastly different modes of literary production and signified within vastly different social contexts. I will examine them in relation to each other and in relation to a third text, Mark Twain's *Captain Stormfield's Visit to Heaven* (1907), in part to see whether such a study is possible. How meaningful, in other words, are such broad generic categories as "spiritualist" and "utopian"? Can texts from widely different cultural contexts be examined in relation to each other? If not, what does such cultural dissonance mean when these texts were produced in the same country within a few decades of each other?

Chapter 4, "Spirits in the Contact Zone," examines the role spiritualism played in two emerging discourses at the turn into the twentieth century. Spiritualism is a neglected element in the local color fiction of white writers like Sarah Orne Jewett, whose domestic and sentimental renderings of ghosts map the limits of her local color world. Spiritualism was equally important in the work of such writers of color as Charles Chesnutt and María Cristina Mena, and I will examine how each used it to extend the borders of the local color universe. While Chesnutt carefully and subtly weaves a spiritualist resonance into his conjure tales in order to make African-American culture more familiar to a white audience, Mena quickly turns local color spiritualism into a revolutionary critique of European-American culture. By the early twentieth century, spiritualism's cultural meaning had become richly textured and vigorously contested.

Chapter 5, "Spirit Nation," juxtaposes two very different accounts of spiritualism in Boston, Henry James's *The Bostonians* (1886) and Pauline Hopkins's *Of One Blood* (1903), in order to show how spiritualism served as a tool for analyzing and contesting national identity in postbellum America. Trance speaking and mediumship were for both writers powerful figures for exploring the multiple ideologies struggling to find a voice in the American subject. The two novels present, however, very different models of ideological critique. James draws on a realist aesthetic to satirize spiritualism as a kind of false consciousness, while Hopkins offers, in her formally disruptive work, a version of identity that is as complex, contradictory, and unstable as America itself at the dawn of the twentieth century.

The conclusion, "The Poetics and Politics of Spiritualism," will follow some of the issues raised in previous chapters into the present, sketching spiritualism's evolution into its late-twentieth-century forms, from New Age channeling to angelmania, with particular attention to spiritualism's literary manifestations across a broad cultural front. I will reconsider in a contemporary setting the questions that framed earlier chapters. How do writers from broadly different cultural contexts deploy the discourses of spiritualism in a national literary culture? How is spiritualism inflected by the continually vexed categories of race, class, and gender? How, finally, did spiritualism build and stretch the fragile bonds that hold America together in a ghostly communion?

Ghostly Communion

Around Rochester

Spiritualism, Reform, and Harriet Jacobs's
Incidents in the Life of a Slave Girl

In March 1849, Harriet Jacobs moved to Rochester, New York, to help her brother John run an antislavery reading room. She had been living in the North as a fugitive slave for seven years, almost exactly the length of time she had spent hidden in the attic of her grandmother's house in North Carolina. The reading room quickly proved a financial failure, but by other standards the year and a half she spent in Rochester was rich indeed. Jacobs read widely in the literature collected in the reading room and was introduced into one of the most influential circles of abolitionists in America; the reading room was located above the offices where Frederick Douglass published his newspaper, the *North Star,* and helped to organize abolitionist activity throughout the North. Jacobs also began a lifelong friendship with Amy Post—a radical Quaker, a long-standing and zealous abolitionist, an early activist in the cause of women's rights, and one of the first proponents of a cultural phenomenon then sweeping across America: spiritualism.[1]

Jacobs's friendship with Post is well documented. Jacobs spent almost nine months of her time in Rochester living in the Post household, and a voluminous correspondence developed between the two women when Jacobs left Rochester to work as a servant in New York. Post first encouraged Jacobs to tell her story and served as Jacobs's trusted adviser in the years it took her to write her manuscript and shepherd it into print. Yet while the many accounts of Jacobs's book duly point out Post's influence on Jacobs, and many more explore how Jacobs both mines and modulates the dominant strands of abolitionist, sentimental, and feminist discourse in writing her narrative, few even note how powerful a hold spiritualism had on the imagination of Jacobs's intended audience and her closest friends.[2] The years between 1849, when Jacobs first told her incredible story to Amy Post, and 1861, when *Inci-*

dents was finally published, were the heyday of spiritualism in America, years when curiosity surrounding odd noises in a farmhouse in upstate New York grew into a quasi-religious movement that counted its supporters in the millions and its spirited detractors in almost equal numbers. Nurtured in the same "burned over" soil that had long supported abolitionism and that had seen the beginnings of the women's rights movement in America, spiritualism quickly became associated with both causes, drawing its leaders from the same pool of radical talent and, despite the often dubious integrity of some of its practitioners, growing into a powerful force for social change in mid-century America.

Jacobs was a writer acutely aware of her audience. As Jean Fagan Yellin and Hazel Carby have shown, she carefully crafted her work to take advantage of sentimental literary conventions; Jennifer Rae Greeson has similarly traced Jacobs's careful adaptation of the urban Gothic in order to draw in readers attuned to antiprostitution rhetoric. It would be remarkable if Jacobs did *not* make use of spiritualism as she shaped her text for a readership that was largely white, middle class, and female. I will argue that spiritualism is in fact a major element woven carefully and critically into the fabric of her text. As she does with the slave narrative and domestic fiction, Jacobs quickly masters the discourse of spiritualism, using it to gain for herself a voice in the social debates of her day while at the same time subtly and carefully reworking that discourse to suit her own ends.

Spiritualism had long been simmering in antebellum American culture. Witchcraft may not have survived the Salem Witchcraft Trials, but the folk occultism of which it was a part remained largely intact into the nineteenth century. Charms, prophecies, and ghosts were a vital part of European-American rural and working-class culture, keeping alive an epistemology and discourse upon which spiritualism would draw and proving open to African and Native American traditions when more elite culture was not. Upper-class European Americans often eschewed folklore as superstition, favoring instead such modern movements from across the Atlantic as mesmerism and Swedenborgianism. Yet as these movements spread across the American cultural landscape, they often merged with the folk beliefs they were meant to supplant.[3] A burgeoning print culture, especially in the form of almanacs and books of wonder, helped drive this process, as did the lyceum circuit that emerged by the early nineteenth century. Religious reform movements, too, often drew on the twin reservoirs of elite and folk spiritualist discourse as they spread through antebellum culture. While a primarily urban elite drew on Swedenborg and the German Idealists as they fashioned Unitarianism, the rural working class that had long sustained European folk culture found much of its energies and discourse rechanneled by the Methodist revivals that sprouted perennially through the countryside. Religious leaders who attracted smaller groups of zealous adherents, from Ann Lee to Jemimah Wilkinson to Joseph Smith, often drew on a very specific nexus of folk beliefs.[4] The reform movements that sprang up in the 1830s and 1840s grew from bewildering combinations of religious, folk, and scientific discourses. Unitarians and Universalists, Freemasons and Free Lovers, Shakers and Hicksite Quakers, Mormons and Millerites and mesmerists, socialists and Swedenborgians, tee-totalers and Thompsonians and transcendentalists—all flourished in the rich loam of European-American culture, and each contributed to an epistemology that inextricably mingled science and religion, materialism and spirituality.

Although these movements flourished especially in upstate New York in the decades preceding the advent of this most recent manifestation of spiritualism, the Rochester Rappings nevertheless sprang up suddenly. On the night of March 31, 1848, two sisters began to interpret the strange knocks that had been heard in their small farmhouse for some nights. Margaret Fox, age thirteen, and her twelve-year-old sister, Kate, determined that the "rappings" were caused by the spirit of a murdered peddler, who could communicate by making a knocking sound in answer to a yes/no question, or at the appropriate letter as the sisters called out the alphabet. The rappings only occurred in the presence of one or both of the sisters. As Margaret would confess on her deathbed forty years later, she and her sister had produced the rappings by cracking their toe joints, and had intended only to tease their superstitious mother (Kerr 4–5).[5]

Whatever their initial intentions, the impact of the rappings quickly ballooned beyond their household. News of the strange occurrences spread to the local papers, and crowds of people began to gather in the small Hydesville farmhouse to witness the rappings for themselves. The Foxes soon left their unquiet home, and interest in the Fox sisters might have died out had not the girls been sent to Rochester to live with their elder sister, Leah Fox Fish—an old family friend of Isaac and Amy Post. The Posts took an early, if skeptical, interest in the two local celebrities, but their interest quickly grew deadly serious as the girls were able to communicate with the recently deceased spirits of friends and relatives of the Post circle. While some of the messages that came over the "spiritual telegraph" were puzzling—one spirit laboriously spelled out the sentence, "Put on as much molasses as he likes"—many more messages offered powerful solace for people grieving for lost loved ones. Isaac Post recorded one such session with Kate and Margaret in November 1848:

> Dr. Chase who had recently lost his mother, asked if Mother's spirit was present. The answer was, she was. Whether she was happy / she was, whether her knowledge had increased since she passed away / it had. Whether she continually watched over him / she did. Then he asked about a sister, whether his suspicions in regard to her death were correct. The answer, they were not. Would she have lived if other means were used? The reply, she would not. Then he asked if [he] could be convinced that there could be spiritual manifestations, then he could get no more answers. (Braude 12)

In the year that followed the Fox sisters' move to Rochester—the same year that Jacobs moved to the city—the Posts opened communications with the deceased spirits of three of Isaac's sisters and with two children that Isaac and Amy had lost years before. Leah Fox Fish soon proved to be a medium to the spirit world as well, and Isaac's investigations of spiritual phenomena were greatly enhanced when he began to "magnetize" the eldest Fox sister, whose trance speaking proved far more facile than the more cumbersome rappings of Margaret and Kate (Braude 11–15). After discovering his own abilities as a trance writer, Isaac Post began collecting the posthumous communications of famous men and women.

Interest in what had become known as the "Rochester Rappings" quickly spread, and in November 1849 the spirits let it be known that they were ready for a wider audience. Isaac Post and his cousin George Willet rented the largest hall in Rochester, and on the night of the fourteenth, four hundred people gathered to hear the mysterious noises. While Catherine and Margaret Fox communed with the spirit world, Amy Post stood by on the podium, lending the teenage girls the strength of her friendship and the authority of her good name; she then accompanied the sisters to a chamber where they were disrobed and examined by a committee of skeptics looking for signs of a hoax. The committee found nothing, and interest in the girls skyrocketed. By June 1850, the three Fox sisters were in New York offering public demonstrations of the spirit rappings three times a day at Barnum's Hotel. Admission was one dollar, and visitors included the most notable members of New York society. One evening demonstration was attended by such figures as James Fenimore Cooper, William Cullen Bryant, Horace Greeley (who gave the girls a great deal of warm publicity in the pages of the

New York Tribune), and George Ripley (formerly of Brook Farm and now Greeley's chief editor). The most skeptical member of the group was the prominent poet and editor Nathaniel Parker Willis, who was to write later of "the disinclination which these spirits seemed to have for any intercourse with editors" (1955, 189). Willis and the Fox sisters had a common acquaintance back in Rochester: Harriet Jacobs had spent a number of years nursing Willis's children, and in a few months would return to her old position.

Unlike Jacobs, who found little financial success in Rochester, the Fox sisters had struck gold. Catherine and Margaret embarked on a tour of American cities that would occupy them for the next few years, while Leah stayed in New York entertaining callers in her séance room. William Lloyd Garrison describe one typical session in 1854: Six men and four women sat around a table with their hands resting on the table top, touching each other's feet to ensure that the raps were genuine. Then the raps commenced, at one point beating time to a popular song, at another spelling out the message that "spiritualism will work miracles in the cause of reform" (Braude 15–17).

Reform was much on people's minds in America at midcentury. By the late 1840s, the slavery question gripped the national consciousness, supplanting such issues as temperance, prison reform, education, and pacifism that had grown out of the religious revivals of the Second Great Awakening. Reform issues tended to overlap, nurtured by an energetic pool of activists whose characters and reputations ranged from earnest respectability to wild-eyed enthusiasm, yet who shared an optimistic sympathy to new and unpopular causes. By the end of the 1840s, though, abolitionism had extended beyond the radical fringe to become *the* reform issue. Spiritualism spread along reformist channels during the years that saw in quick succession the Compromise of 1850, the Fugitive Slave Act, the Dred Scott decision, the Kansas-Nebraska Act, and the quickening spiral of violence that lead from Bleeding Kansas to Harper's Ferry to Civil War. It is no surprise that, given the explosive social context in which it emerged, such a quasi-religious movement would be quickly politicized.

There were other reasons, too, why spiritualism rapidly became allied with reform issues. It arose in Rochester among one of the most influential groups of reformers in the country, whose eclectic interests included virtually every effort to hasten the social and theological millennium eagerly anticipated in mid-century America. Nancy Hewitt has traced the interlocking trajectories of women reformers in nineteenth-century Rochester, from genteel women who gathered in benevolent societies when Rochester was still a growing village to the increasingly radicalized working-class women who began to agitate for labor rights as the village grew into a major industrial center. Free black women formed Rochester's first antislavery society in 1834, though their efforts received little attention from the mainstream press. By the 1840s, however, they had been joined by a group of white reformers drawn from the fringes of Rochester society who were willing to make common cause with their African-American brothers and sisters in an effort to spread the abolitionist gospel. Rochester was one of the few areas of the country where black and white reformers worked together effectively, and in the mid-1840s this cooperative interracial milieu drew a number of prominent African-American abolitionists to the city (by then an important stop on the Underground Railroad), including the popular lecturer John Jacobs and, by 1848, Frederick Douglass. They found a thriving African-American community and a large group of sympathetic white reformers committed to completely reshaping American society. This group, known as "ultraists," formed the core of nascent movements for abolition, women's rights, and eventually spiritualism. When John Jacobs learned that his sister Harriet, long established in the North but still a fugitive, was in danger of being seized and taken back to North Carolina, he found her a place in the household of one of the most prominent ultraist families in the city (Hewitt 40–42).

The Posts were part of a large Quaker population in upstate New York, many of whose members had become radicalized during doctrinal disputes that erupted earlier in the century. Amy Post, for example, was the cousin of Elias Hicks, who organized the Hicksite Separation in 1827 on the grounds that the Quaker establishment had grown too orthodox and too comfortable with the material institutions of the "world," including slavery. The Posts joined the Hicksites initially, but were in turn censured for engaging in antislavery activity with non-Quakers before being banned in 1849 from the Genessee Yearly Meeting, apparently for hosting the wedding of two black friends. Such social mingling between the races was too much for even the relatively liberal Quakers of upstate New York (Hewitt 143). They then helped form an independent congregation of Friends in Waterloo, New York, that allowed for the ultimate freedom of an individual's conscience. Among their foundational principles, they argued that "an unbroken chain of communication" exists "between the Infinite and all beings," and members of the congregation greeted news of the spirit rappings as confirmation that their departure from orthodox Quakerism had reconnected the "spiritual telegraph" to God. Members of the congregation began investigating the spiritual phenomenon in earnest and enthusiastically communicated news of their findings along an informal network of Friends across the country (Braude 13–14).

For Quakers like the Posts, spiritualism confirmed the merits of both abolitionism and women's rights. Confident in the righteousness of their consciences and newly free to engage in social activism, they renewed their reformist efforts; other social activists greeted the new spiritual movement emerging in upstate New York with equal interest. Lucretia Mott was participating in the organization of the Waterloo congregation when she reunited with her old abolitionist colleague, Elizabeth Cady Stanton, and members of the Waterloo Friends turned their attention from their spiritualist investigations long enough to play a prominent role in the Seneca Falls Convention in 1848. Indeed, raps reportedly rocked the very table where Mott and Stanton penned the Declaration of Sentiments. In Braude's words, "[T]he American women's rights movement drew its first breaths in an atmosphere alive with the rumors of angels," and the two movements remained inextricably entwined throughout the following decades. "While not all feminists were Spiritualists," continues Braude, "all Spiritualists advocated women's rights" (58).

It was in the year following the Seneca Falls convention, as Amy Post organized the follow-up convention in Rochester and continued her investigation of spiritualism, that Harriet Jacobs began her acquaintance with the Posts, first as a partner in the abolitionist cause, and then as a close friend and long-term household member of this family Jacobs describes as "practical believers in the Christian doctrine of human brotherhood" (189). Jacobs's year in Rochester—a year spent in the company of her brother, her daughter, and a circle of friends as determined and outspoken in the cause of justice as she, and a year too where she first had the opportunity to educate herself among the books of the antislavery reading room—was a year in which the intertwined causes of abolition and women's rights fell under the watchful gaze of spirits.

Spiritualism quickly proved a powerful tool in the service of both abolitionism and women's rights. Lucretia Mott stated that "all these subjects of reform are kindred in their nature and giving to each its proper consideration, will tend to strengthen and nerve the mind for all" (Hewitt 129). Slavery was high on the list of issues presented to mediums, with spirits (even that of John C. Calhoun) quick to denounce the peculiar institution (Kerr 7). Because such unequivocal endorsements of abolition from departed slaveholders exposed spiritualism to a good deal of amused skepticism, a number of prominent abolitionists felt that some of the overenthusiastic mediums hurt the cause. Yet many garnered strength from spiritualism. Abolitionists like William Lloyd Garrison, negotiating audiences whose attitude toward African Americans ranged from awkward tolerance to virulent racism, found in the movement a powerful basis for belief in the equality of every soul. Every person had equal access to the Creator, and the prevalence of young, uneducated farm girls as mediums proved class, education, and gender irrelevant in gaining access to the spirit world. Spiritualism also offered an important bridge between black and white culture: spiritualism in its European-American form had many affinities with African-American folk practice, and black churches often proved receptive to white mediums when mainstream white churches would not. A handful of African-American mediums even managed to gain audiences among both races (Braude 28–30). Although the belief in a spiritual essence that survives a person's death was a Christian and African commonplace, the notion that these spirits were a constant, if invisible, presence in the world, and that they could at any time and place transgress that boundary between life and death through a spiritual telegraph, was, for European Americans, rather new, and quite radical. Such constant spiritual surveillance undermined the certainties of traditional institutions, unfixing the authority of the dominant discourse by tapping into a higher source of knowledge. Ultimately, as the number of admittedly fraudulent mediums grew and as communication from the spirits proved as fractured, confused, and contradictory as that produced by humans, spiritualism's own claim to truth proved suspect. But it nevertheless remained for many thousands of Americans a potent source of oppositional discourse and alternative knowledge. If, for abolitionists like Garrison or the Posts, the authority of spiritual communication wasn't enough to put pro-slavery forces to rout, spiritualism did offer a means of reifying their beliefs in racial equality and prying apart the rigid ideologies of racial difference.

Spiritualism proved most effective in the movement for women's rights, offering a model of subjectivity that radically altered dominant constructions of both self and gender, and that had significant implications for the writing of the self by a black woman such as Harriet Jacobs. According to Sidonie Smith, the self as it emerged in American ideology at midcentury was rational, disembodied, autonomous, loaded with inalienable political rights, nongendered, and hence invariably male (79–80). Smith argues that the "male" self was defined against its opposite: a "female" self that was confined by its sensuality, its physicality, its passivity, its political subordination, and its social determination. The emerging cult of domesticity increasingly confined women to their bodies and their homes, constructing women's ways of knowing, in George Eliot's phrase, as "emotional, and rhapsodic, and spiritualistic" (Eliot 334). Women who claimed a male voice, speaking in public under the banner of reason, were increasingly chastised as "unwomanly," as monstrous. The women who gathered at Seneca Falls in 1848 were thus forced to negotiate between their demands for a "masculine" subjectivity and their culture's imperative that they remain "respectable" women. Lucretia Mott and Elizabeth Cady Stanton managed this by maintaining a veneer of masculine control over the convention, asking a male president to submit their Declaration of Sentiments. Smith argues that when Stanton wrote her autobiography many years later, she "use[d] her position as wife and mother to screen her self-asserting presentation of herself as 'individual,' as 'man,' as 'metaphysical self'" (90). But if Stanton's tentative construction of her self serves as one model of resistance to the discourse of domesticity, the spiritualism that emerged alongside the first women's rights convention offered another—a strategy of resistance that was, perhaps, more radical and elusive, and one that Jacobs draws on heavily when fashioning her own version of the female self.

Most obviously, spiritualism contested dominant constructions of women through its insistence on spiritual essence; the willingness of female spirits to communicate the insights they had gained in the afterlife testified to the existence of a disembodied female selfhood. Yet this focus on female spiritual essence was not the principal means by which spiritualism worked to gain women a voice, since the existence of female spirits was quite in line with Christian beliefs and, in any event, spirit communications often divided along gender lines, with male spirits like Ben Franklin's pronouncing on issues of science, philosophy, and public policy while female spirits generally voiced reassurances of their contentment to concerned family members. Spiritualism did, however, offer women's rights advocates one more means of challenging patriarchal norms. Isaac Post, for example, projected a patriarchal gendering of selfhood into his representation of spiritualism, recording a son's anxious queries to his departed mother in an early séance in the private letter cited on page 4, above, while devoting most of his book of spirit communications, *Voices from the Spirit World* (1852), to the spectral words of such public men as Franklin, Washington, and Jefferson.

Yet Post's spirit world critiqued patriarchal conventions as well. The Dr. Chase described in the séance stands remarkably infantilized before his cryptic, authoritative, and ever-vigilant "Mother," and in *Voices from the Spirit World,* Post gives significant (if not quite equal) time to public women like Margaret Fuller. Spiritualists like Post and the Fox sisters could thus undermine strict gender roles while seeming to uphold them. More importantly, though communications from the séance or trance lecture came wrapped in relatively familiar and comforting formulas, they nevertheless profoundly unsettled traditional epistemologies, offering reformers an opportunity to spread radically different visions of society. Knowledge gained through the spiritual telegraph threatened the authority of both the orthodox (and patriarchal) ministry and the increasingly regularized (and patriarchal) scientific community simultaneously. Dr. Chase's conversation with his recently deceased mother brought questions as well as comfort, and such questions gave reformers like Isaac Post and, I will argue, Harriet Jacobs, broader opportunities to speak.

This nuanced strategy for claiming voice bore significant similarities to the approach used by women's rights advocates, who knew when it would behoove them to speak through sympathetic men and cannily shaped their message to take advantage of popular conventions. Not a spiritualist, Stanton wrote to Elizabeth Smith Miller in 1850, "The spirits seem to be making some new manifestations! I am convinced it is all humbug" (Stanton 42). Yet she was careful not to alienate those who were believers. Indeed, the letter following this sharp dismissal of the spirits is addressed to Amy Post herself, and Stanton would champion the famous spiritualist Victoria Woodhull after the Civil War in order to further the cause of women's rights.

Stanton also proved willing to adopt a more relational model of feminine selfhood. If the Declaration of Sentiments claims for women the "masculine" selfhood characteristic of the Declaration of Independence, other women's rights forums drew on other models of selfhood. After the Seneca Falls convention, Stanton established a conversation club modeled on the conversations Margaret Fuller had held a decade earlier in Boston. The conversation club, poised between social entertainment and social reform, structured around a relational identity, and set in the woman's sphere of the parlor, proved a powerful mechanism for women's advancement, and anticipated closely the séances that would spread throughout the country in the 1850s. The mingled ideologies of selfhood characteristic of the women's rights movement and spiritualism, too, point to Stanton's debt to Fuller. Looking back in *The History of Women's Suffrage,* Stanton portrays Fuller as both rational (masculine) and spiritual (feminine): "[W]hether we look upon her as critic, creator, or seer, she was thoroughly a woman" (802). Faced with adopting an ideology of selfhood that was either masculine, rational, and disembodied, or feminine, mystical, and embodied, Stanton, like Jacobs, chose both.

Like women's rights activists, spiritualists appropriated dominant constructions of femininity for their own purposes. The great majority of mediums were, like Catherine and Margaret Fox, among the most abject members of white America: poor teenage girls. They gained their agency not by speaking *as* metaphysical subjects, but by speaking *for* metaphysical subjects. That is, the medium gained voice and subjectivity, paradoxically, by posing as transparent subjects, as mere conduits for the disembodied voices of the spirit world, as mere machinery of the spiritual telegraph. Mediums identified themselves with the very ideals of the domestic ideology they contested, making themselves exquisitely sensitive, preternaturally passive, the very apotheosis of spirituality; and by their being so, the most powerful men of the nation might sit humble at their feet. The trance speakers who followed in the wake of the Foxes gained large audiences across the country at a time when women campaigning for abolition and women's rights had a difficult time booking a hall anywhere; once on the stage, mediums were free to swear like sailors or speak on the most explosive topics of the day, depending on the spirits that spoke through them.

Cora Hatch, for example, who rose to fame as a trance speaker in the 1850s, was widely noted as pioneering and as being somewhat shocking and, ultimately, enchanting. Nathaniel Parker Willis, writing in 1859, described Hatch as "a delicate-featured blond, of seventeen or eighteen, flaxen ringlets falling over her shoulders, movements deliberate and self-possessed, voice calm and deep" (306). He then observes how "very curious it was to see a long haired young woman standing alone in a pulpit, her face turned upwards, her delicate bare arms raised in a clergyman's attitude of devotion, and a church full of people listening attentively while she prayed." Willis became, if not a convert to women's rights, at least less of a reactionary. Though still uncomfortable with a woman lecturer, he confesses "I was prepared to believe her an exception—either that a male spirit was speaking through her lips, or that the relative position of the sexes is not the same as in the days of St. Paul" (309). In such canny manipulation and exaggeration of nineteenth-century conventions of womanhood lay the radical impact of spiritualism. Women like Cora Hatch claimed a level of agency by simultaneously pointing to their bodies and away from them, mastering the male gaze by turning their bodies into a mask, contesting the embodying gaze by turning against it the gaze of spirits. The medium on the stage served as both a projection of the dominant ideology and resistance to it, a site of multiplicity and contradiction where the conflicting strands of gendered interpellation found an apt figure in the woman speaking with / being spoken by multifarious voices. An externalization of the contending forces within the female subject, the medium burst the increasingly narrow confines into which the female subject was placed.[6]

While Willis sat entranced before Cora Hatch, Jacobs was quietly crafting a performance of her own, drafting her manuscript in hours stolen from her domestic duties in the Willis household. She, too, gained her voice by writing from the ideological fissures of mid-century America, and the complexity of her narrative strategy matched the depths of the discursive abjection from which she had to wrest her selfhood. Barbara Johnson offers one useful map of the ideological landscape in which Jacobs moved in Rochester. If white men such as Isaac Post enjoyed the status of universality, subjectivity could be imagined by black men like Frederick Douglass and John Jacobs in their claim of manhood and their status as respectable citizens. Likewise, white women could begin to claim subjectivity by stressing an essential universality and appropriating male roles (as reformers, as public speakers). The black woman, however, remained twice removed from a disembodied subjectivity (168–69). Henry Louis Gates Jr. notes the doubly embodied status of the black woman in antebellum America: tied already to the female body, the black woman was additionally inscribed within a racial body that placed her even further down the chain of being (1986, 3–5). Jacobs consequently needed to work doubly hard to write herself out of this double bind.

Many of the strategies Jacobs used have been thoroughly catalogued. Jean Fagan Yellin presents a writer actively contesting the taboos against female sexuality—Jacobs borrows from the popular tradition of seduction tales (in which the heroine's sexual sin invariably leads to her death) in order to reject it. Jacobs presents Linda's sexual sin instead as a calculated move designed to procure her freedom (xxx). Hazel Carby argues that Jacobs's writing of a narrative that resists so many conventions of domesticity "revealed the concept of true womanhood to be an ideology, not a lived set of social relations" (49). Once Jacobs has shaken off the shackles of patriarchal ideology, Elizabeth Fox-Genovese argues, she stakes a claim to universal selfhood: at the center of the narrative lies not Brent's body, but her will—an essential, disembodied site of agency from which Brent draws her power of resistance. She becomes the avatar of the "self-made man" in a manner that shares powerful resonances with Frederick Douglass's own narrative of the triumph of the will (Fox-Genovese, 171–72).

Yet such a direct claim to a self-constructed "will" was neither wholly successful nor, in Jacobs's case, wholly desirable. William L. Andrews has argued that the slave narrative, however much focused on the self-determination of its hero, invariably conflated a narrative self with a racial self—the former slave could only write, and could only be read, as a representative of his or her race. Thus figurations of the black body continually accrued to an essential, disembodied selfhood that was continually asserted against that black body in an anxious and never-ending game of discursive tag (6–7). Jacobs, a black woman determined to write herself into the pervasive discourse of "polite" femininity, was more willing to modulate her claims to such a "male" selfhood. Sidonie Smith among others has pointed out that Jacobs revises the male slave narrative convention of the "isolato," defining both her self and her rebellion against an oppressive master and the institution of slavery itself as profoundly shaped by networks of friends and family. Indeed, Smith argues that the marginal location from which Jacobs writes and the fluidity of the identities that she constructs throughout *Incidents* problematize the fixed binary of male and female selfhood as is was defined at midcentury: "Life-storytelling becomes the site of 'selfhood,' now understood as discursive, contextual, communicative, and ultimately 'fictive.' Thus Jacobs's narrative testifies to the ambiguities of any core of irreducible, essentialist 'selfhood'" (102). In Smith's reading, *Incidents* figures as the quintessential poststructuralist text, artfully deconstructing categories of race, gender, and identity itself. Similarly, Michelle Burnham argues that Jacobs's narrative, particularly the chapter "The Loophole of Retreat," exemplifies resistance to an oppressive, panoptical gaze that offers a useful gloss to Foucault, and models agency that doesn't depend on dominant constructions of subjectivity. Brent's retreat to her grandmother's garret, posits Burnham, exploits the blind spot of slavery, functioning not by claiming a subjectivity that can oppose an oppressive structure, but "by relocating agency in the juncture between the structure and the subject, in sites that elude the gaze not because they are outside the structure . . . but because they are so clearly and centrally a part of it" (64).

Jacobs wrote, in her own words, to "arouse the women of the North to a realizing sense of the condition of two millions of women at the South, still in bondage, suffering what I suffered, and most of them far worse" (1). One could argue that Jacobs simply adapted the oppositional discourse of the slave narrative by mixing it with the more conventional and palatable discourse of sentimental fiction in a textual algebra whose end result was to be the arousal of sympathy in the hearts of a million northern, white, female breasts. However, such a reading would not do justice to the complexity of Jacobs's narrative; nor would it comprehend the incredible complexity of the self Jacobs constructed in the text—a self that simultaneously exploited and resisted dominant social constructions of race and gender, a self that was in turns embodied and disembodied, singular and communal, racial and universal, easily identifiable and utterly out of reach. I will argue that, in addition to formulating masterfully realized discourses of the slave narrative and the sentimental novel, Jacobs wove spiritualism into *Incidents in the Life of a Slave Girl* to strike a sympathetic chord with her chosen audience—while at the same time offering a model of agency more fluid than the rigid femininity of the sentimental novel and more subtle than the willful opposition of the slave narrative. This discourse of spiritualism, found at the juncture of disembodied subjectivity and patriarchal structures of power, offered Jacobs the possibility of a radical and elusive agency.

While it is easy to locate Jacobs at the origins of American spiritualism, her views on the topic are a bit more obscure. There are no obvious references to spiritualism in *Incidents* either as an interpretive frame for the events that took place before 1848 or in chapters that chronicle the years after her initial acquaintance with the Posts. There are some good reasons for this: by end of the 1850s, as Jacobs composed her manuscript, spiritualism had begun to decline from the crest of popularity it had enjoyed in the early 1850s. The initial enthusiasm that propelled spiritualism had lessened (though it would continue to be a strong presence in the American cultural landscape through the end of the century), and the combined weight of good-humored ridicule and sober skepticism undermined a good deal of mainstream interest in the movement. If Jacobs were to align herself openly with spiritualism, she would risk alienating much of the mainstream audience at which she aimed. There were more personal reasons as well. Spiritualism complicated the already strained relationship between the many reformers committed to abolition; for people struggling to balance the personal rivalries, racial tensions, alternative strategies, and differing priorities that helped fracture the abolitionist movement in the 1850s, spiritualism could prove one more point of conflict. Jacobs may have found herself caught between friends and supporters like the Posts, who actively endorsed spiritualism, and those who, like Frederick Douglass, remained equivocal.[7]

During the months Jacobs encountered spiritualism in the Post household, she busily educated herself in the antislavery reading room she ran with her brother. The books she encountered there must have shaped her response to the movement. The Jacobs stocked "the latest and best books on slavery and other moral questions," according to advertisements in the *North Star,* whose offices were downstairs in the same building. Titles included "Spooner on the Unconditionality of Slavery," *Slavery Illustrated by Its Effects on Women, The Branded Hand, Archy Moore,* and, clearly set apart, *The Narrative of the Life of Frederick Douglass.* This group of texts that fired Jacobs's imagination and informed every page of *Incidents* served as an alternative interpretive community to the circles who gathered in the Post household to explore the abolitionism, women's rights, and spiritualism. Although we don't know exactly which texts Jacobs admired most, her own autobiography reveals a studied familiarity with abolitionist literature in general and the growing tradition of slave narratives in particular. From earlier slave narratives, Jacobs developed not only the tropes, phrases, and plots that lent her own story such discursive richness, but also a well-developed spiritualist sensibility quite different from the spiritualism taking shape in the Posts' parlor. Former slaves beginning with Olaudah Equiano had structured the stories of their lives around the conversion narrative, seeking to win converts to the abolitionist cause by making the story of their own escapes from bondage indistinguishable from orthodox narratives of the religious experience. Much of the power of Frederick Douglass's 1845 *Narrative,* and indeed of Douglass's public persona, hinged on his self-representation as a respectable, righteous Christian; and two more narratives that would have reached Jacob's reading room during her tenure in 1850, those by Henry Bibb and Sojourner Truth, are likewise self-consciously Christian slave narratives. An orthodox representation of spirituality was a crucial part of a slave narrative's appeal. African Americans trying to reach beyond narrow abolitionist circles to a wider white audience that was, at best, wary of abolitionist radicalism tended to choose a spiritual frame of reference that would be familiar to their readers. Often devout Christians themselves, the authors of slave narratives used Christianity to build common ground with their readers.

Consequently, former slaves tended to downplay the spiritual aspect of their stories that would be most alien to a European-American audience, the uniquely African-American spirituality that shaped slave culture in the antebellum South. When, for example, Equiano describes Igbo religious beliefs, he lapses into an uncharacteristic "they"—a word that affirms his European acculturation by turning an ethnographic gaze on his own homeland (19). Henry Bibb echoes this narrative ploy, noting that "there is much superstition among the slaves. Many of them believe in what they call 'conjuration,' tricking, and witchcraft" (25). Yet black writers did not wholly dismiss such moments, either. Frederick Douglass's equivocal story of the root that helped

give him the strength to resist the slave-breaker, Covey, is perhaps the most famous example of a spiritual discourse understandable to a white audience yet
marked by an African difference. Such a carefully modulated spiritual stance
draws affinities with orthodox Protestant Christianity and more heterodox
movements such as the Rochester Rappings while remaining rooted in the
distinct spiritual sensibilities slaves formed in the New World. This suggests
that Jacobs learned from the community of writers gathered about the shelves
of her reading room a set of spiritual priorities at once similar to and very different from those taking shape at the séance table.

Jacobs's literary consciousness took shape in an abolitionist culture just
beginning to fracture. Douglass had moved to Rochester largely to escape the
often patronizing (and sometimes blatantly racist) treatment he was given by
white abolitionists in Massachusetts (McFeeley 146–50); indeed, his move
reflected the growing schism between white and black opponents of slavery.
The Rochester abolitionist community, though it remained unusually integrated, would itself soon fall to arguing about whether to focus solely on the
plight of the slaves or whether to yoke abolition to a wider array of social reforms. Jacobs straddled both camps, on the one hand struggling to keep the
abolitionist reading room viable in a largely indifferent city while her brother
traveled and lectured for the cause before hostile crowds, and on the other living in a household that embraced, it seemed, every new movement that
sprouted in upstate New York's fertile reformist soil. The lines dividing the
North Star offices and the Post household were anything but sharp, of
course. Even during the brief schism between Douglass and the Posts in the
late 1850s, there remained a core of friendship that kept them united in a way
that Douglass and Garrison were not.[8]

Still, differences between the groups remained. While Douglass welcomed
the struggle for women's rights, abolition unmistakably remained his primary
goal, a goal reinforced by the racial slights he was forced to endure in Rochester and in his travels. The account Douglass published in the *North Star* of
the spiritualist exhibition at Rochester's Corinthian Hall (written not by him
but by "J.D.") is markedly skeptical and remarkably anonymous. The article
mentions neither the Fox sisters nor the Posts by name, a striking omission
given that Amy Post had been advertising an upcoming antislavery meeting in
the paper for weeks. Either Douglass or his reporter was carefully playing
down the connections between abolitionism and spiritualism. The Posts,
confined to the margins of polite Rochester society by their radicalism, were
nevertheless secure in their white privilege, and may have felt freer to give
more of their attention to other concerns. Like other white abolitionists who

experimented with spiritualism, including Horace Greeley, Harriet Beecher Stowe, Lydia Maria Child, and William Lloyd Garrison himself, the Posts had no trouble reconciling their investigations of the spirit world with their efforts for social reform.

As Jacobs immersed herself in the world of reform and the literature that sprang from it, she had immediately before her two very different models of authorship. Douglass tended a newspaper that grew into the most influential African-American voice in print, delivered some of the most stirring anti-slavery orations ever given, and began updating his 1845 *Narrative*. Meanwhile, Isaac Post began compiling transcripts of spirit communications from the likes of Benjamin Franklin, John C. Calhoun, Emmanuel Swedenborg, and George Washington, who offer advice on every reformist agenda of the day. The Founding Fathers appear in Douglass's work as well, but their message is more focused. In "The Heroic Slave" (1853), the spirit of 1776 speaks through the aptly named slave Madison Washington, whose oratory fuels his bid for freedom and convinces all but his most base listeners of his humanity. Douglass was not averse to heightening the spiritualist resonance of his work. In *My Bondage and My Freedom* (1855), he expands the story of the root from a matter-of-fact recital of event to a more contemplative exploration of spiritual truth. "I found Sandy an old advisor. He was not only a religious man, but he professed to believe in a system for which I have no name. He was a genuine African, and had inherited some of the so called magical powers, said to be possessed by African and eastern nations" (280). Douglass's refusal to name Sandy's African-American vernacular religion is striking given the range of terms available to him. Yet naming the spirituality at the heart of his narrative would have forced him to take sides in the increasingly heated debates about spirit communication. Rather than align himself either with or against people like Isaac Post, he equivocates, acknowledging the rich provenance of Sandy's spirituality without clearly endorsing it. While this passage suggests sympathy for unorthodox spirituality, Douglass ultimately portrays it as a distraction from his main antislavery theme: "I now forgot my *roots, and remembered to stand up in my own defense"* (283). For Douglass, spiritualist inquiry and abolitionist zeal couldn't exist on equal terms, and Jacobs, as she began contemplating her own foray into print, had to choose her focus as well.

Jacobs chose not to embrace spiritualism, at least not in the manner of Isaac Post. If she wished to exploit a discourse that held the potential of opening powerful bonds of sympathy among a wide portion of her readership, she would do so guardedly. Her reticence must have been reinforced when, after declaring the reading room a financial bust, she left the Post household and returned to New York City in 1850, two months before the Fox sisters made their trip to P. T. Barnum's hotel in the same city. Jacobs returned to domestic service in the house of Nathaniel Parker Willis, an employer who bore not a few resemblances to the master she had fled, Dr. Norcom. Although Willis was a famous journalist and editor of the popular magazine *The Home Journal,* his chief occupation was social climbing, a goal he pursued in part by assiduously cultivating an aristocratic lifestyle.[9] Anxious to maintain his social ties with the southern gentry and saturated with racial and class privilege, Willis supported slavery at least until the Civil War—one of his biographers noted that even then "he retained a secret sympathy with the South" (Beers 342). In New York Jacobs found conditions distressingly like those she had fled in North Carolina, balancing an unsavory patriarch with a nurturing maternal figure, in this case Cornelia Grinnell Willis, a committed abolitionist who would eventually purchase Jacobs's freedom. Before that day, however, Jacobs had to suffer through the terror of the newly passed Fugitive Slave Law. For over a year, she became a virtual prisoner in Willis's home, hardly daring to venture outside during daylight and constantly aware that she could be snatched at any moment back to the horrors of slavery (Jacobs 190–93).[10]

In such a setting, spiritualism was sure to lose any appeal it might have had for Jacobs, especially since it had been taken up briefly by Willis himself. Whereas spiritualism for the Posts was one more weapon in the struggle for reform, for Willis it was genteel amusement and good copy. His most well-regarded poem, "Unseen Spirits" (1843), was collected with Willis's other poetry in 1850, just as Jacobs returned from Rochester; it used spirits as a Gothic metaphor to heighten the pathos of a Broadway scene. Soon after the arrival of the Fox sisters in New York, Willis wrote a long account of the séance he attended along with a group of other literati. His tone was one of amused indulgence and pseudoscientific speculation, far removed indeed from the earnest credulity of Isaac Post, and certainly not calculated to appeal to people like Jacobs. Willis's article, indeed, marked spiritualism's transformation from radical reform to fashionable entertainment. While Isaac Post consulted the spirits on the most weighty social issues of the day, the Fox sisters used their mediumship to transcribe messages calculated to help them scale New York's social ladder, and Willis gleefully transcribed his invitation to the séance: "'Mrs. Fox and her daughters, having received communication from the Spiritual world, would be happy to see Mr. Willis at Barnum's Hotel, at any hour most convenient to himself.' What a whirl we live in," gushed Willis in reaction, as he noted the arrival of spirits into the already crowded fashionable circles of New York City (Willis 1855, 190). Jacobs's re-action to the whims of New York society was different, though it echoed Willis's prose: "The great city rushed on in its whirl of excitement, taking no note of the 'short and simple annals of the poor.' But while the fashionables were listening to the voice of Jenny Lind in Metropolitan Hall, the thrilling voices of poor hunted colored people went up, in an agony of supplication, to the Lord, from Zion's church" (191). Jacobs here refers to the gathering of a thousand black and white activists organizing against the Fugitive Slave Law, an occasion far more compelling to her than the fads and fancies that oc-cupied what Willis termed "the upper ten thousand."

Jacobs began her own authorial self-fashioning in self-conscious opposi-tion to Willis, choosing to enter print not with an account geared to the whims and prejudices of polite society but with her own story, carefully crafted to in-fluence political opinion in the first tumultuous days of the Fugitive Slave Law. A letter published in the *New York Tribune* in 1853 offered a spare ac-count of her time in slavery; in style and substance, Jacobs's first published writing admonished Willis's entire literary career. The *Tribune's* editor, Ho-race Greeley, had also charted a very different literary course from Willis's. Greeley was well known for his espousal of radical causes including aboli-tion, women's rights, and spiritualism, and Jacobs may have known him from his trip to Rochester in 1850, when he came to invite the Fox sisters to New York City.[11] As she continued to contemplate expanding her brief autobio-graphical letters into a full-fledged book, she had before her other models of antislavery writing that made use of spiritualism. The most prominent was by Willis's one-time teacher, Harriet Beecher Stowe. *Uncle Tom's Cabin* (1852), though hardly a spiritualist text, makes effective use of ghosts (or at least be-lief in them), particularly in Cassie's escape from Simon Legree, which had all the marks of a fraudulent séance. Jacobs admired Stowe enough to ask for her help in drafting her own story, and while Jacobs recoiled from Stowe's callous handling of her request, she nevertheless may have continued to fol-low the famous author's career.

If Jacobs came upon *Dred* (1856) during the years when she secretly penned her own manuscript in her attic room, she would have read Stowe's portrayal the mystical visions of an escaped slave who haunted the swamps near Jacobs's own hometown of Edenton, North Carolina. Stowe's *Dred* was neither an entirely successful representation of a rebellious slave nor an en-tirely successful book, but it did offer an image of African-American spiritu-ality far removed from the respectable orthodoxy writers like Douglass and Bibb used to frame their own sometimes less-than-orthodox religious beliefs.

In *Dred,* Stowe tried to imagine a distinctly African-American Christianity practiced far from white eyes, but the failure of Dred to emerge as anything more than a flat and wooden updating of an Old Testament prophet signaled the difficulties of yoking unorthodox spirituality to abolitionist literature. Stowe sought to make Dred (and his model, Nat Turner) recognizable to her white, middle-class audience by wrapping him in Judaic cadences. Stowe couldn't have represented him within the context of African-American spirituality, partly because she herself had little access to its forms and traditions, and partly because such a tack would have made Dred unrecognizable to her audience. The Judaic spiritualism Stowe used in *Dred* proved clumsy, though useful. If Jacobs were to weave spiritualism (African or European American) into her own story, she would have to proceed carefully. Yet as she drafted her story, the possibilities of spiritualism as a bridge to a broad white audience would prove hard to ignore, for it saturated her literary environment. Like Stowe herself, Jacobs's ultimate editor, Lydia Maria Child (a onetime paramour of Willis's), was an enthusiastic spiritualist (Karcher 403).

Jacobs's measured use of spiritualism is most evident in some of the letters she wrote to Amy Post, which show her absorption of many of the symbols and subjects common in spiritualist discourse. In March 1854, as Jacobs began writing her narrative, she noted: "[J]ust now the poor Book is in its Chrysalis-state and though I can never make it a butterfly I am satisfied to have it creep meekly among some of the humbler bugs" (238). Long a popular figure in Swedenborgian literature, the chrysalis was quickly adopted by spiritualists as a metaphor for a person's translation from an earthly to a spiritual existence.[12] Jacobs, however, carefully keeps the figure grounded, refusing to head off into the further reaches of pseudoscientific reform. After quickly referring to phrenology (as well as to both Rip Van Winkle and *Uncle Tom's Cabin*—Jacobs was clearly steeped in American popular literary culture), the letter ends with ominous musings on the Nebraska Bill, encouragement for Isaac Post in his efforts to organize against it, references to recent issues of the *Liberator,* and plans to win more time for her own work in the service of abolition. The letter is noteworthy for its breadth of reference and for the insight it gives into Jacobs's authorial stew. Phrenology, biblical and American literature, the abolitionist press, and the details of contemporary politics were all on her mind as she crafted her own story, and whether the chrysalis metaphor was explicitly spiritualist or not, Jacobs likely remembered the séances from her Rochester days as she wrote to Post. Jacobs was weaving a complicated work indeed.

Her measured view of spiritualism in this process is more evident in a letter she wrote to Post in 1861:

[T]he trouble is I begin to find out we poor Women has always been too meek,— when I hear a Man call a woman an Angel when she is out of sight—I begin to think about poor Leah of the Bible, not Leah of the spirits [. . .] I told our spirit friend it was better to be born lucky than rich— (*Incidents* 248)

This passage, the only explicit reference to spiritualism in Jacobs's published writing, illustrates her sophisticated handling of spiritualist discourse. "Leah of the spirits" was most likely the medium Leah Fox Underhill (by 1861 she had remarried), eldest of the three Fox sisters and close friend of the Posts, who had moved to New York City at the same time Jacobs had rejoined the Willis household. "Leah of the Bible" was the wife of Jacob, whose vision of angels was commonly cited as an Old Testament precursor to nineteenth-century spiritualist phenomena.[13] As the story unfolds in *Genesis,* Jacob passes by the "blear-eyed" Leah in favor of her younger sister, Rachel; Leah's father, however, sneaks his elder daughter into the bridal chamber on the wedding night. Leah remains Jacob's fruitful but unloved spouse, and the model of the long-suffering wife.

Jacobs's reference to the story in her letter hardly offers a ringing endorsement of spiritual investigation. By giving priority to the biblical rather than the spiritualist Leah, Jacobs gives priority to the lived relations between the sexes in the earthly sphere rather than celestial visions. "Angel" for Jacobs signifies primarily the sentimental ideal epitomized by Coventry Patmore's poetry and Stowe's Little Eva—in other words, the domestic ideology so exhaustively critiqued in *Incidents*. The biblical Leah, like the fictionalized Linda, wrestled with the materiality of sexual politics rather than with the mysteries of angels, and Jacobs has no qualms about holding biblical patriarchs, the cult of domesticity, or spiritualism itself to material standards. Thus, while Jacobs clearly rejects the saintly meekness of the biblical Leah and her nineteenth-century counterparts, her comment suggests that spiritualism had done little to better women's status or even to undercut the power of domesticity. Men, she argues, still use the discourse of angels to reinforce women's passivity. Indeed, by setting the two Leahs in binary opposition, Jacobs seems to argue that spiritualism as a social reform movement had largely failed to advance women's status.

Yet while Jacobs seems skeptical about the social import of spiritualism, her rather cryptic message to "our spirit friend"—"it is better to be born lucky than rich"—suggests that Jacobs was not wholly dismissive of the movement. Though the identity of the spirit friend is not entirely clear (it may have been Leah Fox Underhill or, perhaps, a spirit she had channeled), her message sheds a great deal of light on Jacobs's attitude toward spiritualist mediums and, indeed, her own self-fashioning. Jacobs was certainly in a position to understand the value of luck, but she also knew well that luck was too important to be left to chance ("we poor Women has always been too meek"). The binary structure of the letter aligns "rich" with "meek," suggesting that the cult of domesticity flourished best among women of wealth and status, and suggesting as well that such women are anything but enviable—they are, in Jacobs's word, "poor." "Lucky," on the other hand, signifies not the passive acceptance of good fortune, but the very opposite of meekness, an assertive subjectivity that exploits every opportunity and bends every situation to its advantage. Jacobs offers here not the logocentric, metaphysical, Enlightenment subjectivity claimed, for example, by Douglass and Stanton, but a subjectivity rooted in the margins of dominant nineteenth-century ideology. In place of the meek angel of the house, Jacobs posits not the self-made woman, but a more slippery subjectivity that had a great deal in common with the spiritualist medium: the trickster.[14]

In alluding to the story of Jacob and Leah, Jacobs highlights two biblical episodes where trickery gained God's favor. Indeed, Jacob's angelic vision occurred precisely because he had tricked his father into giving him his blessing, and that blessing in turn led to Jacob's wealth. Leah, too, won God's blessing and her many children as much through her father's nuptial bait-and-switch as through her patient suffering. Jacobs's coy message to her "spirit friend" may have been a knowing (and punning) wink from one trickster to another, a sign that she knew that the angelic postures of both the biblical and spiritualist Leah were not, in fact, entirely meek. The passage is complicated, presenting a nuanced position on women's social status by referencing both biblical and contemporary spiritualism, given from a perspective shaped by Jacobs's own years of enslavement and hard-won freedom. Her position at the end of this passage has a flavor of Dickinsonian inscrutability that allows Jacobs to hold open several discursive possibilities at once.

Although the subtext of spiritualism in *Incidents in the Life of a Slave Girl* is even more guarded than it is in Jacobs's letters to Amy Post, it could not have been missed by readers in the know. For those who were, the obscurity of the spiritualist subtext would function as a shared secret, strengthening the bonds between the knowing audience and the author while at the same time excluding those who lacked such special knowledge. Such a rhetorical strategy offered Jacobs a chance to build solidarity with an audience on lines other than race and gender, while at the same time maintaining the more traditional lines of sympathy inherent in the slave narrative and the sentimental novel. She could have things three ways at once.

The first references to spiritualism are so oblique as to be virtually insubstantial, and would be unconvincing but for Jacobs's immersion in spiritualist circles and the more powerful references later in the text. Their presence begins a faint spiritualist resonance upon which Jacobs will build. In Chapter 2, Aunt Marthy is described as "a very spirited woman," and at the chapter's end we have, after the bitter death of a slave girl in childbirth, the prospect of a spiritual reunion between mother and child (such reunions served as a ubiquitous spiritualist—and slave narrative—trope) (11–13). The neighbor who spots Brent's brother Ben in Baltimore during his second escape is described as "not quite deaf to that mystic clock," and then promptly compares Ben to a ghost (24). In the chapter entitled "Sketches of Neighboring Slaveholders," Jacobs says the benevolent actions of slaveholders are "'Like angels' visits—few and far between.'" Earlier in the same chapter she also refers to ghosts, with characteristic ambiguity: "He might have believed in ghosts," she says of a master who habitually murdered his slaves and, consequently, feared to walk alone at night; a paragraph later she describes the repeated disinterring of his body, an act of cold-blooded treasure seeking (he was rumored to have been buried with his money), with overtones of a gruesome supernatural ritual (47).

Jacobs draws on a wide variety of supernatural tropes—Christian spirituality, Gothic horror, enlightenment mysticism, and folk wisdom and ritual—and as a result, her tropes figure across generic boundaries. Angels and ghosts and mystic clocks are not squeezed into a single spiritualist framework, but gain resonance instead through their interconnections. Such scattered yet linked language enables Jacobs to maintain her appeal to a number of different audiences at once without tipping her narrative hand—a classic strategy of a writer working at the margins of a number of competing strands of discourse. While Jacobs won't be tied to a spiritualist ideology even as loosely constructed as that forged in Rochester in 1848, spiritualism of a broader stripe manifests itself throughout her text.

These subtle references to spiritualism culminate in the most spectacular section of *Incidents,* the moment that stands as the dark center of Jacobs's

text and the curious pivot of Linda Brent's journey to freedom. That section
is the seven-year period Brent hides in the crawl space above her grandmother's storage shed, a few hundred yards away from the master she is flee-
ing. The "loophole of retreat" has been read, variously, as the "dark night of
the soul" that structures both the conversion narrative and the slave narrative;
as the metaphoric death that follows the traditional seduction narrative; as the
literalization of the abject status of the black woman in American society; as
the (dis)embodiment of the self-less mother in the cult of domesticity; as the
figurative return of Brent to the "womb" of her grandmother; and as a strategy of Foucaultian resistance.[15] Rather than choose among these various
interpretive models, I'll add a reading of my own. A significant portion of
Jacobs's audience would recognize Brent's years in the loophole as analogous
to the status of a recently departed spirit, disembodied and invisible, yet
ceaselessly watching over her loved ones, able (with the aid of a sympathetic
medium) to speak from beyond the grave, and able to use her spiritual insight
to shape the course of earthly events. Such a reading of the loophole cannot,
of course, be authoritative, any more than it can render the brief catalog of
readings listed above untrue. It can, however, add to the richness of Jacobs's
text and offer some valuable insight into how this text might have functioned
in its initial context.

The loophole episode begins, significantly, with Brent's initiating her own
contact with spirits beyond the grave. Before making her final decision to flee
from Dr. Flint, she visits the cemetery where her mother lies buried, for "in
many an hour of tribulation I had seemed to hear her voice, sometimes chid-
ing me, sometimes whispering loving words into my wounded heart" (90).
She kneels by her parents' graves in "the death-like stillness," her "spirit over-
awed by the solemnity of the scene." Then,

As I passed the wreck of the old meeting house, where, before Nat Turner's time, the
slaves had been allowed to meet for worship, I seemed to hear my father's voice come
from it, bidding me not to tarry till I reached freedom or the grave. I rushed out with
renovated hopes. My trust in God had been strengthened by that prayer among the
graves. (91)

In this moment of prosopopoeia, powerfully resonant with the voice from beyond the grave speaking through the Fox family's gatherings in Hydesville or
through Isaac Post's eager pen, Brent gains the spiritual advice she seeks. The
sacred solemnity of the location, the seeking of reassurance and guidance
from the dead, the Christian context of the communication, and even the age

and gender of the medium (the teenaged Linda), are all characteristic of spiritualist practice, and easily recognizable as such to a readership that had been
anxiously exploring such communications for the better part of a decade—
only the word "seemed" insulates her from an explicit claim of spirit contact.
Brent's visit to the graveyard revises the sexually and racially embodying gaze
of Dr. Flint in a manner that would have been recognizable, too, to the young
white female mediums plying their trade across the country. The spiritual
communication restores an essential, metaphysical selfhood to Brent that
gives her a masculine agency in resisting Dr. Flint—her father's voice stiffens
her will. This agency is carefully (if barely) masked by her mother's domestic
consolations and the communal identity signified (and critiqued) by the ru-
ined church.

Emboldened, Brent goes into hiding, first in a friend's house, and then in
an attic at the home of one of her grandmother's friends. Once there, she virtually disappears; Dr. Flint, believing she has fled for good, agrees to sell her
children to Mr. Sands, who, unbeknownst to Dr. Flint, is Brent's lover and the
children's father. The day the sale is completed, Jacobs relates a second, even
more explicit, spiritualist episode:

And now I will tell you something that happened to me; though you will, perhaps,
think it illustrates the superstition of slaves. I sat in my usual place on the floor near
the window, where I could hear much of that was said in the street without being
seen. The family had retired for the night, and all was still. I sat there thinking of my
children, when I heard a low strain of music. A band of serenaders were under the
window, playing "Home, sweet home." I listened till the sounds did not seem like
music, but like the moaning of children. It seemed as if my heart would burst. I rose
from my sitting posture, and knelt. A streak of moonlight was on the floor before me,
and in the midst of it appeared the forms of my two children. They vanished; but I
had seen them distinctly. Some will call it a dream, others a vision. (107–8)

Spectral music was a common feature in spiritualist gatherings, and in Brent's
yearning for a sign from her lost children, many of Jacobs's readers would
doubtless recognize their own desires at the séance table. Jacobs makes recognizable a spiritual phenomenon that might have distanced her from her
white readers ("*you* will think it illustrates the superstition of slaves") by
cloaking it in the trappings of domesticity and spiritualism. By the end of the
passage, what might have been read as a slave's superstition is something
"[s]ome will call a dream, others a vision," but none will dismiss. Jacobs has
established a common spiritualist ground.

Moreover, the sudden transformation of the strains of music into the moans of her children figures her own transformation into a disembodied, invisible, seeing presence of the spirit world. Like the mediums familiar to readers across the country, Jacobs asserts her independence by emptying out her subjectivity, gaining power by surrendering her will. From this point until her flight to New York, Brent will hover at the margins of her North Carolina town, casting a spectral eye over the doings of her enemies and her loved ones; a presence often felt if rarely seen, though able, in a limited way, to use the knowledge she gains from her vantage point to intercede in the affairs of the living. She becomes, in a manner so literal as to be radically unnerving, the angel of her grandmother's house.

If Brent doesn't quite speak from beyond the grave, she certainly comes close, for the garret in which she subsequently hides quickly becomes her figurative tomb. Inside this "hole," "the air was stifling; the darkness total" (114). It is full of vermin who run at will over her body, and daylight offers no relief—only the sound of her children, dimly heard, provides comfort. Soon Brent's anxiety melts into the timelessness of long confinement, a gravelike eternity: "Sometimes it appeared to me as if ages had rolled away since I entered that gloomy, monotonous existence" (148). Yet like the restless spirits so determined to be heard at séances across the country, Brent soon manages to make use of her invisible vantage point. The small hole she makes in the wall of her garret (by boring three rows of three holes) grants her the power of surveillance, of functioning as the disembodied gaze over both Dr. Flint and her children. As the angel of the house, she shares an angel's limited powers—she can thwart the wicked intentions of Dr. Flint by orchestrating "sightings" of herself in distant cities, and she can influence the sympathetic (if spotted) heart of Mr. Sands by whispering, angel-like, moral imperatives into his ear. Most powerfully, she can appear herself as if by magic in the arms of her children the night before they are taken away, offering the very same spiritual comfort Brent had gained from her own vanished mother. If Aunt Nancy, lying on her deathbed and remembering her two children who died in infancy, can look forward only to the chance to "meet their little spirits in heaven" (144), Brent can enact the longing so many of her readers (black and white) shared—she can return from her own "death" to nestle in the arms of her babes.

Brent embodies the same longing for mother-child reunion that drove so many women to the séance table. Indeed, the operative metaphor in the loophole section of *Incidents is* the séance. Centered squarely in the home, dependent upon the close cooperation of participants of mixed gender, and self-consciously passive and "feminine" in character, the séance in mid-century

America mimicked domestic ideology while at the same time contesting the authority of patriarchal institutions like the church and the university in spiritual and philosophical matters. In the words of one spiritualist, "Not in the church, not in the capitol, but in the family, came the first demonstrable recognition of immortal life and immortal love—the holiest truth to the holiest place" (Braude 24). Brent's family, from her youngest child to her uncannily sensitive son to her grandmother to the uncles and friends who keep her secret, cooperate faultlessly in their efforts to tend the willful spirit locked away in their own house, contesting at every turn in this domestic rebellion the patriarchal powers of "the peculiar institution."

Yet for all the care with which Jacobs builds resonances between her narrative of slavery and escape and the spiritualist movement, she is careful, too, to keep the analogy a tentative one: by writing into it irreducible marks of difference, Jacobs prevents her narrative from collapsing into a mere allegory of a movement that was overwhelmingly northern and white. For example, drawing on the multiple traditions of the picaresque adventure, the slave narrative, the sentimental novel, the Gothic tale, and others, her narrative couldn't possibly be tied into any one discursive tradition. Her text inhabits the margins of too many literatures to be fixed within the bounds of a single one. In addition, for all the moments when Jacobs constructs a disembodied selfhood in the garret of her grandmother's house, there are other moments where she points to her self in the garret as distinctly *em*bodied. The crippling disorders that plague Brent during her years in hiding, and indeed throughout the remainder of her life, physically testify to her efforts to thwart the sexual predation of Dr. Flint by turning herself into pure will. In resisting, she loses the "masculine" physical potency that was such a determining part of the identity of such former slaves as Sojourner Truth and Frederick Douglass, actually becoming the frail female body in her effort to refuse being constructed as such. During Brent's second winter especially, the sheer physicality of her identity threatens to overwhelm her:

My limbs were benumbed by inaction, and the cold filled them with cramp. I had a very painful sensation of coldness in my head; even my face and tongue stiffened, and I lost the power of speech. . . . [My brother] afterwards told me he thought I was dying, for I had been in an unconscious state sixteen hours. I next became delirious, and was in great danger of betraying myself and my friends. To prevent this, they stupefied me with drugs. I remained in bed six weeks, weary in body and sick at heart. (122)

Such description of physical torture overwhelms any simple identification of her status with that of a disembodied spirit; it underscores instead the figurality of Jacobs's metaphor. In those dark six weeks she problematizes the possibilities of disembodiment by coming close to literal disembodiment. Brent (and Jacobs) operate instead at the very margins between the models of physical and spiritual self, wavering constantly between the will and the body that it inhabits, drawing on the strengths and weaknesses of both. In this respect, she is closer to the mediums who operated at the borderland between spirit and body than she is to the spirits themselves, using her doubled identity to layer her voice.

Indeed, a useful term for Jacobs's (mis)use of the discourse of spiritualism would be Henry Louis Gates Jr.'s "signifyin(g)," a term he defines in *The Signifying Monkey* as "the slave's trope" (52): "Signifyin(g), in Lacan's sense, is the Other of discourse; but it also constitutes the black Other's discourse as its rhetoric." For Gates, the black Other is not so much independent from white "master" discourse as it is interimplicated with it in a "symbiotic . . . vertiginous relationship" (50). Drawing on Frederick Douglass's description of the doubled meaning of the slave songs, sung with quite distinct significance for a black and white audience, Gates argues that "the language of blackness encodes and names its sense of independence through a rhetorical process that we might think of as the Signifyin(g) black difference" (66). "Signifyin(g)" is for Gates the very figure of the doubled discourse of African-American speech; in the context of the slave narrative especially, it is a rhetorical device by which African-American writers were able to master the dominant discourses of their literary milieu while at the same time maintaining their difference from that community by reifying the boundaries of a shared African-American cultural practice. Jacobs's signifyin(g) in her narrative thus places her within the dominant discourse of spiritualism and at the same time cements her allegiance to an African-American discursive community that operated within and against spiritualist discourse.

The Other that Jacobs weaves into her spiritualist discourse is a distinctly African heritage that reaches back across the Middle Passage, a non-European spiritualist tradition that contributed both a unique vocabulary and a non-Christian context for her narrative. Since slaves weren't actively converted to Christianity in America until the late eighteenth century, traditional African religious beliefs and practices managed to survive in the plantation system more intact than many other cultural practices. Though slaves were taken from a great many West African societies with very divergent spiritual beliefs during the two hundred years of the active slave trade, Sandra Greene has shown that there was a robust exchange of religious beliefs and practices between West African cultures in this era, particularly in divination rites. Differences between African cultures tended to blur during the trauma of the Middle Passage, and slaves were most likely to build communities in the New World out of the broader beliefs and customs that members of different tribes and cultures had in common. Vodou, hoodoo, Santería, and umbanga are just some of the syncretic religions that emerged in the crucible of the New World. These African-American vernacular religions included a variety of such elements as herbal healing, magic charms, and secret signs, that weren't necessarily spiritualist. At the same time, like most West African religions, they shared a belief in a spiritual world intimately connected with the material one, in which lesser gods, nature spirits, and ancestors watched over, rewarded, or punished people in due course, depending on the fidelity or negligence of their devotees.

Alice Eley Jones argues that in America "West African spiritualism thrived because wherever the African went, the spirits accompanied him" (94). Spirits could be contacted through a variety of means of divination or through highly stylized rituals of spirit possession (Raboteau 7–11). Margaret Washington Creel, writing about Gullah culture as a paradigm for African cultural survival in American slave communities, states that "spiritual concerns could not be set apart from secular or communal ones. . . . Ancestral patriarchs, matriarchs, diviners, the living dead, and other spirits were daily guardians of human behavior" (72). Spirits were an integral part of African and African-American religion, as Lawrence Levine notes:

Ghosts were conceived of in the African tradition as spirits at a certain stage of their being. That is, they were natural phenomena and by no means invariably a source of fear. The ghosts of loved ones frequently returned to render aid and protection, give counsel, and even occasionally point the way to hidden treasure. (79)

Sacred folk beliefs existed quite comfortably alongside Christianity in the black community; many former slaves who condemned hoodoo still believed firmly in charms, signs, and ghosts.

While spiritualism in white popular culture provided a means of subverting dominant ideology from the fringe, spiritualism in black culture provided a means of unifying a dispersed population and resisting white domination. Conjure played an important part in a great many slave rebellions—from an insurrection in New York in 1712 where slaves sucked each other's blood to bind themselves to secrecy and used a powder that conferred invisibility, to the use of crab claws as charms against wounding in Denmark Vesey's conspiracy of 1822, to the prophetic visions that inspired Nat Turner's rebellion in 1831 (Levine 75–77). In one North Carolina plantation dating from the early nineteenth century, archeologists have found divining rods, ritual walking sticks, cowrie shells, and other traditional African artefacts hidden around the plantations buildings, testifying to a robust and covert African-American religion that helped unite slaves and resist white dominance (Jones). Jacobs had powerful literary antecedents for her spiritualist signifyin(g), as well, in the many slave narratives that touch on African-American vernacular religion. Though all are mindful of their white, Christian audience, most signify an African difference. Jacobs engages the same rhetorical strategy, carefully downplaying the rebellious tradition of African-American spiritualism in presenting her narrative to a mainstream audience. While recognizable to a white audience familiar with the Rochester Rappings and the séance, Jacobs's spiritualism for black readers remains firmly embedded in the fundamentally different heritage of an African-American past. This narrative strategy allowed Jacobs's white readers to identify with her experience, without their appropriating it as simply another addition to the familiar discourse of spiritualism.

It is thus possible to read against the spiritualist subtext of the loophole section of *Incidents* yet another subtext of African-American folk belief. The graveyard scene, for example, signifies quite differently in this context. Burial practices have long been a locus of West African cultural survivals, and Jacobs may have remembered Olaudah Equiano's description of visits to a graveyard with his mother in Africa: "When she went to make these oblations at her mother's tomb, which was a kind of small solitary thatched house, I sometimes attended her. There she made her libations, and spent most of the night in cries and lamentations" (41). Jacobs further signals a subtext of difference and resistance by quietly setting the scene near "the wreck of the old meeting house, where, before Nat Turner's time, the slaves had been allowed to meet for worship" (91). Here Jacobs marks her spirit communion with her parents with the most powerful signifier of slavery and resistance available in mid-century America—Nat Turner. The episode, in addition to establishing a European-American spiritualist resonance, preserves an African cast. Writing about West African and Gullah attitudes toward death, Creel notes that "death was not the end of life nor the cemetery a final resting place; it was a door (*mwelo*) between two worlds" (82). The graveyard episode in *Incidents,* where Brent seeks and finds wisdom from her dead parents, shows that this sensibility survived the Middle Passage. Moreover, Creel's door is an apt figure for Jacobs's own situation as a writer, poised between two audiences, two cultures, and two distinct, though analogous, visions of the spirit world.

Other elements in *Incidents* reveal how thoroughly Jacobs was rooted in African culture. Creel notes that a loosely organized group of tribes in an area of West Africa that provided a large portion of America's slaves shared initiation rites and secret societies. Called Poro (for men) and Sande (for women), these societies served as powerful forces for social cohesion even across the Atlantic:

Nearly all Africans brought to America came from groups that practiced some type of initiation process. While none contained the distinctive structurally inclusive elements of Poro and Sande, one can still argue for the tenacity of the practice. The bush experience was a shared memory instilling loyalty, bonds of attachments, and unity that neither Christianity nor Islam could destroy, even today. (78)

Creel then describes an initiation ceremony and philosophy that share some startling resemblances to Jacobs's account of her escape. The ceremony impressed upon the initiate his or her duty to the community:

To this end the youths underwent a *travel*, a series of terrifying dreams in which they were symbolically eaten by the Poro or Sande spirit—the devil—and were then reborn by the same spiritual force. Once rebirth in the bush occurred, each individual was bound to the society and vowed to uphold the secrecy of the initiation and abide by Poro-Sande authority. (77)

Initiated, a person was more fully able to appreciate the mystical nature of the world:

Poro-Sande spiritual significance was pervasive. Spirits dwelled in the sacred grove; among them were ancestral spirits, bush and water spirits, spirits of associations, and Poro-Sande spirits, all with particular functions. Ancestral spirits, for example, explained life after death, were concerned with the family and the larger group's well-being, and were protectors. Poro-Sande spirits, of whom the "bush devil" was the most important, were worldly representations of supernatural forces, personifying the will of God and mysteries of life. While other spirits in the pantheon were of the unseen world, Poro-Sande spirits represented the supernatural sphere and earthly manifestations of supernatural power. . . . One aim [of the societies] was spirit control . . . [enabling] society's religious leaders to contact the spirit world and interpret it to the people. (78)

Jacobs's description of Brent's flight from Dr. Flint bears striking similarities to these initiation rites. While in her first hiding place, Brent is forced to flee into a nearby "thicket of bushes" when her pursuers come to the house; there she is bitten by "a reptile of some kind," and can only be cured through re-course to a conjure woman's remedy.

While the episode might simply be a suspense-filled event that helps ex-plain the extraordinary fear of snakes that pervades the narrative, it may also contain a memory of the snake-god cult that flourished in the African king-dom of Dahomey in the eighteenth century and arrived relatively intact in New Orleans at the beginning of the nineteenth century as vodou (Raboteau 75–76). The scene's African resonance is underscored by a second journey ("travel"?) into a snake-infested bush. Snakes were important symbols in West African religions, signs of fertility and potent of omens of good or evil fortune. Particularly central in vodou, they retained an important status throughout African-American culture (Blassingame 41). In Whydah, a prin-cipal slave-trading port, one of the last things slaves would have seen was the celebrated snake temple, where priests tended sacred pythons and mediums went into trances to contact the spirits (Segal 429).[16]

Brent's circuitous move from her second hiding place to her final one in her grandmother's garret via a walk through town (in drag), a short boat ride, and a night in Snaky Swamp, is one of the more curious moments in the narrative. Yet the excursion carries a tremendous psychic charge, both as the emotional nadir of Brent's long journey to freedom and as a surrealistic passage full of supernatural resonance. Once hidden in the swamp, Brent, under the guidance of her Aunt Nancy's husband, faces her worst fears:

As the light increased, I saw snake after snake crawling round us. I had been accus-tomed to the sight of snakes all my life, but these were larger than any I had ever seen. To this day I shudder when I remember that morning. As evening approached, the number of snakes increased so much that we were continually obliged to thrash them with sticks to keep them from crawling over us. The bamboos were so high and so thick that it was impossible to see beyond a very short distance. . . . But even those large, venomous snakes were less dreadful to my imagination than the white men in that community called civilized. (112–13)

Devoured by mosquitoes and confronted by a devilish gathering of reptiles, Brent survives this dark night of the soul with her will intact, even affirmed. It is impossible to know the exact nature of whatever African beliefs survived in Edenton, North Carolina, circa 1835, but similarities between Jacobs's retelling of the episode and the general outlines of the Sande travel—the journey to the bush, the horrible dreams, the symbolic devouring by the "bush devil"—are more than striking. Snakes not only threaten Brent's life;

they symbolize as well the horrors of the slavery from which she flees. The "white men called civilized" are as terrible for her as the bush devils that remained a potent African memory. Perhaps most important, the episode functions as a version of an initiation, one that Jacobs's spiritualist friends might have described as the transformation of a "chrysalis." The episode also bears uncanny similarities to a vodou initiation ceremony, where snakes were used to bless sacred garments and the initiate would fall into a trance for days, during which he or she would journey to the spirit world (Jones 102–3). While Jacobs makes no claims to being a vodou priestess, once through this terrifying ritual she becomes more firmly cemented than ever into her secret community—one that functions powerfully and cohesively while remaining invisible to the wider society around it.

The Snaky Swamp episode has literary as well as religious referents: Anne Bradford Warner argues that Jacobs's representation of her nightmarish visit to the swamp counters Stowe's romanticized image of Dred's maroon hideaway in the Great Dismal Swamp, where grape arbors swaddle a secure and bucolic settlement. Warner reads the swamp as part of Jacobs's larger struggle to wrest control over the literary representation of African-American slavery away from northern, white writers. Jacobs's swamp thus aligns with the horrific wasteland portrayed by Henry Bibb in his 1850 slave narrative. After escaping, Bibb's family (Bibb, his wife, and his small daughter) makes its way to the Red River swamp "among the buzzing insects and wild beasts of the forest. We wandered about in the wilderness for eight or ten days before we were apprehended, striving to make our way from slavery; but it was all in vain" (123). While Jacobs and Bibb may, as Warner argues, be countering a popular conception that blacks were particularly at home in swamps and forests, their strategies are equally remarkable for their difference. Jacobs's marshy sojourn is drenched in an African resonance that would have remained opaque to her white readers, while Bibb's is overlaid upon Judeo-Christian mythology consonant with Stowe's portrayal of Dred. Bibb's efforts to cast himself as a failed Moses would have been easily recognized by both black and white readers. Jacobs's representation of Snaky Swamp, shrouded in African spiritualist difference, remains irreducible to European-American norms.

Jacobs's years spent hiding in her grandmother's attic were both the most remarkable and the most incomprehensible part of her story; the Willis family met it with wonder, while a number of other readers found it simply implausible (Beers 285; Yellin 1987). While spiritualists, as I have argued above, would have seen the loophole as analogous to the spirit world, Jacobs also resisted such an analogy by stressing her materiality, by unflinchingly re-counting the details of her bodily suffering during her years in hiding. Such a representational tack might have been quite familiar to readers versed in Af-rican spiritualism. Brent, carefully watching over her children, fits readily into the category of ancestor spirit. "The ancestors are watchful guardians," notes Raboteau (13). Or consider the statement of Equiano, who describes the Igbo beliefs he remembered from childhood: "Those spirits which were not transmigrated, such as their dear friends and relations, they believe always attend them, and guard them from bad spirits or their foes" (41). Relatives offer oblations at the graves of their loved ones primarily to relieve their su-ffering in the afterlife; so Brent's family tends to her needs while she watches over her children, anxiously crafting strategies to protect them from the power of Dr. Flint. My point is that Jacobs's narrative, and the loophole section especially, is a spiritualist text only if "spiritualism" is read cross-culturally. *Incidents* belongs partly to the world the Fox sisters and Isaac and Amy Post discovered or created in the parlors and exhibition halls of white, middle-class America, and it belongs partly to the world the displaced Africans reconstructed in the slave quarters of the South. Jacobs's spiritual-ism is resonant with the Rochester Rappings, but not consonant with them; it instead seeks to mediate between two rich spiritualist traditions. Both Afri-can and European spirits speak through Jacobs's pen.

This culturally doubled spiritualism is best exemplified, perhaps, in a sec-tion of *Incidents* that has nothing to do with spirits—the puzzling chapter that follows Brent's retreat to her loophole. At the onset of the most remark-able period of her life, Jacobs opts to describe the African-American Christ-mas tradition of Johnkannaus. It is a valuable piece of autoethnography in its own right, a rare description of a cultural practice that spanned the Atlantic, with roots in West Africa and versions performed in the West Indies, New Or-leans, and the Carolinas (277–78). The description is another example of sig-nifyin(g), this time on the significance of Christmas festivities. The chapter establishes Jacobs's commonality with any reader, white or black, who re-membered with nostalgia the holiday customs of her childhood; the chapter, indeed, is an early example of a local color aesthetic that sought to build a shared national identity across lines of regional and, at times, racial differ-ence. But the chapter also underscores Jacobs's strong allegiance to African-American culture. While Frederick Douglass scorned African-American holiday rituals as a powerful check on slave resistance, Jacobs asserts both the universality of African-American folk practice ("Every child rises early on Christmas morning to see the Johnkannaus. Without them Christmas would be shorn of its greatest attraction") (118) and the importance of loyalty within the African-American community (she is warned that day to be quiet due to the presence of "a free colored man, who tried to pass himself off for white, and who was always ready to do any mean work for the sake of currying favor with white people") (118–19). Superfluous in terms of narrative momentum, the chapter ("Christmas Festivities") testifies to Jacobs's own loyalties, and serves as further evidence that no matter how skillfully she exploited the discourses of white society, her work remained firmly rooted in the richness and strength of her own community.[17] As with Christmas, so with spirits. *Incidents* powerfully marshals the discourse of European-American spiritualism, for it offered a means of reaching an audience that was widespread, sympathetic, and politically engaged, but it draws equal strength from the African-American spiritualism that shaped and sustained Jacobs's long journey to freedom.

Chapter 2

Public Spirits

Spiritualism in American Periodicals, 1848–1861

Like any cultural phenomenon that rises from obscurity to nationwide prominence in a few years, the brand of spiritualism that swept America in the middle of the nineteenth century built its appeal by synthesizing a great many strands of long-established discourses. As it grew from a local curiosity centering on odd noises in a New York farmhouse to a movement that numbered its practitioners in the thousands and its believers in the millions, spiritualism began to signify in contexts far removed from the folk sensibilities and revivalist traditions that nurtured the Fox sisters. This occurred primarily because of the medium by which spiritualism spread: the growing flood of newspapers, magazines, and books that served, by the 1850s, an increasingly national market.[1] Because of that burgeoning print culture, spiritualism became available to many groups who adapted it to their own ends.

Tracing the transformation of the Rochester Rappings into spiritualism helps map the discursive world of America at midcentury. Spiritualism gained adherents across the social spectrum in every state and territory of the country. It thrived on the crossing of boundaries—of region, class, gender, race, religion, public and private, life and death. By attending to its modulations as it crossed these borders, we can begin to retrace how American identities in this era were constructed—and how they changed. Further, spiritualism can shed light on the interaction of the centripetal and centrifugal forces that played out in American print culture in the early 1850s. How powerful a social glue was spiritualism? How did its appropriation by groups on the fringes of American society intersect with the many mainstream elements of popular culture with which spiritualism became allied? How did groups forced to the margins—especially Native American tribes struggling for political and cultural survival and African Americans struggling for freedom—

manipulate spiritualism in order to claim a public voice? And finally, how does the tangled trajectory of spiritualism in antebellum print illustrate the unraveling of a unified public sphere in the years leading to the Civil War?

I will begin by turning to one of the most powerfully unifying forces in American print culture at midcentury, the national literary magazines. In a period dominated by partisan papers, an increasingly lurid penny press, and a proliferation of printed organs for narrowly defined interest groups, magazines like *Putnam's*, the *Knickerbocker*, the *North American Review*, *Graham's*, and *Harper's* self-consciously strove to reach a national audience. Editors addressed the readership of these magazines as a nonpartisan, rational, and genteel American public that harked back to the disembodied public spirits who filled the papers of the eighteenth century above pseudonyms like "Cato" and "Publius." The national literary magazines, indeed, were in many ways the last American refuge of the republican ideal of the public sphere as theorized by Jürgen Habermas. Destroyed as a political ideal by the emergence of democratic factionalism in the early nineteenth century, an ideology of a unified national high culture operating above partisan interest nevertheless remained the dominant discourse of the American press.

Interestingly, this republican rhetoric proved a crucial tool in the efforts of marginalized groups to gain access to an antebellum public sphere that had long been predicated on the exclusion of its nonwhite, non-Protestant others. In a small but significant number of newspapers and magazines, African-American and Indian editors mimicked the republican ideal in order to legitimate their cultural perspective in European-American society—and to complicate mainstream print culture. By exploring how the spiritualist movement, with is marginal origins, radical sympathies, and broad social appeal, played in the national imaginary constructed by periodical print culture, we can begin to respond to Thomas Bender's call for a history organized around the struggle of various groups to define a unified "public culture" (126). The intersection of the literary magazine and spiritualism offers an opportunity to assess the effectiveness of periodicals in shaping a national consensus—and to assess the possibilities and limits of national consensus itself.

Periodicals and the Public Sphere

The explosion of print in antebellum America at once expanded the power of the press and changed forever the means by which the public sphere was defined, thus transforming the machinery of national consensus as well. Print had long acted as one means of binding together a far-flung and diverse group of European settlers. By the 1850s, as spiritualism began to spread, periodicals extended the reach of print to unprecedented breadth. While only a handful of books sold more than a hundred thousand copies before the Civil War, a number of periodicals reached that many readers with every issue. In an era of informal literary societies and widely shared copies, periodicals alone claimed a truly national audience.[2]

Yet more important than raw numbers was the imagined audience for the magazines I will consider. While most of these magazines were published in New York, all were explicitly national in focus, even those most associated with specific regions or interest groups. Each projected itself as an arbiter of public culture, as a voice for a disinterested public sensibility best suited to shepherding the national interest. In an era in which the political process was increasingly seen as incapable of holding the country together, reform movements confined themselves to northern strongholds, religious institutions settled into discrete contours of class and region, and politically charged literature was faced with a blockade at the Mason-Dixon line, national periodicals remained one of the few cultural institutions that struggled to maintain an "American" voice. For a short period before the Civil War, American periodicals occupied a pivotal place in the national imaginary, acting as a de facto public sphere that helped pull the country together at a time when other forces were pulling it apart.

The public sphere as formulated by Habermas describes the emergence in eighteenth-century Europe of bourgeois civil society firmly based in the medium of "public opinion" as established by a new periodical press. Journals quickly established a rational, anonymous, and disembodied voice in contrast to the embodied, deeply personal public voice of a pre-print political paradigm (1-26). In the United States, the editors and writers of magazines like *Harper's, Graham's,* and *Putnam's,* carefully preserving the standards of rational-critical debate established a century earlier, were striking in their invisibility, operating from what Michael Warner calls the "principle of negativity." "It is a ground rule of argument in a public discourse that it defines its norms as abstract and universal, but it is also a political resource available only in this discourse, and available only to those participants whose social role allows such self-abnegation (that is, to those persons defined by whiteness, maleness and capital). . . . Virtue comes to be defined by the negation of other traits of personhood, in particular as rational and disinterested concern for the public good" (42). Tracing the development of the public sphere in the emerging magazine print culture of the early republic, Carroll

Smith-Rosenberg illustrates how these new periodicals interpellated a national subject, a *homo Americanus* who was white, male, and middle class, against a growing list of "negative others" that included (though was not limited to) white women, Native Americans, and African Americans (841–55).

Habermas was not particularly interested in the cross-cultural dimensions of the public sphere.[3] Yet as groups marginalized by the dominant culture gained increasing access to print, print culture began to take on a more heterogeneous texture. Print served as an engine of unity and difference. Nancy Fraser notes that from the beginnings of the public sphere marginal social groups formed "subaltern counterpublics" that preserved their distinct sensibilities even as they entered a broader social discourse (110). Such counterpublics were, for Mary Ryan, always present in the American public sphere, whose origins she finds amidst the populist factionalism of the Jacksonian era. Ryan notes that various marginalized groups fought their way into the public sphere by locating "proliferating points of access to political discussion where established authority could be challenged" (283–84). Such points included public rallies, social reform work, and, most notably, print. Publication, as the word itself implies, was a vital avenue to participation in the public sphere. The anxieties and contradictions that Smith-Rosenberg reads in what was at the turn of the century still a relatively confined and elite print culture could only be intensified with the explosion of publishing that accompanied the industrialization of printing at midcentury. If the editors and writers of the national literary magazines were the self-appointed guardians of the public sphere, they ruled, in the wake of Jacksonian politics and the emergence of a burgeoning press, over a shrinking realm, and they ruled jealously.

Such jealousy in regards to spiritualism was not unfounded. People attending séances most frequently sought to communicate with deceased family members, but serious spiritualists frequently invoked the spirits of eminent public figures to marshal authority for their work. The strategy drew a great deal of merry satire from spiritualism's critics, but the humor typically had an anxious edge. The attempt to draw on the authority of former philosophers and political heroes had the effect of both enlarging the public sphere and deconstructing it. The role of public sphere as a mechanism for the disembodied, disinterested surveillance of society was certainly reinforced by invoking the ranks of a literally disembodied corps of spirits, yet such a move also turned discourse in the public sphere away from an authorized and elitist interpretation of phenomena. Equally threatening to the smooth functioning of a public sphere were the complications mediumship posed to traditional attitudes of subjectivity. Subjects interpellated by the public sphere were invariably disembodied and privileged, produced against a series of embodied and underprivileged others. When adolescent women (or, for that matter, supreme court judges) began speaking with the voices of long-dead philosophers and statesmen, the stable binaries of republican subjectivity begin to collapse. Thus as spiritualism entered the realm of print culture, it came under the surveillance of this increasingly anxious public gaze.

While a few elite eighteenth-century literary quarterlies survived into the 1850s, their regional distribution and small circulations undercut their national influence. Among the most notable was the *North American Review*, a quarterly published in Boston and long settled in a close orbit around Harvard, and the *Knickerbocker*, published in New York to serve as the intellectual organ of a deeply rooted regional elite. Other periodicals, however, flourished in the transformed publishing industry and transformed, in turn, the nature of the public sphere. *Godey's Lady's Book*, founded in the 1830s in self-conscious opposition to the elitist, erudite, analytical, and masculinist magazines that long characterized the American periodical scene, tailored its moralistic and sentimental contents to a growing female readership. Its phenomenal success inspired the periodicals that rose to national prominence in the 1850s. *Harper's Magazine* began publishing in New York, aiming to capture the broad middle-class reading public by studiously avoiding the controversial political and social issues of midcentury, serving instead a steady diet of sentimental and moralistic fiction and nonfiction. *Putnam's Monthly* and the *Atlantic Monthly*, based in New York and Boston, respectively, shared a more erudite and socially critical editorial stance, and hence counted their readers in the tens of thousands rather than the hundreds of thousands that *Harper's* enjoyed.[4] These three periodicals, despite their slightly different emphases, helped sustain the ideals of the earlier republican public sphere while extending its reach to a far broader population.

They were joined in print by thousands of other periodicals whose circulation was more limited, but whose claims for national representativeness were no less insistent. Such periodicals as *DeBow's* and the *Southern Literary Messenger*, both closely associated with an ossifying southern regional identity, nevertheless insisted on their claims for a representative American voice in contradistinction to the emerging metropolitan sensibilities of the periodicals published in the Northeast. While no Native American literary magazines were founded in the mid-nineteenth century, a number of newspapers were; of these, the *Cherokee Advocate* was the most notable effort to lay claim to an Indian nationhood by marshaling all the apparatus of European-

American print culture. By the 1850s, the *Cherokee Advocate* had been long established in the Cherokee reservation in what would become Oklahoma— resuming publication was, indeed, one of the first priorities of the tribal government after the forced removal of the Cherokees in 1839. By the 1850s, the newspaper had become the best written and best edited paper on the frontier.[5] Published weekly, its six to eight pages included two or three in Cherokee syllabery, and were compiled from reprints of national news stories, reports of local events, poetry, collections of folklore from other Indian and non-Indian cultures, and, most prominently, dispatches from the delegations sent each year to Washington to lobby on the Cherokee nation's behalf, all presented from the perspective of a rational, disembodied elite. The newspaper tried to accomplish through rhetorical means what Cherokee leaders tried to accomplish through politics: claim a full voice in the American public sphere. A useful counter example to the *Cherokee Advocate* (though a much shorter lived one) is *Copway's American Indian,* a weekly founded (and folded) by the Ojibwa George Copway in New York City in 1851. While the *Cherokee Advocate* sought to forge a distinct national and cultural identity modeled on Anglo-American terms, Copway took an assimilationist editorial line that positioned Native Americans very differently within the public sphere; his treatment of spiritual issues followed suit.

Also important are a pair of African-American publications from the antebellum period, the abolitionist newspaper the *North Star* (later *Frederick Douglass's Paper*), and the short-lived but remarkable *Anglo-African Magazine.* The former was the most successful effort by a black abolitionist to establish a voice independent of the whites who had long retained control of the abolitionist press, if not of the broader movement. Though Douglass's move was not well received by many of his white colleagues, it was a crucial part of his effort to claim equal status for blacks in the public discourse; indeed, the highly rational and politically engaged editorial tone Douglass set for his paper conveyed a commitment to the American public sphere that the contrarian zeal of Garrison often failed to match. The *Anglo-African Magazine,* founded in 1859 in New York City, tried to broaden the narrow focus of Douglass's paper by publishing the literary efforts of its black contributors. Though the magazine was not a commercial success, undergoing a number of format changes in the the Civil War years before ceasing publication, it nevertheless established a distinctly African-American voice in the most influential medium of mid-century print culture. In the editorial responses of this magazine and others to spiritualism, we can trace the efforts of a variety of marginalized groups to gain access to and shape the public sphere.

The ideology and rhetoric of republican literary culture was one of the

few things most Americans could agree upon at midcentury, and as spiritualism entered the public realm it became a useful vehicle for gauging the strength
of that agreement, for measuring its openness to new parties, and for marking
its strains. I will begin by sketching spiritualism's reception at the heart of the
public sphere—the metropolitan periodicals—before tracing its trajectory in
more marginal periodical venues. For spiritualism, arising at the margins of
mainstream European-American culture and resonant with the central beliefs
of many of the peoples disenfranchised by that mainstream, would prove
an elusive subject within the public sphere, and would help contribute to its
unraveling.

Public Skepticism

At first, the national magazines ignored spiritualism. While stories of séances
and spiritual manifestations filled newspapers beginning with the first reports
of the Fox demonstrations in Rochester in 1849 and continuing throughout
the following decade, accounts of spiritualism were surprisingly slow to appear in the national magazines. A brief reference in a *Harper's* review and two
poems—one satirical and one serious—were the extent of spiritualism's presence in the national literary press until the end of 1852. Almost three years
after reports of strange happenings in upstate New York began filtering into
newspapers across the country, and two years after the Rochester Rappings
had risen to national prominence, spiritualism remained banished from the
arena of the public sphere policed by the editors of the national magazines.

When spiritualism did appear, it was handled in a matter befitting the disembodied gentility of the eighteenth-century public sphere. *Harper's* weighed
in with a gentle dig at the phenomenon in the summer of 1850 in review of an
American reprint of the French book *The Phantom World,*

a general survey of the history and philosophy of spirits, apparitions, ghosts, elves,
fairies, spooks, bogles, bugaboos and hobgoblins. It will probably meet with an extensive circulation in these days when Connecticut divines are haunted by infernal
visits, and the Rochester sibyls are on exhibition in New York. (428)

By casting the Fox sisters as the Rochester sibyls, the editorial both pins them
to a peripheral region and contains them within a context of classical reference underscored by the continental learning of *The Phantom World.* The
unlocated, educated, and satirical voice of the editorial constructs an equally

(un)situated reader, who can recognize *him*self or *her*self only in opposition to the unlettered provincial femininity of the Rochester sibyls and Connecticut divines. The underlying accusation of crass hucksterism inherent in the phrase "on exhibition" serves merely to reinforce the comfortable, and therefore invisible, economic status of both the editor and his ideal audience.

James Russell Lowell's attack on spiritualism followed a similar line. After a friend sent him an account of a Rochester séance in January 1850, he responded that "only foolish little men . . . are fond of mysteries and fusses" (Kerr 23). He soon worked his masculinist distaste for the movement into nine hundred lines of satirical verse entitled "The Unhappy Lot of Mr. Knott," published in *Graham's* in the spring of 1851. A credulous, newly moneyed, and rather effeminate widower, Mr. Knott, is persuaded by the rapping voices of spirits to break off his daughter's engagement to an unsavory old colonel and allow her to marry the man of her choosing—a man who, Mr. Knott's more skeptical neighbors suspect, was responsible for the rapping noises all along (Kerr 23–24). Howard Kerr reads Lowell's piece as an example of a gleeful exploitation of comic literary potential, but the satire may well cover a more serious anxiety. The poem is remarkable for its recasting of the almost universally female spiritualist medium as a male on the make—a modification that may have masked Lowell's apprehension about the prospect of young female mediums manipulating public discourse.

Satire was carried to a more explicitly conservative extreme in a piece from the "Editor's Table" in the *Knickerbocker* of August 1854, in which the fictional editor of the *Bunkum Flag-Staff,* now settled in Nebraska, writes back East. "I'm a *mejum*—a writing, tipping, knocking, rapping and speaking mejum; which is as true as the Nebrasky bill has passed both houses." Regional satire and political commentary have merged, with both frontier hicks and Washington politicians constructed as irrational buffoons against smug chuckles of a rational elite embodied in a figure resembling James Russell Lowell. The solution to the foolishness inherent in politics and poltergeists is a rejection of both, with the message driven home at the end: "If I am a mejum, it will be mejum of common sense, and I do n't [*sic*] want to see the slavery of superstition settin' its cloven foot on the Nebraska Territory before we get the first crop of corn reaped" (190–91). The loaded phrase "slavery of superstition" manages to lump slaveholders and spiritualists into a class even less reasonable and refined than the former editor of the *Bunkum*—a class far removed from the genteel imaginary of the *Knickerbocker's* ideal audience. This aggressively apolitical piece manages to cast the militant migrants to Nebraska as delusional spiritualists with low-class superstitions while at the same time advocating a know-nothing stance in relation to the most compelling public issue of the time, slavery.

By 1852, as spiritualism proved more than a passing fad, the national magazines began to take a different tack. While satirical treatments of séances and suspect mediumship remained a popular filler and a useful point of reference for more traditional ghost stories throughout the decade, serious accounts of spiritualism appeared that gathered it under the mantle of science or philosophy at the expense of the often radical ideology formulated by spiritualists themselves. Thus *Harper's,* in April of 1852, published a long disquisition in the Editor's Table section considering spirituality, materiality, and communication at great length, and ultimately resolved them with orthodox views on science and Christianity without any reference to spiritualism. The tone is learned, level, and absolutely straight:

Homer, indeed, had long ago compared thought to lightning; but how much more definite, and, on this account, more effective, is the kindred simile drawn from the discovery of the electric telegraph. And yet, is there not here something more than simile? Is not the communication from soul to soul literally, as well as figuratively *telegraphic,* that is, *far-writing,* or *writing from afar?* We hope to interest our readers by a brief examination of the query we have started. (699)

A vain hope, perhaps, but the appropriation of the language of spiritualism into a disembodied, professorial discourse is quite in keeping with Warner's principle of negativity—though in this case its aggression, albeit not explicit, is unmistakable. The guardians of the public sphere are, here, on the attack, marshaling their privileged learning ("Homer, indeed") in a tone so authoritative that they hope to be unanswerable.

Other magazines soon published similar accounts. Horace Greeley's "Modern 'Spiritualism,'" in the January 1853 issue of *Putman's,* was the most sympathetic—an appropriate stance from a man who embraced a wide array of radical causes, and who was largely responsible for bringing the Fox sisters to New York (Goldsmith 55). In his article, a brief and skeptical account of occult history precedes a number of anecdotes about spiritual manifestations and an equal number of clear hoaxes, reprinted verbatim (trial-like) from Greeley's sources. His concludes with a scientific equivocation: "Let us not fear to open our eyes lest we see something contrary to our preconceptions of Nature and Providence; for if these preconceptions are at war with *facts,* it is high time they were revised and corrected" (63). Greeley places spiritualism squarely within the rational-skeptical discourse of the classic public sphere, with his trial rhetoric belying the essential conservatism of his method. The jury of the public sphere, he implies, would find far different resonances for spiritualism than the radical reformers who champion it (including Greeley himself, who keeps his devotion to radical causes and his personal enthusiasm for spiritualism under wraps). Greeley closes with an assertion that a reasonable investigation will surely lead directly back to a very familiar God. Articles in *Harper's,* the *Knickerbocker, Putnam's,* and the *North American Review* in the year or two following continued this approach. By directing attention away from the mediums and popularizers of spiritualism, with their often inconvenient ideological baggage, and toward the pure and uncorruptable world of facts, the national magazine culture worked to sever spiritualism from its social and political moorings.

Even the southern journals that disputed the right of northern editors to speak for the national public sphere based their attacks on the same terms. The *Southern Literary Messenger*'s response to Greeley's very tentative (and anonymous) endorsement of spiritualism in *Putman's* is a good example. In the 1853 article "Spiritual Manifestations," the *Messenger* quickly leveled a viscious attack on Greeley's personal beliefs and person, claiming at one point that "Mr. Greeley's credulity has as large a gullet as the natural orifice of the great giant Gargantua" (387). Sectional politics here tear at the public sphere—Greeley's effort to refashion spiritualism in republican terms is met with an attempt to undercut his role as an arbiter of the public sphere by attacking both his anonymity and his rationality. Greeley becomes, in the pages of the *Southern Literary Messenger,* an exemplar of northern faddishness against which the literary men of the South could stake their claim to a public sphere fashioned distinctly against the bodies of northern editors.

In short, by midcentury the public sphere, long organized around the personal authority of rational, learned men, had begun to place great emphasis on the depersonalized discourse of facts, an emphasis most apparent in the conundrum posed by Judge John Worth Edmonds, a New York Supreme Court justice whose embrace of spiritualism undermined the very republican public sphere he represented. Edmonds's career as a politician and jurist had reached its pinnacle when, grief-stricken at the death of his wife, he began attending séances lead by Margaret Fox. By 1853 he had become a true believer and published a highly popular account of spiritualist phenomena and ideology (Kerr 12–13). Not female, non-white, or lower class, Judge Edmonds (the title ever preceding his name as a standard-bearer of orthodox authority) was someone to be reckoned with, as the writings of another reviewer in *Putnam's* in December 1853 nicely illustrate. The review ("Spiritualism") begins with a glance back to a public sphere shaped by the personal embodiment of power:

The reputation of such an indorser [sic] as Judge Edmonds too—a lawyer of great sagacity, accustomed to weighing evidence, and a man of the most exemplary integrity, whose words on a matter of fact cannot be doubted, ought to commend the subject to an impartial investigation, or at least shield it from the flippant commentaries of the lower order of journalists. (680)

The glance is nostalgic—while Judge Edmonds's integrity *ought* to put the matter to rest, at least to the extent of quieting mere journalists, it doesn't. The paradigm of personal politics has clearly (if regrettably) vanished. The review goes on to note that "the most exalted of men have fallen into the grossest errors," citing the judgment of the esteemed Sir Matthew Hale in the Salem Witchcraft Trials. Like Greeley, the review posits a public sphere governed not by persons, but by the cold impartiality of facts:

The book of Judge Edmonds must be judged on its face. The facts he narrates, we have no doubt, are just as they occurred. His singular experiences are faithfully recorded; and the only point for the world to discuss, is the meaning of those facts (681).

The locus of authority here has shifted. The trope of judging a (judge's) book on its face points to the depersonalization of authority in a world of print culture. "Face," in this context, signifies not Judge Edmonds's personal integrity but the reliability of his data. The name "Judge Edmonds" signifies authority, but is no longer sufficient to command it. Judgment resides instead in the more anonymous, disembodied, and rational realm of elite print culture.

After questioning whether spiritualist phenomena arise from natural or supernatural causes, the review defers judgment, for "the observations in respect to [the subject], which have thus far been made by *reliable minds,* are not numerous" (emphasis mine). The question of authority is deferred to the nebulous "world" of "reliable minds" who do in fact have the power to judge. That world, unidentified in terms of race, class, and gender, was invariably white, propertied, and male. "They" hold the power of interpretation, which is vested in "their" control of the word. When confronted by a phenomenon like spiritualism, arising out of a folk culture through the agency of a pair of teenage girls and their radical handlers, the custodians of the public sphere in national magazines sought to preserve their prerogative by systematically excluding spiritualist ideas and advocates. They invoked mockery and satire, rationality, and "reliable minds" to keep spiritualism away from the centers of discursive power. Ironically, this formula would provide the means of access for a variety of groups who had long sought access to the American public sphere.

Peripheral Publics

One primary means of gaining access to the public sphere was to imitate the forms used by Europeans to shape it. Thus, the very act of publishing a periodical proclaimed a group's entitlement to participate in the public discourse. The *Cherokee Advocate* was, for the Cherokee nation, a crucial element in their struggle for sovereignty, among the most compelling proofs the tribe could offer it was fit to take part in the structures of Western civilization. *Copway's American Indian* appealed to a white public sphere with far less ambivalence than its Cherokee cousin. Copway's newspaper was endorsed by a number of well-established public men of letters whose names were blazoned on the front page of the first issue, from the "Hon. J. R. Chandler, Philadelphia" to H. R. Schoolcraft, Francis Parkman, James Fenimore Cooper, John Neal, William Cullen Bryant, Washington Irving, and N. P. Willis. In gaining access to such an exclusive club, apparently, it helped to have the right friends. Such friendship had its price, however. Copway's quid pro quo was his acceptance of the discourse of the vanishing Indian. After thanking his white friends for their support in his "Prospectus," he justified a periodical devoted to Indians by stating:

That race is fast vanishing away; a few years more and its existence will be found only in the history of the past: may not an Indian, then, hope for countenance and support in a modest and unambitious effort to preserve, while yet he may, the still lingering memorials of his own people, once numerous and strong, and interesting alike to the Christian, the philanthropist, the philosopher, and the general reader? (1)

Copway has cast his lot not with the vanishing member of his own race, but with the "Christian, the philosopher and the general reader"—the white people for whom he writes.

Like these two Native American publications, both Frederick Douglass's *North Star* and the *Anglo-African Magazine* were clearly patterned after mainstream periodicals, and because both emanated from major metropolitan centers, both were able to address a substantial number of black and white readers. Again like their Native American counterparts, both were published in part to prove that they could be published, that African Americans could command the same public voice as their white compatriots. Spiritualism proved a useful topic with which to demonstrate that voice.

While the *Anglo-African* began its short run ten years after the Fox sisters rose to fame and included no direct commentaries on spiritualism (I will consider more indirect ones below), Frederick Douglass published his paper near the epicenter of the Rochester Rappings and responded to this spiritualist episode with rational skepticism. As I argued earlier, Douglass's cool reception of the Fox sisters, especially in the guarded reporting of their exhibition in Rochester's Corinthian Hall in 1849, was part of a strategy to appeal to a wider audience of abolitionists and sympathizers without expressly attacking his spiritualist friends. His appeal to the facts, indeed, echoes that of Greeley, who also suppressed his personal ties to the spiritualist movement in favor of the dispassionate, disembodied persona appropriate to the public sphere. The *Cherokee Advocate* took this rationalist position even further, promulgating a discourse of scientism that proved far more interested in reporting on the wonders of the mechanical telegraph than on its spiritual cousin. "We were never more impressed with the power of the telegraph," proclaimed the editors in 1850, "to annihilate space, and bring to instant mental communication individuals separated by hundreds of miles" (3). None reported on the Rochester Rappings. Science, not spiritualism, would be the common ground claimed by the Cherokee in their effort to enter the public sphere.

The *Cherokee Advocate* adopted the same satiric voice toward spiritualist phenomena as that used by the metropolitan press. Although careful not to offend the evangelical sensibilities of the missionaries who played a central role in Cherokee society, the newspaper tended to adopt an elitist stance when describing trances, unexplained phenomena, and ecstatic religion. While the Rochester Rappings never fell under the paper's editorial gaze, an article published in December 1849 described a "tranced child" of Bangor who, when stricken with cholera, described visiting relatives in heaven, two of whom the child hadn't known were dead. The story is presented as an unadorned riddle, not as a harbinger of a new revelation, and is the magazine's most sympathetic account of a spiritualist phenomenon. Indeed, other articles of the period turn an intense, satiric skepticism toward those who built doctrines out of such elusive material. The *Advocate* had reprinted a scathing article about the Millerites in 1844 that spoke of "this deluded set of fanatics . . . playing all sorts of strange pranks" (4). In 1849 an unattributed article entitled "Strange Religious Possession" similarly parsed the more extreme forms of Christian revivalism, detailing such phenomena as the "falling exercise," the "jerking exercise," the "rolling exercise," the "hugging exercise," and the "Holy Laugh." The piece draws a familiar moral:

> The extraordinary scenes at camp-meeting have been the subject of much speculation.—Nervous excitement may be extended throughout the masses, affecting all in the most singular manner. . . . Mesmerism, imagination, or whatever it may be called, the peculiar state can be turned to good or evil, and a full knowledge of it is essential. (1)

The skepticism of this article would be right at home in the elitist pages of the *Knickerbocker* or the *Atlantic Monthly,* where the spiritual excesses of the masses were to be met with cool, scientific inquiry. That such a superior stance toward popular Christianity emanated from a nation deemed by the U.S. government as too primitive for self-government was an irony entirely to the point.

Both the editors of the *Cherokee Advocate* and George Copway were even more anxious to fashion their elite, rationalist sensibility against traditional Indian spiritualism than they were against nonelite whites. I noted above that Copway's intention was to capture the culture and religion of what he deemed "vanishing peoples," and hence prominently featured in his pages were ethnographic descriptions of various tribal beliefs, some gathered by white observers and some reported in great detail by Copway himself. Copway's position in relation to these articles is somewhat ambiguous. While he adopts the stance of detached (and superior) observer, he clearly takes tribal legends seriously. His second issue juxtaposes a careful account of an Algonquin legend, an essay by Lewis Henry Morgan on the education and Christianization of the Iroquois, and a short piece on a contemporary young woman who receives wisdom in her dreams. In this delicate editorial balancing act, Copway seems as anxious to assert the validity of Indian religions as he is to demonstrate his own superiority to them. He attempts to resolve this bind in the following issue, where, in an article that would have made a transcendentalist proud, he posits the commonality of creation myths in all cultures.

The editors of the *Cherokee Advocate* adopted a similar approach to traditional Indian religions. They occasionally reprinted Copway's renditions of

Indian traditions along with other accounts of different tribes, in each case presenting such religious beliefs more as ethnographic curiosities than as viable spiritual traditions. One 1850 article, "Indian Customs," is typical:

> The Senecas believe that there is a land of spirits, and that most of their people are enjoying those objects there which they delighted to pursue while in the land of mortality. The dog which they sacrifice is, according to their notion, only sent as a messenger to their ancient chiefs and people.

The Senecas here occupy a position of otherness, of curious spirituality quite akin the Kentucky revivalists, against which the Cherokee editors can establish their cultural superiority, their disinterested rationality, and hence their entitlement to a place in the public sphere.

Divisive Spirits

The irony of such attempts by marginalized groups to enter the public sphere is that by the 1850s print culture had become far too heterodox to serve as a unified public sphere. What had entered the century as a coherent ideological chorus of rational voices threatened to become, by the century's midpoint, a cacophony. Spiritualism's literary manifestation was symptomatic of this trend. It had spread so widely and so quickly that by the time the editors of *Putnam's* and other periodicals began a concerted effort to appropriate the movement into the more tidy and depoliticized world of rational, scientific discourse, spiritualism had become far too slippery to control. It soon proved a vehicle for the forces pulling the public sphere apart.

One such force was ubiquitous within the very print culture seeking to preserve the rational-skeptical mode. Nearly every periodical of the day, no matter how staid, included some poetry in its columns, sometimes as a principal feature, sometimes as filler. While some poetry, including satiric portrayals of spiritualism like Lowell's "The Unhappy Lot of Mr. Knott," reinforced inherited public sphere norms, much more of it worked against them. One reason was poetry's wider field of signification—unlike the learned, tightly controlled rationality of most of the nonfiction prose found in periodicals, mid-century verse tended to signify more widely, to draw on a broader range of traditions and cultural forms, and hence to carry a richer resonance. Poetry that drew on the same cultural currents from which the Rochester Rappings flowed, from evangelical Christianity to English folklore to Native American traditions to European Gothic, reinforced a spiritualist sensibility even as the periodicals publishing these poems decried spiritualism as a hoax or worse. Moreover, the sentimentalism that became a dominant poetic form at mid-century provided a powerful alternative to the rational, erudite discourse then typical of the public sphere. The staples of sentimental poetry, especially the deaths of children and the visions of loved ones looking fondly on from heaven, were also the staples of the séance table.[6] Such poetry helped fracture the brittle rationalist facade of the public sphere that so many mainstream periodicals tried to present, and that so many marginal periodicals tried to join.

One of the earliest poems specifically to address spiritualism is "To the Rapping Spirits," published in the *Knickerbocker* of April 1851. As unusual as it is flat, it offers little more than an indifferently versified version of the open-minded skepticism of the editorial comments:

> Ye, of the Spirit-Land,
> How, with a boneless hand,
> Rap ye so loudly and
>   Baffle our vision?
> Why are ye wandering?
> Tell us the news ye bring:
> Come ye from the realms of Spring,
>   Regions Elysian? (311)

The ode, while hardly a masterpiece, offers a discursive pivot away from the carefully policed realm of scientific speculation carried on by learned men and toward the far less tidy world of literature, where the recent vogue for the tortured syntax and fevered imaginings of Gothic verse made the revelations of the séance table read like old news. Poetry especially was a discourse that moved easily in a wide variety of circles, from learned and disembodied elitism to the most engaged of politics, and the attribution of the poem above aptly figures the mingled status of poetry. Next to the initials "E.L.B." the town of Schoolcraft, Michigan, is listed. The origin of the poem is *almost* located, fixed enough to signify an historical context for the words (and, not incidentally, the national scope of the magazine), unfixed enough to participate in an unlocated public sphere.

More importantly, the recasting of spiritualism in verse signifies in the direction of other publics than the one promulgated by the editors of the major periodicals. If the editorial pages of the mid-century magazines gave scant serious attention to spiritualism in its first years, many of the poems in the magazines were far more sympathetic. The Gothic romanticism and Christian sentimentalism that had long been popular modes of composition gained a spiritualist resonance once the news of the Fox sisters had swept the country. Such poetry wasn't necessarily composed with rapping spirits in mind—it may even have been written years before in countries far removed from the cultural landscapes of Rochester and New York City at midcentury. Yet once such poetry entered American print culture after 1849, it became embedded in an interpretive community in which spiritualism figured significantly. The very broad community of all print media throughout the states and territories can, of course, be usefully broken down; different groups read different things. Yet even in a relatively broad readership like that of the national literary magazines, it is important to keep in mind the different perspectives from which the magazines were read, and how those perspectives might have been brought to bear in different ways on any given poem. In periodicals with narrower circulation among distinct interest groups, such overdetermination takes on a distinctly politicized resonance.

If "To the Rapping Spirits," in its bemused interest, is rather transparent, "Angel Eve," a poem from the January 1852 *Knickerbocker,* is totally sincere. It imagines a baby girl who dies in infancy as an angel sent to earth by God on a brief mission of love, and marshals all the conventions of sentimental piety to wrest an orthodox moral from what was an all-too-common tragedy:

> Our little Eve's smile beamed upon us,
>   As it never beamed before,
> And she straightway left the earthly
>   For the distant Eden-shore. (47)

Although such a central sentimental trope as communication with a dead child precedes the Rochester Rappings, it soon became the driving force behind the séance. And spiritualism of this sentimental variety managed to evade the rationalist scrutiny that the Rochester Rappings and its many descendants received. The emotional, spiritual, domestic, and feminine touchstones of sentimental literature have been well charted as a coherent alternative to the rational, materialist, public, and masculine discourse that competed for attention in antebellum print culture.[7] Less commonly noted is how frequently both discourses shared space in the pages of the same periodicals. The result was a bifurcation in the print culture of the day in which sentimental and republican sensibilities operated side by side, cultivating overlapping publics. Thus spiritualism was met with rationalist skepticism on the one hand and sentimental sympathy on the other. The result was a further crumbling of an elite republican edifice.

This bifurcation carried through to the marginal periodicals trying to gain a foothold in the mainstream public. Writers from minority ethnic groups had long couched their appeals to a wider audience in sentimental terms; slave narratives especially often mingled rational and sentimental arguments in an effort to appeal to both the minds and hearts of white readers. The periodicals under consideration here were no different. The *Cherokee Advocate* often published unattributed poetry, most of which probably originated in the many schools that dotted the Oklahoma reservation. Much of the poetry was indistinguishable in tone and subject from that which appeared in metropolitan magazines. One 1850 poem, entitled "The Angel Watcher" (1), details a deathbed scene in which an angel takes the place of a daughter at her mother's bedside; the mother awakes, mistakes the angel for her daughter, and professes her love before dying. If the poem was in fact reprinted from mainstream periodicals, the effect would have been equally jarring. In pages that had rigorously gathered a wide range of spiritual phenomena, from ecstatic revivals to traditional Indian spiritual narrative, under the watchful gaze of scientific inquiry, this example of sentimental spiritualism chastened the rational discourse around it. Copway, too, balanced sentimental spiritualism and science, reprinting a poem by William Cullen Bryant entitled "The Future Life" (3), in which the narrator addresses a friend now dwelling in the sphere of spirits, alongside an ethnographic account of an Ojibwa legend in which warriors called on spirits to clear a fog during a war with the Iroquois.

The *Anglo-African* also published sentimental spiritualism uncritically. Frances Harper's poetry, which presented abolitionist and other reformist themes in sentimental terms, was a staple of the new magazine. Amos Gerry Beman wrote the most clearly spiritualist story in this vein. In "A Visit to my Mother's Grave," the narrator reports a remarkable vision: "[T]he Genius of the Bible, with her flaming torch of inspiration, stood before me. She spoke, and her beaming features were irradiated with a seraphic smile. 'Thy feelings are from the dust,' said she; 'this light illuminates the grave; it dissipates the darkness of the tomb; it opens a bright vision; it discovers a nobler state of existence, a brighter world'" (12). Such a vision, framed by the Bible and by filial obligations to a deceased mother, remains free of the critical eye of science and rationality; the learned, disembodied editorial persona could, if it chose, contextualize the story with scholarship and shunt the vision off to the margins of scientific inquiry, but it doesn't. The story instead lingers in the uncertain realm between literary metaphor and numinous prophecy, in neither case answerable to the policing gaze of the republican public sphere.

While sentimental spiritualism's ability to cut across cultural lines provided one alternative to the republican public sphere, other poems and stories rich with spiritualist resonance signified with far more cultural specificity, emphasizing cultural difference and hence further undermining a monolithic national public sphere. A poem like Frances Osgood's "The Spirit-Harp," in the *Southern Literary Messenger* of January 1850, is an example of a work that helped ossify cultural divisions. The poem tells the story of a murdered sister whose spirit speaks in harp strings made from her hair:

> A maid's sweet voice, thro' the gold strings sighed—
> "Be hushed the harp!" said the haughty bride.
> "Now listen—now listen!" the minstrel sang,
> "There's a wondrous tale in the chord's sweet clang,"
> And wild thro' the hall the melody rang—
> "Young bride, dost thou listen?" the minstrel sang.
> "With my golden wreath, is the bride's hair bound!"
> Pleading and soft does the second chord ring—
> "To my loved bridegroom, the bride doth cling!"
> And madly the terrible tempest beat
> At the lattice high like a fierce Afrite!
> And a wild, sad wail the third chord gave—
> "My sister drowned me in the deep, deep wave!" (27)

Though Osgood's poem centers on spectral music rather than rapping spirits—the phenomenon of a spirit speaking through a musical instrument wouldn't become a spiritualist commonplace until later in the decade—it nevertheless conveys a strong spiritualist resonance that is ethnically European American. Set in a mythic Anglo-Saxon past and ostensibly translated from German, the poem might well have appealed to the type of nineteenth-century student of folklore who also collected traditional Indian stories as relics of a vanishing race. Poems like "The Spirit-Harp," however, are cast as part of a living heritage now flourishing in America, designed to appeal, perhaps, to a white reader anxiously tracing an Anglo-Saxon past in order to shore up his or her identity against a tide of immigration—or, perhaps, against the "Afrites," a word that signifies, along with its primary meaning of evil djinns, those whose continued enslavement the southern press insisted upon with increasing vehemence. Thus, while the poem echoes other stories of communication from beyond the grave and anticipates the phenomenon of spectral music, it also signifies a rich European inheritance flourishing in America. The poem posits a nativist spiritualism against the more polyglot, reformist version spread by spiritualism's earliest adherents. And like the southern press in general, the poem signifies an allegiance to an English heritage very much in line with a southern ideology that cast the South as a bulwark of tradition against the modernizing zeal of the North.

If "The Spirit-Harp" uses spiritualism to recall an ethnic homeland, poems and stories from other cultural groups did likewise, often in counterpoint to the editorial line in the periodicals in which they appeared. *Copway's American Indian*, the *Cherokee Advocate*, and the *Anglo-African Magazine* each provide examples. A very minor piece Copway included in his first issue (1851), entitled "Legend of the Mongaup, Sullivan Co., N.Y.," by F. L. Waddell, follows the ideological line laid out in *Hiawatha*. The only role imagined for Indians in an America settled by whites is that of dispossessed, and hence disembodied, spirits. Waddell's poem baldly states that the way for surviving Indians to contact their dead is to join them:

> Alas! alas! where is now their home?
> Like birds of the air they houseless roam.
> They are gone to the lands of the setting sun,
> Like trout from Pike compelled to run.
> "The Manetoo's just," the Indian said,
> "In my own land I'll join the dead:"
> Then from the high and dizzy peak
> In solemn pomp he made the leap. (3)

The only good Indian, in short, was an Indian spirit, and the trip to the spirit land was one-way. The myriad recastings of Indian stories into European idioms, of which this poem is but an example and Longfellow's *Hiawatha* the apotheosis, mystifies the European conquest of America. The poem illustrates the cost of Copway's position. An Indian who sought to secure his status by aligning himself with Anglo-Saxon nativism had first to surrender ties to a cultural homeland, and surrender as well the ties between ancestral spirits and living members that had nurtured tribes even in the face of white colonialism.[8] Not surprisingly, he found few readers.

Unlike Copway, the editors of the *Cherokee Advocate* tried to carve out a more ambiguous position, using their newspaper on the one hand to show that the Cherokees belonged fully in the mainstream of the national public sphere and, on the other hand, to argue for a separate nation for the Cherokee people. While many of the articles in the newspaper adopted a skeptical stance toward spiritualist phenomena in keeping with metropolitan norms, some of the spiritualist poetry the newspaper printed tended to reinforce the separatist agenda. The best example is an untitled poem by C. N. Wigwam (a pseudonym, most likely, of a Cherokee student or teacher in the reservation's extensive school system). The poem is in the idiom of conventional European verse representations of Indian experience, but its resonance is quite different from, for example, the poem from *Copway's American Indian* quoted above. It tells the story of an Indian who has lost his home, his friends, and his wife, and cannot find happiness even in the beautiful natural surroundings in which he wanders:

> East of old oou-gill-o-gee's darkened shore,
> A steep hill rears its rocky brow high o'er—
> Hill, stream and forest all in confusion there,
> So sweetly blended, so divinely fair,
> That angels, descending from bright realms of bliss,
> Hung entranced o'er a scene like this.
> There floating in the balmy zephered air,
> Gazed with delight upon a scene so fair. (1)

Like the poem printed by Copway, this poem echoes the mid-century European-American representation of Indian sensibilities (it is, indeed, a good deal less wooden than most). Its differences in both content and context, however, are significant. The first is that the poem does not end with its hero happily departing to the hereafter; instead, he manages to survive in a world of loss. A second is that the poem's spiritual texture is not Indian religion refracted through white ethnocentrism, but instead genuinely Christian. (No angels appear in the *Song of Hiawatha,* however frequently they grace the lines of Longfellow's more conventional verse.) Instead of projecting Indian spiritualism as one more signifier of unbridgeable cultural difference, the poem imagines an Indian in a seamless Christian spiritualist context.

These differences, of Indian survival and accommodation to a Judeo-Christian spiritual sensibility, are significant in the context of the *Cherokee Advocate,* a periodical devoted to a people who had been torn from their own homeland after failing to vanish, who had lost as many as half their number on the Trail of Tears, and who nevertheless clung to their own version of the faith of their conquerors. A poem drenched in loss and full of spiritual wonder for a mountain homeland peopled by angels and painted according to European poetics powerfully complements the tribe's effort to secure its sovereignty. To its white readers, the poem demonstrates the tribe's "civilized" status, particularly when compared to the ethnographic curiosities of other tribes detailed in the paper's pages. To its own readers, the poem illustrates the emotive potential of a European form to express a Cherokee sensibility—a point that the Western-educated half-blood leaders of the Cherokees made again and again to the full-blood majority of the tribe. Angels, this poem argues, can speak to Indians—even if only in English (the poem wasn't included in the page translated into Sequoyan syllabery).

While the *Anglo-African Magazine* didn't have recourse to its own alphabet, it presented a version of spiritualism in its pages that reified the cultural divide between blacks and whites on the eve of the Civil War. If the article "A Visit to my Mother's Grave" tapped into the sentimental spiritualism common throughout mid-century America, an article appearing in the previous issue sounded a more divisive note. "The Nat Turner Insurrection" (1859), published hard on the heels of John Brown's attack on Harper's Ferry, responded to the abolitionist martyr by reprinting Nat Turner's *Confessions* and then speculating about the relationship between these two most controversial figures of the antislavery movement. Interestingly, the article highlights their spiritual connections:

There are many points of similarity between the two men: they were both idealists; both governed by their views of the teachings of the Bible; both harbored for years the purpose to which they gave up their lives; both felt themselves swayed by some divine, or at least, spiritual influence; the one seeking in the air, the earth and the heavens, for signs which came at last; and the other, obeying impulses which he believes to have been fore-ordained from the eternal past. (386)

Such an argument was hardly meant to help bring John Brown and his militant abolitionism into the mainstream of the American public sphere, as writings by such white abolitionists as Lydia Maria Child and Henry David Thoreau sought to do. The article instead pulls Brown's more recognizable evangelistic spiritualism into the orbit of the visionary Turner, whose direct communication with the spirit world occupied the center of his bloody narrative.

Like the editors of the *Anglo-African,* and indeed like the editors of the *Cherokee Advocate* and the poet C. N. Wigwam cited above, Turner rooted his spiritualism in an avowedly Christian context: he stressed in his *Confessions* that he gained his influence "not by means of conjuring and such like tricks . . . but by the communion of the spirit." Yet Turner's spiritualism, and hence by association Brown's, is not a mechanism by which a marginalized group can gain access to the public sphere, but instead a means of fueling a race war. As if to underscore this fracturing consensus, the introduction to Turner's reprinted *Confessions* assigns to the illiterate slave the qualities more often associated with republican virtue, arguing that had John Brown been "governed by [Turner's] inexorable logic and cool daring, the soil of Virginia and Maryland and the far South, would by this time be drenched in blood, and the wild and sanguinary course of these men, no earthly power could then stay" (386). Reason and selfless courage, here joined to Turner's Old Testament spiritualism, serve not to bind a fractured country, but to set it awash in violence.

Tracing spiritualism's modulations across a diverse segment of antebellum print culture offers some useful insights into how oppositional discourses signify in the public sphere. Spiritualism spread through sympathetic interpretive communities that exploited its multiple resonances in order to evade the interpretive control of authorities like the national magazine press. Long before spiritualism was taken seriously by editors of literary magazines, spiritualist resonances had been infiltrating the print culture those editors had created, smuggled in by the overdetermined resonance of the sentimental and gothic literature that filled these magazines' pages. Satirical and scientific attacks on spiritualism often occupied the same pages as poems and stories about ghosts and angels, and the effect, ultimately, was to drive a wedge into the increasingly brittle facade of a unified public sphere. Yet the loose cohesion of sympathetic cultural forms offered by spiritualism proved unable to cohere into a stabilizing social force. Ultimately, spiritualism proved more useful to the contest of identities within mid-century American culture than to unifying the voice of the public sphere. Ethnic groups and sectional interests found in spiritualism a means of celebrating not the disembodied essence of all humanity, but the ancestral spirits who preserved the distinct cultural identities pulling America toward civil war. Just as spirits entered the antebellum public sphere, they helped tear it apart.

Chapter 3

The Politics of Heaven

The Ghost Dance, The Gates Ajar, *and* Captain Stormfield's Visit to Heaven

The spread of the Ghost Dance among the tribes of the Great Basin and Great Plains in 1890 precipitated a crises not only in the United States's Indian policy, but in white representations of Native American culture as well. In the first accounts of the Ghost Dance to appear in the *New York Times* (late 1890), we see a metropolitan newspaper struggling to comprehend a visionary Indian theology by stretching the resonance of "heaven." The first report, published on November 16 and titled "The New Indian Messiah," describes the experience of the Arapaho medicine man Sitting Bull as a "vision, for such it appears to have been," in which Christ appeared, promised "the restoration of the old order of things," and fed him buffalo meat (11). The writer won't use the term "heaven" to describe this distinctly Indian spirit world, but he does report that when the messiah later appeared before a group of believers, he told them "he had just returned from heaven, where he had seen God." The location of Sitting Bull's vision and the messiah's heaven are different places in this article's lexicon, due perhaps to anxiety on the part of a writer in conflating European and Indian notions of the afterlife.[1] This opposition continued in an article published in the same newspaper two weeks later, entitled "Weird Things in Dreams" (8) which summarized the proceedings of a meeting of the American Folklore Society devoted to the Ghost Dance. The anthropologists gathered at Columbia University, including Frank Boas, refer to the movement as a "craze" characterized by visions of a "spirit land" or "luminous place" full of dead Indians; a number drew links to other religious revivals among people safely removed from modern European-American society, including medieval Europeans, contemporary Arabs, and African Americans during the Civil War. "There seems to be a strong impulse," noted one professor, "to excitements like this Indian craze among all oppressed races." Yet the effort to segregate the Ghost Dance from the quite viable belief in heaven among turn-of-the-century whites did not succeed. The very next day (November 30) another *New York Times* article appeared, accurately citing Jack Wilson, or "Wo-vo-Kar," as the Ghost Dance prophet, an "intelligent, fine-looking Indian" who tells his followers that "he has been to heaven and that the Messiah is coming to the earth again, and will put the Indians in possession of this country; that he has seen in heaven a heap of Indians, some of them dressed in white man's clothes" (9). Heaven in this account, at least, is broad enough to include the Ghost Dance, and while "spirit world" in this context is not synonymous with the spirit world central to European-American religion, they share their signifier.

In this chapter, I will examine three versions of heaven that took shape in the United States in the latter half of the nineteenth century. Rooted in very different cultural contexts, these representations of the spirit world featured recognizably American landscapes. Both the Ghost Dance and the *Gates* novels (*The Gates Ajar, Beyond the Gates,* and *The Gates Between*) of Elizabeth Stuart Phelps, published between 1867 and 1888, offered elaborate, compelling, and strikingly similar portraits of heaven. Yet both emerged out of distinct cultural traditions at opposite ends of the continent without apparent reference to each other. Indeed, their visions of heaven bear the marks of the struggle for the very land under their authors' feet. A third text, Mark Twain's *Extracts from Captain Stormfield's Visit to Heaven,* had gone through forty years of revisions before it saw print in 1907; begun as a simple satire of *The Gates Ajar,* it eventually used its heavenly setting to grapple with some of the very questions raised by juxtaposing the *Gates* novels and the Ghost Dance. How are we to read the connections between peoples who simply happen to share the same land? Can beliefs from such widely different cultures be examined in relation to each other? If not, what does such cultural dissonance mean when these texts were produced in the same country in the space of a few decades? What, finally, do these heavenly portraits have to tell us about the meaning of culture, nationality, and identity in nineteenth-century America? These visions of heaven are, ultimately, visions of America; what unites and divides them to a large degree unites and divides the different cultures that share this land.

The Ghost Dance, Revitalization, and Visionary Nostalgia

Despite the best efforts of the *New York Times* circa 1890, the term "heaven" applies imperfectly at best to Native American religions. Although the hundreds of Indian cultures in the United States differ greatly in the tenor and terms of their religious beliefs, none share the Judeo-Christian duality of a perfect heaven defined against a fallen creation; nor do they share the sense of heaven stressed by most nineteenth-century Christian missionaries to various Indian tribes, that of a paradise reserved for an elect few in contradistinction to the more ecumenical horrors of hell. Most Indian cultures instead share a conception of the world as fundamentally sacred, where material and spiritual elements seamlessly coexist, and where communion between the living and the dead, the earthly and the spiritual, is a central fact of life. While Indian religious sensibilities certainly evolved over centuries of contact with European Americans, this world view remained remarkably intact when white anthropologists began to take native religions seriously at the end of the nineteenth century—an interest greatly spurred by the Ghost Dance.[2]

The spirit world in this cosmology is an extension of earthly life, closely modeled on its forms and contiguous with its terrain. Spirits can wander between the two worlds, and indeed frequently linger among the living, who can, in trances, sojourn among the spirits. Such a cosmology, too, enjoys a flexibility and adaptability quite distinct from the more rigorously codified European-American religions.[3] The tribes that adopted the Ghost Dance share what Lee Irwin calls a "visionary episteme," a cosmology "based in religious world views that are enhanced and qualified according to individual visionary experiences, which are integrated into broadly shared repertoires of behaviors, attitudes and enactments that are found throughout the Plains area" (6). As a result, Native American religions proved tremendously adaptable, evolving to reflect the various cultural influences and pressures the various tribes confronted over time. Thus the Ghost Dance of 1890 was, though novel in many ways, very much in line with traditional Indian conceptions of the spirit world.

Of course, the Ghost Dance itself was not entirely new in 1890. James Mooney's classic *The Ghost Dance Religion and Wounded Knee* (1896) is the first of many histories to treat the Ghost Dance not as one movement, but as many, beginning with the Pueblo Revolt of 1680 and continuing through a long series of traditional religious revivals among the tribes resisting U.S. westward expansion. The Delaware Prophet in the 1760s, the Shawano medicine man Tenskwatawa around 1810, Känakuk of the Kickapoo in the 1830s and 1840s, Tä'vibo of the Paiute in 1869, and Smohalla among the Columbia River tribes in the 1870s offered a spiritual counterpart to the military resistance with which Indians met encroaching white settlement. Though these medicine men often borrowed theological elements from Christian missionaries, their doctrines were firmly rooted in traditional beliefs and ceremonies.[4] All told of visions of a heaven reserved for Indians that abounded in game and the fruits of the earth; all promised that this heaven could be brought to earth if quarreling tribes would unite, perform certain rituals, and resist white encroachment. Most of these movements ended with military defeat or the forced removal of tribes to reservations far from their homelands; a few dissipated after failing to attract a wide following; many left indelible marks on tribal memories.

By 1890, the last of the Indian wars had been fought; every major tribe had been confined to reservations, and those reservations had long been carved up for white settlement. The Dawes Act of 1887 had instituted as policy the long-standing U.S. government goal of acculturation. Indian agents, when they didn't enrich themselves out of meager government allotments, insisted Indians abandon their communal economy for small farms and sent Indian children to distant boarding schools where they were forced to eat, dress, speak, learn, and worship like whites. Reeducation tried to accomplish what a century of literary myth and military brutality had not: the vanishing of the American Indian.

Thus when news began to spread among Indians of the Great Basin and Plains that a young Paiute named Wovoka had been to heaven and brought back the promise of a new millennium, tribal delegations flocked to hear the words from the prophet himself. Wovoka's message was clear and compelling: follow the Ghost Dance and see your tribe return to its precontact glory.

He fell asleep in the daytime and was taken up to the other world. Here he saw God, with all the people who had died long ago engaged in their oldtime sports and occupations, all happy and forever young. It was a pleasant land and full of game. After showing him all, God told him he must go back and tell his people they must be good and love one another, have no quarreling, and live in peace with the whites; that they must work, and not lie or steal; that they must put away all the old practices that savored of war; that if they faithfully obeyed his instructions, they would at last be reunited with their friends in this other world, where there would be no more death or sickness or old age. He was there given the dance which he was commanded to bring back to his people. By performing this dance at intervals, for five consecutive days each time, they would secure this happiness to themselves and hasten the event. (Mooney 771–72)

The dance involved a circle of believers adorned with body paints and bearing sacred feathers singing special "ghost songs" for hours; dancers regularly collapsed and, while fellow dancers stepped around their fallen bodies, journeyed to a spirit world devoid of whites, where they were greeted by deceased relatives and friends and supplied with new songs for future dances.

The Paiute dancers were soon joined by members of tribes from all parts of the American West, from the Bannock to the north to the Hopi to the south to the Arapaho, Cheyenne, and Sioux of the Eastern Plains. Although a few delegates were skeptical, most enthusiastically embraced the new revelation, which they quickly adapted to the traditions of their respective tribes. By the fall of 1890, Indian nations all over the West participated in the dance, visiting the spirit world in trances and hoping to hasten its coming. Most believed it would arrive with the green grass of spring in the following year, sliding atop the old world and burying both whites and Indian unbelievers under an avalanche or wall of fire, while the dancers themselves would be carried to a new world teeming with game and full of the vast ranks of Indians who had gone before.

Whites who heard of the dance grew uneasy, and in the late fall of 1890, when a few bands of Sioux, disgusted with short rations and false promises on their Dakota reservations and wary of increasing numbers of federal troops, headed toward the Black Hills, they were met by the U.S. cavalry. One band was intercepted at Wounded Knee Creek on December 29, and when federal troops began disarming the warriors, a medicine man named Yellow Bird urged them to resist—the ghosts shirts they wore, he said, would make them invulnerable to the white man's bullets. When one warrior did resist, the cavalry opened fire with light artillery and machine guns, killing about a hundred warriors and a hundred and twenty women and children, many of whom were shot down as they sought refuge in the creek bed or as they fled—their bodies were found as far as two miles from the scene. With the slaughter died most of the enthusiasm for the Ghost Dance, and the movement thereafter dwindled rapidly.[5]

Though white Americans had been slow to notice the spread of the Ghost Dance, the events surrounding Wounded Knee focused a great deal of attention on the movement. While many other Indian spiritual revivals had followed the course of European-American expansion, none had spread as far and as fast as Wovoka's Ghost Dance, and reservation missionaries, federal agents and newly commissioned anthropologists from the Bureau of Ethnology quickly spread throughout the West searching for explanations. Most whites and some Indians saw the Ghost Dance as the last gasp of a dying culture. American anthropology had long worked from a model of cultural evolution most fully developed by Lewis Henry Morgan in the 1870s, in which primitive societies inevitably yielded before more developed civilization. The

Bureau of Ethnology itself had been recently formed both to gather tribal artifacts before the cultures that produced them finally crumbled and to guide government policies designed to hasten Indian assimilation to European-American norms. From this perspective, the Ghost Dance was doomed from the start, and most observers who decried the massacre at Wounded Knee argued that the government had followed poor policy toward a movement that should have been left to wither of its own accord. Theodore Roosevelt, reviewing a book on Indian warfare for the *Atlantic Monthly* in 1892, praises the author for "all his remarks in relation to breaking up the tribal system, the absolute need of treating the Indians with justice, and the folly of waging war upon every tribe where there happens to be an epidemic of dancing and ghost-seeing" (272). Roosevelt's view was shared by at least one Indian who had adopted Western culture. Charles Eastman, a Santee Sioux who witnessed the aftermath of Wounded Knee, described the Ghost Dance as "a religious craze" that "meant that the last hope of the race had entirely departed, and my people were groping blindly after spiritual relief in their bewilderment and misery" (748). Writers like Eastman and Roosevelt felt sympathy for the victims of the massacre, but little for the culture to which those victims had tried to cling.

As a result, whites who tried to study the Ghost Dance made little progress among Indians deeply distrustful of government motives and wary of discussing religious doctrines with unsympathetic listeners. Wovoka's identity as "the Ghost Dance messiah" was not firmly established among whites until James Mooney traveled to the Walker River valley to meet him over a year after Wounded Knee—despite a letter from the local agent swearing the local Paiutes had nothing to do with Ghost Dance (Mooney 767). Mooney was rather more successful at gaining the confidence of people who had adopted the Ghost Dance. The book that emerged from his extensive study not only remains the standard text on the movement, but also marked a turning point in anthropology from efforts to chart the stages of human culture to attempts to understand the workings of human culture in general by exploring its myriad manifestations.[6] Accounts of the movement since Mooney have tended to waver between stressing the movement's cross-cultural elements and its cultural specificity. Black Elk's narrative is the first account of the Ghost Dance rooted firmly in a Sioux context. Though John Neihardt presents the Oglala Sioux holy man's account of the events leading to Wounded Knee as an Indian Passion that brought the Sioux closer to Christianity, Black Elk's unedited transcripts place a greater emphasis on the role the Ghost Dance played in his later efforts to recuperate more traditional Lakota spirituality. Later studies, especially Alice Beck Kehoe's, have picked up on Black Elk's theme, reading the Ghost Dance as a catalyst in renewing traditional culture.

Kehoe, in fact, cites the Ghost Dance as a classic example of what A. F. C. Wallace in 1956 termed a "revitalization movement." Out of a context of cultural disintegration, a prophet arises promising a return of a community's prestige and integrity if members adopt a new code of beliefs. The new code is nativistic in orientation, but incorporates enough new elements to address the changes that led to the cultural distortions in the first place, a process Kehoe calls "creative pruning" (48). Wallace formulated his concept in reference to the preaching of Handsome Lake among the Seneca at the end of the eighteenth century, a movement with strong parallels to Wovoka and the Ghost Dance. The concept of revitalization also provided a corrective to earlier ethnographies of such Indian spiritual movements, portraying them as something more than the last gasps of cultures inevitably losing in their evolutionary struggle. Such a shift in focus sees the Ghost Dance and related movements as entirely normal reactions of cultures under stress adapting to meet changing conditions. Indeed, one sociologist, Russell Thornton, managed to establish a rough correlation between a tribe's recent depopulation and its enthusiasm for the Ghost Dance; moreover, the tactic, on some level, worked. Tribes that adopted the Ghost Dance saw their populations rise. Equally importantly, those tribes saw a strengthening of tribal identity despite the increasing pressures of assimilation. The rituals of the Ghost Dance brought Indians together within and across tribal lines, strengthening social ties and renewing the participants' focus on the many elements of traditional religious practice that the Ghost Dance preserved.

While contemporary white observers tended to read the Ghost Dance as bastardized Christianity—with a messiah preaching a gospel of an Indian Father colored by the apocalyptic strains of the Book of Revelation—and while James Mooney himself stressed what he saw as the universal elements of the movement, the Ghost Dance was nevertheless fashioned out of Native American materials. Of the 160 Ghost Dance songs from almost a dozen tribes recorded by Mooney, almost 50 center on traditional religious elements. Some, like this example from the Arapahoe, feature animal spirits (in this case, the crow is the traditional messenger to the spirit world) and their totems:

> The crow is circling above me,
> The crow is circling above me.
> He says he will give me a hawk feather,
> He says he will give me a hawk feather. (991)

Others, like this example from the Cheyenne, involve ritual body paints:

> The crow—Ehe'e'e'ye'!
> The crow—Ehe'e'e'ye'!
> The grease paint—He'e'ye'!
> The grease paint—He'e'ye'!
> He brings it to me,
> He brings it to me.
> The red paint—He'e'ye'!
> The red paint—He'e'ye'!
> He brings it,
> He brings it. (1037)

Still others rehearse the individual traditions of the tribes who took up the Ghost Dance (for instance, the Cheyenne's origins on the Turtle River [1029]), cite particularly sacred animals and the dances devoted to them (1033), illustrate traditional medicine (1083), or reference myths whose meanings remain opaque even to as diligent an observer as Mooney. The songs whose referents he can trace, however, offer enough material for Mooney to recreate dense summaries of the various tribal belief systems—and more than enough to show that for members of the tribes themselves, the Ghost Dance provided a rich opportunity to preserve and rehearse their traditions.

Such traditions, of course, were saved under the most dismaying of conditions. It is no surprise that studies of the Ghost Dance focus quite understandably on the massacre at Wounded Knee; the battlefield horrors have a tremendous narrative pull and lend a powerful focus to the human stakes of the movement. The carnage also highlights the apocalyptic dimension of the Ghost Dance, the promise of a new earth that would bury or burn all the whites and Indian unbelievers. From the vantage point of Wounded Knee, the Ghost Dance appears as a last-ditch effort to accomplish through spiritual means what people had failed to accomplish through politics or war—a final attempt to outflank the technological and numerical superiority of whites by calling on an unanswerable, uncompromising power that would once and for all restore the power of those who had clung most tenaciously to their traditional life. This was, indeed, an important part of the movement; Mooney collected songs featuring the coming apocalypse from all but one tribe. Arapaho ghost dancers thus sing of triumph over whites while confined to their reservation: "I'yehe! we have rendered them desolate—*Eye'de'yuhe'yu!* / The whites are crazy—*he'yuhe'yu!*" (972), and *"He'yoho'ho! He'yoho'ho! /* The yellow-hide, the white-skin (man)/I have now put him aside!" (978). The

Kiowa, in turn, sang, "The spirit army is approaching, / The whole world is moving onward" (1082), while one Sioux song promised to confer military invincibility to earthly warriors: "The shirt will cause you to live, / Says the father, says the father" (1073). Such songs do much to explain the appeal of the Ghost Dance at this nadir in the history of the Plains tribes, especially to the Sioux band camped under the Hotchkiss guns by Wounded Knee Creek. Yet such explicitly militaristic elements make up a remarkably small portion of the Ghost Dance movement. Of the songs recorded by Mooney, only forty or so concern the arrival of the new earth, and only two, both from the Arapaho, contain references to the destruction of the whites. To be sure, ghost dancers in the early 1890s, especially among the Sioux, may have been reluctant to share their most incendiary songs with a white anthropologist on the government payroll; the ability to collect two such songs from the Arapaho, indeed, illustrates the depth of the confidence Mooney had won from his informants.

The centrality of Wounded Knee skews our understanding of the Ghost Dance toward its apocalyptic dimension, while the songs themselves indicate that the crucial impact of the movement lay neither in the unfulfilled promise of a cataclysm arriving with the green grass of spring nor with the unimagined cataclysm that did occur in the bitter cold of winter. It was instead the vivid visions of heaven that held the key to the Ghost Dance's power. Of the 160 songs in Mooney's *Ghost Dance Religion,* almost 60 contain representations of a spirit land identical to the world Indians remembered from before the era of white expansion. Another 25 describe the meeting of deceased friends and relatives. Thus over half of the songs detail a heaven that is explicit, detailed, intimately familiar, and close at hand—accessible to any willing to believe and able to participate in the rituals of the dance. A Sioux woman could visit the spirit land and return to sing,

> *E'yaye'ye'! E'yaye'ye'!*
> It is my own child,
> It is my own child. (1069)

Other dancers woke from their trances to tell of seeing fathers and mothers and hosts of friends, all living according to lifeways that had vanished from the reservations. An Arapaho woman returned to sing of a camp full of buffalo skin teepees:

> *E'yehe'!* they are new—
> The bed coverings,
> The bed coverings. (963)

A Sioux woman, joining her spirit friends as they began to butcher buffalo, sang,

> Give me my knife,
> I shall hang up the meat to dry—*Yĕ'ye'!*
> When it is dry I shall make pemmican. (1066)

Still others sing of playing traditional games—the "awl game," the "dice game," a ball-and-stick game called "shinny," games involving buttons and tops, hoops and arrows. All this occurs in a verdant landscape abounding with each tribe's favorite traditional foods: the *wai-va,* or wild millet, of the Paiute; the cottonwood of the Arapaho; the thunderberries of the Kiowa; the buffalo that fed, clothed, and housed all the Plains tribes.

Such specific descriptions of the spirit land contrast sharply with the more traditional visionary experiences of the western Indian nations, where contact with spirits was marked by strangeness. Among the Sioux, things *wakan* were by definition extraordinary, beyond the bounds of daily experience. "Wakan was anything that was hard to understand," the Lakota Good Seat told James Walker. "If the thing done was what no one could understand, it was Wakan Tanka" (70). While spirits were a regular presence in the communal life of the Sioux and other tribes, the spirit land itself was far away "beyond the pines," in a mystical northern world that the living did not visit. Visions occurred seldom in the lives of ordinary people, usually at moments of great personal crisis and even then only after elaborate preparation—never on the frequent intervals enjoyed by the ghost dancers. And finally, visions came couched in a highly charged, richly symbolic language quite distinct from the idiom of daily life. Most depended on holy men and women for interpretation: "A wakan man knows things that the people do not know. . . . He can tell people what their visions mean" (Walker 69). One who received a vision might, like Black Elk, spend a lifetime trying to unravel its import or, like the Paiute Tä'vibo, who started a Ghost Dance movement in 1869, decide after some years that the vision was the work of evil spirits (Kehoe).

Such ambiguity and interpretive apparatus were strikingly absent from the Ghost Dance songs. Dancers instead had immediate and regular access to visions, whose meanings were direct and clear. Indeed, the Ghost Dance inverted the traditional Indian cosmology; where contact with the spirit world had previously given a numinous charge to the ordinary world, lending mystery and power to a familiar environment, in the Ghost Dance people turned from a physical world grown alien and strange to find, in the spirit world, the familiar environs of home. The visionary has become nostalgic. Irwin argues that the traditional visions of the Plains tribes are a "sacred praxis" in which "cultural identity is strengthened through . . . enactment, and individual symbolization of dream and visionary contents contribute an emergent quality to this identity" (186). Such an ongoing cultural fashioning is also apparent in the Ghost Dance, but the terms have shifted: rather than mystifying ordinary social relations, the visionary nostalgia of the Ghost Dance songs helped preserve a structure of traditional social relations that threatened to vanish. Ghost dancers journeyed to heaven to save the earth they knew.

The Gates Novels and White Revitalization

While heaven was hardly a new concept in nineteenth-century European America, it too evolved considerably before and after the Civil War. Protestant religions had been tempering Calvinist visions of hellfire since the eighteenth century, gradually shifting from the threat of damnation to the promise of salvation in their efforts to attract believers. Yet like the spirit land in most Native American religions, heaven in most denominations remained a thinly sketched promise whose pleasures were incomprehensible to earthbound minds; most Protestant faiths emphasized, the cardinal experience of personal conversion over the promise of heaven.[7] With the advent of spiritualism at midcentury, however, heaven became a more central category of religious experience. Once spirits had established their otherworldly credentials at a typical séance, they were peppered with questions about their surroundings. Most described an afterlife that conformed to the Swedenborgian beliefs common among the progressives and free-thinkers who made up the early core of spiritualist mediums and advocates. The spirit world consisted of a succession of spheres surrounding the mortal earth, through which spirits ascended according to their virtue and learning, as described here in an 1854 séance:

I remained near my body until it was interred. Then they [the spirit's father, grandfather, and grandmother] took me, hand-in-hand, and led me to a grand enclosure planted with trees, that Heavenly eyes only can appreciate. This they called the First Sphere. The Spirits there seemed happy, but not so happy as many I have seen since. I remained here till—but we do not count time as you do—say a very short time. Then we passed to another Sphere, where I met still larger numbers of still happier Spirits, upon a glorious stadium, hedged in with evergreens. Here bands associated in close-bound affinity, who sang, and taught, and chanted the high notes of Knowledge and Love, and blessed each other together. (Ferguson 41– 42)

Thus spirits progress towards "eternal Brotherhood," ever advancing in spiritual wisdom and frequently looking over and encouraging spirits and mortals mired in lower spheres. Although this version of heaven was not entirely new—it was, indeed, old when Dante wrote—two aspects are worth noting. First, it presented a seamless connection between the earthly and spiritual worlds. The spirits of the dead continually watch over and, through the "spiritual telegraph," interact with the living. Second, this version of the spirit land is not presented as an allegory for a transcendent reality, but as an actual representation of heaven, a vivid portrait of a real world. As other spiritualists elaborated on the landscape of heaven, an increasingly vivid image emerged to supplement the Swedenborgian notion of a succession of spheres, one more fully limned with the pigments of an idealized American landscape. "Summerland," as this ubiquitous version of heaven came to be known, portrayed heaven as a more earthly paradise, drawing as much from the iconography of the Hudson River School painters as from the ideology of Swedenborg:

I see a towering mount covered over by animals of all descriptions. It is festooned with vines and blooming wildflowers. A broad river flows by its side and winds around its base, presenting every variety of cascade and cataract, before moving on into a wide and undulating valley. The sweetest strains of music pour forth from myriad voices, accompanied by innumerable instruments, while hosts of happy Spirits move to the melodious notes, in offices of duty and ecstasies of love. (Ferguson 34)

Such an effort to domesticate heaven, to chart its pleasures in terms immediately recognizable to a still rural nation, became widespread, and indeed still persists in the lush garden cemeteries that began appearing across the country in the years before the Civil War. Inaugurated by Mount Auburn Cemetery founded outside of Boston, these cemeteries replaced the spartan Puritan graveyards squeezed onto spare bits of town land; they are instead rolling pastoral landscapes covered with flowering trees and dotted with Greek temples, Gothic chapels, and tombs ornamented with graceful statuary rather than the grim memento morias typical of older graves. These heavenly simulacra soon became popular attractions in their own right.[8] By the time Elizabeth Stuart Phelps began sketching her own version of heaven in the *Gates* novels, white Americans had long been accustomed to contemplating the pleasures of the afterlife.

Phelps was in her early twenties when the Civil War ended. She had spent the war years in the relative sanctity of Andover, Massachusetts, where her father was a professor of theology at one of the last redoubts of conservative

Calvinism left in the United States, the Andover Theological Seminary. She had seen the majority of Andover students march off to Southern battlefields and been engaged to one who didn't come back; like the Native American peoples devastated by war, Phelps's mind was on those left on the battlefields. "The Grand Review passed through Washington," she wrote, looking back on the years following the war; "four hundred thousand ghosts of murdered men kept invisible march to the drumbeats" (1896, 96). Such metaphors came naturally to Phelps. Though never an avowed spiritualist, she happily advertised her works in the spiritualist press and invariably spoke kindly of the movement, a stance she traced to her affection for her grandfather, the Reverend Eliakim Phelps, whose home was the scene of the widely reported Stratford Rappings in 1850. Coming hard on the heels of the Rochester Rappings, this small storm of airborne candlesticks, bent forks, strangely marked turnips dropped from the ceiling, and mysterious rappings demanding squash pie was attributed by some to the minister's stepchildren, but by others to a genuine, if rather impish, spirit. Eliakim Phelps continued to believe the phenomena genuine; his granddaughter somewhat equivocally agreed (6–9).

Phelps's relative openness to new theological ideas was typical of mainstream white reactions to spiritualism. Indeed, even while staunch Calvinist ministers held sway at Andover, a number of their wives helped popularize a more genial version of Christianity. Among them was Phelps's mother, who shared her daughter's name and anticipated her career as a best-selling author, publishing two idyllic novels about life in a country parsonage. Harriet Beecher Stowe, who was a neighbor and friend of the Phelps family in the late 1850s, not only tempered the orthodox Calvinism of her father and husband, but also proved a cautious proponent of spiritualism, publishing her own investigations of the planchette alongside Austin Phelps's earnest account of the Stratford Rappings in Charles Beecher's *Spirit Manifestations* (1879). Thus as Phelps began drafting her version of heaven in the years after the Civil War, she had before her models of the afterlife that clothed the vivid details drawn from séances in the more familiar trappings of traditional Protestant Christianity.

The Gates Ajar (1868), a novel published some twenty-five years before Wovoka's vision spread across the West, consists of diary entries written by a young woman, Mary, whose brother dies in battle. Sunk deep into grief, she finds consolation not in the stern doctrines of the deacon or minister—whose sermon on heaven follows the abstract syllogisms of classic Puritan theology—but in the vivid images of heaven lovingly offered by her aunt, Winifred, who promises a heaven full of friends and loved ones and cozy homes surrounded by gardens. While Phelps rigorously documents her ideas with biblical and scholarly texts, her model for heaven is clearly the idealized Andover of her childhood, close-knit, genteel, intellectual, and homogeneous. Although the deceased do not spend their time communicating with the living through rappings and Ouija boards, they do look over loved ones still on earth—"I cannot doubt that our absent dead are very present with us," says Winifred (60). When not haunting the earth, the spirits of the dead pursue their earthly interests in heaven, from writing poetry to playing piano to, in one case, tinkering on improvements to carpet sweepers.

The specificity with which she imagined heaven was novel indeed, and when *The Gates Ajar* was published in 1868 the response was overwhelming. The first printing of four thousand copies sold out in a few weeks; over two hundred thousand were sold in the United States and abroad by the century's end. The book was also subject to one of the first mass-marketing campaigns of modern times, infiltrating every corner of American popular culture through the medium of *Gates Ajar* clothing, cigars, funeral wreaths, and patent medicines (H. Smith vi). Having become a literary celebrity, Phelps quickly embraced a variety of social causes, writing a series of novels (including *The Silent Partner* [1871], *The Story of Avis* [1877], and *Doctor Zay* [1882]) strongly advocating women's rights, temperance, and reforms to protect the working class.

Her modest contemporary reputation as an early feminist and social realist rests largely on these works, but they were poorly received by her contemporaries, and Phelps returned later in her career to the heavenly fictions upon which that career had been built. She wrote two sequels to *The Gates Ajar*. *Beyond the Gates* (1885) is narrated by another Mary, an unmarried school teacher active in the variety of social causes near and dear to her author's heart. She lives in a Massachusetts factory town with her mother until stricken with a brain fever; one night her long-dead father appears at her bedside to lead her to the heavenly sphere located far above the earth. Once greeted by the lost waifs and wounded soldiers she had helped on earth, and by Christ himself, she settles, after a quick return to visit her funeral, into the business of heaven. She moves into her father's neatly appointed cottage, located in the suburbs of ᶜ city complete with schools (for both men and women), museums, parks, a hospital (for those sick in their souls), and a concert hall where Beethoven and Mendelssohn premier their latest work. Just as she begins to settle in, she wakes to find her vision the result of a fevered dream.

No such device frames the third heaven novel, *The Gates Between* (1887). Esmereld Thorne, a gruff and successful doctor, finds himself utterly bewildered after being thrown from his horse and killed—unable to accept his death, he wanders miserably around the city for days until a former patient, a pious invalid happily named Mrs. Faith, points the way to heaven. He finds his scientific and worldly knowledge a handicap in a world in which sensitive and spiritual matriarchs have the upper hand; his redemption comes only when he learns to humble himself before his child and long-abused wife.

Phelps's widely popular portrait of heaven has long been read as the culmination of the liberal reaction to Calvinism in the nineteenth century, the endpoint in an ongoing effort to construct a cosmology in opposition to such stern Puritan representations as Michael Wigglesworth's *Day of Doom* (1662), which unapologetically consigns unbaptized infants to hell and dwells as carefully on the torments of damnation as the *Gates* novels dwell on the pleasures of salvation.[9] Such a reading places Phelps squarely in the context of her former neighbor, Harriet Beecher Stowe, and the other members of her formidable family who emphasized the gospel of love in their efforts to fashion a mainstream Christianity fit for the burly optimism of nineteenth-century America. This reading also places Phelps in the context of the literary movement known as the Mount Auburn School, with its graveyard meditations on the deaths of children predicated on the promise of heavenly reunion. *The Gates Ajar* neatly joins both movements. Mary finds comfort in the refulgent, picturesque landscape around her brother's grave, while Dr. Bland's sermon on heaven, with its "illustrations, metaphors, proof-texts, learning and eloquence" (50), is no match for the reassurance of Aunt Winifred's hand: "Ah, Dr. Bland, if you had known how that little soft touch was preaching against you!" (49).

That the "soft touch" was a woman's mattered greatly, and indeed most efforts to recuperate Phelps's reputation have focused on the feminist valence of her work, with assessments of the *Gates* novels roughly tracking recent efforts to reassess the cultural meanings of sentimental writing in general. Thus while Ann Douglass, writing in 1975, damns Phelps as "always a sentimental, often a sloppy writer, seldom likable, her talents sapped by her need for self-justification" (66–67), Douglass sees as well an undercurrent of assertiveness, even revenge, in Phelps's genial portrait of heaven. Phelps and her followers "had an immense interest in visualizing the afterlife as one scaled to their domestic and pastoral proportions, as a place where they would dominate rather than be dominated" (68). Carol Kessler, writing in the 1980s, foregrounds Phelps's assertiveness, arguing that the *Gates* novels should be read as a protofeminist utopia rather than a sentimental Christian fantasy of revenge. Lisa Long, in a more recent article (1997), argues that *The*

Gates Ajar is best read not as one example of feminine consolation literature but as an integral part of Civil War literature, an effort to reimagine a fractured European-American ontology through the prism of the woman's sphere. The vivid embodiment of spirits in heaven, Long argues, counters an American identity shown by the devastation of civil war to be fragile indeed. Life on earth, dominated by nationalist rhetoric and scientific epistemology, is for Phelps only a shadow of the ultimate reality of heaven.

By the third installment of the *Gates* novels, Phelps's protofeminism has grown rather more than "proto." Like Wovoka and his followers, who forbade warfare, welcomed women, and highlighted the domestic pleasures of the spirit land, Phelps centered the promise of heaven on the hearth. The first two *Gates* novels abound in models of gentle, even womanly, men; in the final novel she systematically removes the masculine touchstones of Esmereld Thorne's personality—from his professional status to his financial success to his gruff egocentrism—and remakes him, via the machinery of heaven, into a meek, tender, and all but genderless soul. Such gender blending was hardly new. As women made up a rising percentage of members in mainstream Protestant churches in the nineteenth century, ministers increasingly cultivated their "feminine" attributes. Spiritualism was especially known for its mingling of gender attributes. Mediums male and female were described in equivalent terms, as particularly passive receptors of whatever magnetic currents carried the voices of the dead, and while departed spirits retained their interest in their earthly pursuits, séance after séance underscored the importance of domestic virtues in the afterlife. *The Gates Between* is unusual, however, in its determination to render the spirit of the successful doctor utterly powerless in the very settings he once dominated. In her determination to show that the social structures that empower men like Thorne on earth are poor tools with which to fashion a heavenly soul, Phelps shows that her principal focus is not the heaven for which Thorne must be made fit, but the world that rewarded such an unfit soul as he.

The most striking connection between the Ghost Dance and the *Gates* novels also sets them apart from earlier European-American representations of the afterlife. While most writers draw on occult rhetoric to capture the numinous, inexpressible quality of the other world, Phelps, like most spiritualists and like most ghost dancers, insists on the recognizable, even ordinary, nature of the afterlife. Indeed, the earthly texture of Phelps's heaven made it more compelling than the visionary, highly figurative, and relentlessly allegorical descriptions of heaven that appeared regularly in séances and reached their spiritualist apogee in the work of Andrew Jackson Davis. Phelps insists on what I term "visionary realism," a device that applies the techniques of social realism to spiritual visions. "The Father's house are many mansions," says Winifred in *The Gates Ajar*. "Sometimes I fancy those words have a literal meaning which the simple men who heard them may have understood better than we, and that Christ is truly 'preparing' my home for me" (94). Like the ghost dancers, Phelps creates in the *Gates* novels a heaven that sought to set within a visionary frame an utterly concrete representation of lived reality. Whereas previous representations—biblical prophecy, Dantean allegory, Swedenborgian mysticism—gained power by stressing heaven's otherness, its distance from the mundane minutiae and pains petty and profound that characterized earthly life, the visionary realism in the *Gates* novels works by refracting earthly reality through a idealized lens.

Heaven, for Phelps as for the ghost dancers, functions as a cultural ideal, a utopia, a means for imagining a prosperous and harmonious society that had proven elusive on earth.[10] Heaven, in other words, is politics by other means. Frederick Jameson has argued that the utopian impulse depends on social morass: "[T]he vocation of Utopia lies in failure. . . . [I]ts epistemological value lies in the walls it allows us to detect by sheerest inductions, the mirings of our imaginations in the mode of production itself, the mud of the present age in which winged Utopian shoes stick, imagining that to be the force of gravity itself" (75). Phelps looks forward by facing back. Failed or frustrated social reform movements (as those urging the feminist, temperance, and socialist causes) managed to regroup in heaven when beaten back on earth. Phelps builds her vision of the heavenly city in *The Gates Between* out of fragments salvaged from the wreckage of an industrial reform movement she had worked on for more than a decade. Thus the rhythm of the *Gates* novels: heaven seemed particularly appealing every dozen years or so, roughly following the boom and bust cycle of social reform movements centered in the East. *The Gates Ajar* has long been tied to the social disruption that followed the Civil War; *The Gates Between* and *Beyond the Gates* appeared in the years following the end of Reconstruction and the economic recession of the late 1870s, when reform movements were in a serious retreat that only ended with the Progressive movement at the turn of the century.

In psychoanalytic terms, heaven in the Ghost Dance and the *Gates* novels is an example of wish fulfillment or, better still, an *objet petit a*, a fantasized lost object whose endlessly deferred attainment promises to restore wholeness to the fractured subject. Phelps formulates a particularly vivid heaven in order to resolve the psychic anxieties of earth. In *The Gates Ajar,* Winifred's vivid portraits of heaven cathect Mary's desires from a narcissistic death drive toward a deferred ideal, and likewise shift the desires of other characters from channels frustrated by social realities (poverty in one case, an overbearing father in another; a deceased wife in a third) toward less destructive channels oriented toward the endlessly deferred pleasures of heaven. By making heaven real, by recasting (or misrecognizing) orthodox Christian doctrines of the afterlife, by making heaven, in other words, into an *objet petit a,* Phelps manages to transform her characters' subjectivity. And so with her readers: for women especially, who formed her most devoted readership, *The Gates Ajar* offered a new setting for an ego ideal structured around Victorian domesticity. Desire for sentimental love and family fractured by the Civil War were reborn in heaven. In her later novels, the increasingly detailed utopias imagined in the afterlife served as substitutes for thwarted reformist ideals. While local colorists frequently resolved the anxieties inherent in the industrializing and diversifying terrain of New England by summoning an idealized vision of the New England past to take its place, Phelps located her ego ideal in the afterworld.

Yet while the origins of the *Gates* novels may have been rooted in the failure of central cultural aspirations, their utopian retreats may also be read, like the Ghost Dance, as strategic withdrawals. Although few anthropologists have turned their attention to European-American society, the concept of revitalization, developed in regard to an Indian culture Phelps's own society had displaced, applies equally well to Phelps's own work. Her *Gates* novels neatly follow Wallace's model. From a satisfactory adaptation to a social and economic milieu, best exemplified in Phelps's case by the antebellum idyll sketched in her mother's *Sunnyside,* European-American culture underwent the wrenching distortions of civil war and industrialization. These episodes clearly match the phases sketched by Wallace of individual stress and cultural distortion, when traditional rituals and beliefs failed to answer people's physical and emotional needs. To the extent that *The Gates Ajar* offered a "reformulation of a cultural pattern" to meet the disruption of middle-class mourning rituals, as Long argues, or that *The Gates Between* and *Beyond the Gates* offer reformulated versions of reform movements disrupted by political corruption, industrialization, and economic panic, Phelps's novels are part of a postbellum revitalization movement of European-American bourgeois culture. Indeed, the progress of Phelps's representations of heaven reflect Wallace's concept of movement from individual stress to cultural dislocation: whereas *The Gates Ajar* centers on the fate of the individual body in the afterlife, Phelps's focus broadened in the later *Gates* novels to embrace the wide array of problems facing a modernizing America.

Thus Phelps revitalizes a European-American society in crises by weaving together ideologies that were increasingly at odds in postbellum culture. Upon a traditional Protestant Christian tradition Phelps grafted a radical spiritualist sensibility and used the result to reimagine modernity. The heavenly utopias hinted at in *The Gates Ajar* and more fully developed in *Beyond the Gates* and *The Gates Between* posit an America revitalized through a pious modernity, a society full of the material abundance promised by capitalism. The vague promise in *The Gates Ajar* of "organized society" evolves in *Beyond the Gates* into a description of a heavenly city that reads more like the travel report of an urban planner than the raptures of a visionary: "The width and shining cleanliness of the streets, the beauty and glittering material of the houses, the frequent presence of libraries, museums, public gardens, signs of attention to the wants of animals, and places of shelter for travelers such as I had never seen in the most advanced and benevolent of cities below" (118). Mary continues on to the suburbs and stops before "a small and quiet house built of curiously inlaid wood," perfectly set in a picturesque landscape of trees and flowers. She enters, admires "certain useful articles . . . and works of art," and finds the house belongs to her father. "Heaven itself seemed to have been ransacked to bring together the daintiest, the most delicate, the purest thoughts and fancies that celestial skill or art could create" (128–29). Phelps's description of heaven as a bourgeois fantasy sprung from the pages of a home and garden magazine, though frequently mocked, nevertheless bespeaks her effort to imagine a modern, capitalist, consumer society that remained profoundly spiritual at its core.

The visionary realism of the *Gates* novels helped revitalize postbellum America by casting (or better, mystifying) the furthest extremes of consumerism as sacrifices laid upon the alter of domesticity. Her efforts were not alone. Of the many attempts to reformulate the excesses and abuses of late-nineteenth-century capitalism, the most popular, Edward Bellamy's *Looking Backward* (1887), owes the deepest debt to Phelps's work. Yet Bellamy's twentieth-century Boston is distinctly secular. While Phelps's work did not spawn a national political movement, it did anticipate in a way that Bellamy did not the Christian undercurrents of the Progressive movement that tried to put so many of her ideas into practice. Though the Progressives may not have recreated Phelps's heavenly city on earth, they did manage to achieve the final stage of Wallace's revitalization: a satisfactory adaptation to a changed world.

Heaven and Empire

The Ghost Dance and the *Gates* novels share a number of fundamental similarities. Yet to argue that Wovoka and Phelps both participated in revitalization movements merely underscores the cultural divisions between them.
Each emerged in vastly different political contexts, and each responded to
those contexts by attempting to strengthen a distinct cultural identity. Indeed, one result of juxtaposing the Ghost Dance and the *Gates* novels is to
chart the cultural divide that existed in the late nineteenth century between
white and Indian America. How, then, are we to read across the cultural lines
marked by these two conflicting portraits of heaven?

The classic tools of literary history offer some help in reading the relationship between these phenomena. An influence-based criticism might, for
example, look for elements of these heavenly representations that appear to
be borrowed and trace them back to their source. This has been a common
approach to studying the Ghost Dance: some of the first Indian agents to report on the dances to a wider audience attempted to explain items like the
ghost shirts worn by the Sioux by linking them to the endowment robes used
in certain Mormon rituals.[11] Others have tried to explain Wovoka's theology
by assuming he traveled among the Indian Shakers of Puget Sound, a more
Christianized group of Native Americans whose rituals were in turn traced to
Protestant missionaries (Mooney 763). And if we follow those missionaries
back to their New England theological seminaries, we are left one step away
from Elizabeth Stuart Phelps: between *The Gates Ajar* and the Ghost Dance
are, in this case, four degrees of cultural separation.

This approach, typical of classic literary history, at its best has all the finely
tuned allure of good detective work, the sifting for and careful organization of
small clues. But its strength is also its weakness: it tends to imagine that to establish a line of cultural influence (however slight) for a given phenomenon is
to account for it. Such lines, however, are often tenuous, carefully navigating
the gray area between correlation and causation. Explanations of influence
also tend to play into cultural hierarchies, casting Wovoka's prophecies, in
this case, as the debased offspring of Anglo-American religion. Such hierarchies tend to point as well in one direction only, from a "dominant" culture to
an "inferior" one: few readers of Phelps have thought to mine her novel for
examples of Native American influence. Finally, such an approach stresses
similarities between or among various cultures at the expense of differences;
it looks, in an unfamiliar cultural setting, for signs that loom large for the ob-

server because of their familiarity, though they may be quite unremarkable to others.

One of the most striking differences between European-American and the Native American cultures is the medium through which these two representations of heaven spread. The *Gates* novels were products of the newly emerging mass publishing industry in which literature became a capitalist commodity. Phelps began her literary career at a time when relatively informal structures of parlor literature began to give way to a more rigid division of literature into high and low culture, and she managed to gain access at the ground floor to such publishing organs of high culture as the publishing house Ticknor and Fields and the *Atlantic Monthly*. Thus she assumed an emergent (though tenuous) status as an artist, a priestess of culture whose status was affirmed with each batch of fan mail. Such a status tended to separate Phelps from her readers, who themselves began to substitute more solitary reading habits for the more communal reading practices of the antebellum era.

Wovoka, however, neither read nor wrote. While a handful of literate Indians wrote down his prophecies, the Ghost Dance spread primarily through traditional oral channels. Delegations of Indians from tribes across the West visited Wovoka in Nevada, heard his message, danced with his band of Paiutes, and then returned home. Such a mechanism not only allowed the Ghost Dance to spread largely unnoticed by whites fixated on military action and the written word, but also made the doctrines and rituals of the Ghost Dance highly adaptable to the various tribal contexts in which it took root. Thus, while the *Gates* novels remained firmly fixed in the terms set down by their author to be more or less passively consumed by their readers, the Ghost Dance was far more of a communal creation, with Wovoka at one end a chain of creation that encompassed the delegations shaping his message to their tribal audiences, the medicine men who conducted the ceremonies, and the participants whose own visions became the basis of a growing body of Ghost Dance songs. These songs mark a profound difference between the written literature produced by Phelps and the oral literature characteristic of Native American cultures. Karl Kroeber has argued that the short, repetitive, and suggestive nature of traditional Indian songs serves an important cultural function: the songs are participatory in a way that Phelps's conclusively imagined novels are not. "The synecdochic character of Indian song affirms the total group, tribe or nation as the appropriate 'audience' for each individual as poet-singer" (106). Indeed, to treat both the Ghost Dance and the *Gates* novels as literature indicates primarily how diffuse a term "literature" has become in recent years. While a number of Native Americans decided to produce "literature" as it was conceived in the nineteenth century, the many authors of the Ghost Dance were not among them, and juxtaposing the Ghost Dance and the *Gates* novels reveals the depth of the cultural chasm between literate European America and oral Indian America.

Moreover, juxtaposing the heavens of these two cultures illustrates how different economic and religious structures contributed to distinct structures of subjectivity. The people who responded to Wovoka's message sought to reproduce through their religious rituals a communal, tribal subjectivity that was coming under increasing threat from government efforts to promote individual ownership of land and Protestant missionary efforts directed toward individual salvation. The Ghost Dance instead operated largely on a tribal level, with salvation geared toward an entire people and their folkways. "You shall grow to be a nation—Ye'ye'!/Says the father, says the father," sang the Sioux (Mooney 1065). Individual visions were carefully contained within a communal framework, and the songs these worshipers made from their visions typically speak of the tribe or family rather than the individual. Phelps, by contrast, crafts a heaven structured around a highly individualized subjectivity. Mary's greatest horror in *The Gates Ajar* is, curiously, not hell, about which Phelps is silent, but the possibility that her thoughts in heaven will not be private: "I would rather be annihilated than spend eternity with heart laid bare,—the inner temple thrown open to be trampled on by every passing stranger!" (55). Aunt Winifred assures her that in contrast to "this promiscuous theory of refraction," bourgeois notions of privacy will prevail in heaven. Indeed, identity in Phelps's heaven remains closely tied to Protestant notions of individual vocation—people called to be farmers, musicians, social workers, or inventors on earth will pursue those occupations for eternity.

Postcolonial criticism offers a useful model for reading such differences. Carefully attuned to material concerns, it also moves easily from culture to culture, fashioning common critical ground by reading distinct cultural productions through a lens of modern European colonialism and the efforts of native peoples to resist European invasion, settlement, and acculturation on both political and cultural fronts. One strength of this paradigm is its focused cross-culturalism. African, Asian, Latin American, and, more recently, North American literatures are grouped together not by appeals to a universal human nature but by a common historical condition: contact with a more or less monolithic and aggressive western European culture. In such a model, the Ghost Dance and the *Gates* novels stand not as analogous but as antagonistic cultural productions. Phelps, on the one hand, produced novels determined by a metropolitan and imperialist sensibility. Her heaven, described by David S. Reynolds as "a place combining the bucolic beauty of Kansas with the cultured domesticity of Boston" (67), is part of an imperialist ideology that fashions an ideal America that has no place for the people it has displaced. The *Gates* novels thus fit squarely within a visionary tradition in American literature that begins with the anonymous 1785 publication of *The Golden Age,* in which an angel appears to a Revolutionary War veteran to tell him that the seraphim have been watching over the fledgling country, and that the millennium will come when Indians, blacks, and Jews are converted and, along with Spanish and Dutch colonists, are settled in their own states in the Far West. A work published a year after Wounded Knee carries American imperialism to its logical conclusion: in *The Heresy of Mehetabel Clark* (1892), Annie T. Slosson describes a heaven in which God and Jesus live in an exact replica (or prototype?) of the White House. Heaven in these texts is clearly imbued with nationalist ideology.

The Ghost Dance, in this framework, partakes of the same dynamic, emerging in direct response to the political and cultural pressures of U.S. imperialism. The Ghost Dance was, after all, the latest in a series of Native American visionary movements that followed the course of white settlement in the West. Religious doctrine and ritual, in such a reading, are inextricable from the political and economic struggles that provided historical context. In such a reading, distinct tribal histories and traditions fit into a narrative structured by Western imperialism. Yet while the Ghost Dance may have taken shape in response to European-American aggression it hardly imagined a world of interracial harmony. It imagined, instead, a world of Indian autonomy and seperatism. Though Wovoka preached a gospel of peace, and though intertribal cooperation may have been his most powerful legacy, the Ghost Dance was based on an ideology of Indian resurgence. One powerful Sioux song captures this logic:

> The whole world is coming,
> A nation is coming, a nation is coming,
> The Eagle has brought the message to the tribe.
> The father says so, the father says so.
> Over the whole earth they are coming. (Mooney 1072)

In the cosmology embedded in this song, "world," "nation," and "tribe" are equivalent terms. The promise of the Ghost Dance is the promise of one tribe constituting an entire nation, and indeed an entire world.[12] Heaven in both the *Gates* novels and the Ghost Dance may have played a crucial role in revitalizing white and Indian cultures at the end of the nineteenth century, but they did nothing to bring them together.

Captain Stormfield *and Devitalization*

Not every representation of heaven was so culturally monolithic. One, indeed, placed a "heap of Indians" in a heaven patterned explicitly after Phelps's. Though Mark Twain published *Extract from Captain Stormfield's Visit to Heaven* in *Harper's Monthly* in 1907 and 1908, he had begun working on the story as early as 1868 as a rejoinder to *The Gates Ajar,* which he criticized for its "mean little ten-cent heaven about the size of Rhode Island" (1922, 247). His heaven, in contrast, was millions of light-years across, big enough to accommodate billions of terrestrial and extraterrestrial angels of every size, shape, and color, who came from all the worlds of the cosmos. In the tiny section reserved for Americans, white angels find themselves an utterly insignificant minority among the countless Indians who have gone before. Twain's heaven turns the complacent cultural certainties of the *Gates* novels on their head, as critics have long noted. Less noted, despite a recent uptick in interest in *Captain Stormfield,* is the centrality of the Indian presence in Twain's version of heaven. These "brown angels" signify a broader scope to Twain's satire than Phelps's heavenly fictions alone—*Captain Stormfield* belongs as well among the rich vein of anti-imperialist writings that occupied such a central role in Twain's later work. By weaving an Indian presence into his version of heaven, Twain manages not only to unsettle the ideology that drove the European-American conquest of the West, but also to undercut the cultural certainties (both white and Indian) that shaped the afterlife in the *Gates* novels and the Ghost Dance. The ghost dancers and Phelps use heaven as a mechanism to revitalize a threatened culture. Twain, on the other hand, uses heaven to threaten a dominant culture grown dangerously self-assured, as a tool of cultural *de*vitalization designed to counter Anglo-Saxon hegemony on earth with a radically multicultural vision of the afterlife.

Twain first conceived of what would become *Captain Stormfield's Visit to Heaven* soon after his first experiences with U.S. imperialism. He was on his way to New York after visiting the Hawaiian Islands as a San Francisco newspaper correspondent when he first met Captain Ned Wakeman, a veteran sailor and self-taught theologian; they met again when Twain returned to San

Francisco from Europe in 1868. When Wakeman told of a visit to heaven he had made in a dream, Twain began working up the story into a satire of the just-published *Gates Ajar*. Struggling to find an appropriate form, he returned to redraft the story several times, writing much of the present text between 1878 and 1882. Despite the urgings of William Dean Howells, he remained reluctant to publish it, due in part to its unfinished state and in part to the objections of Olivia Clemens, who disapproved of such a direct satire of conventional Christianity. Twain nevertheless returned to the manuscript in 1905, writing chapters that would come before and after the text published in *Harper's*. [13]

The manuscript begins with the captain's death at sea. After watching his shipmates gather around his deathbed, Stormfield finds himself hurtling through space, none too anxious to arrive at what he expects will be a fiery destination. He soon joins the spirits of a Jew, a Republican, and a former slave—a group that sounds like the setup of a bad joke. Yet while Twain draws some ethnic humor from the group, fellowship soon binds the travelers together. Twain makes it clear that racial and ethnic prejudice have no place in the afterlife. "I was trained to a prejudice against Jews," says Stormfield, "but such of it as I had was in my head, there wasn't any in my heart. Dear me, when you are going to—to—where I was going, you are humble-mindeder than you used to be, and thankful for whatever [company] you can get, never mind the quality of it" (142). Twain's multicultural opening sets a clear tone for what follows—*Captain Stormfield* uses heaven not to reify a specific cultural identity, but to humble it.

While the reason Twain dropped the first two chapters when publishing the manuscript remains unclear, the next chapter, the first of the published book, amplifies the unsettling of racial and ethnic pride that occupies the manuscript's beginning. After some thirty years of interstellar travel at the speed of light, interrupted only by passages through the odd star and a brief race with a comet, Stormfield arrives in heaven, though at the wrong gate. The clerks are familiar with the sky blue, seven-headed, one-legged creatures who duly arrive, but have never heard of earth, much less San Francisco, and send him on his way only after much confusion. A quick ride on a magic carpet brings Stormfield to the gates of the earthly heaven, where he is greeted by "a Pi Ute Injun I used to know in Tulare County; mighty good fellow—I remembered being at his funeral" (156). Stormfield soon receives his regulation wings, halo, and harp, only to find that neither his nor the myriad other angels' harp playing and singing have improved since death. He quickly abandons his angelic accoutrements along with all his other preconceptions of the afterlife. Guided by an old, bald-headed angel named Sandy Mc-Williams, Stormfield learns that spirits of the dead live as they wish—studying, visiting, farming, or gossiping as they please. Babies who arrive in heaven grow and change, much to the horror of bereaved mothers who expect to cuddle their infants once again in heaven. Stormfield is startled to learn that unhappiness is an integral part of heaven, a necessary contrast for happiness and a crucial spur to a soul's continued development.

Most jarring, however, is the status of whites. This insignificant corner of heaven, modeled on America but many times larger, is populated almost completely by the spirits of Indians. Tourists from other, more populous parts of heaven, Sandy tells Stormfield, "say this wilderness is populated with a scattering of a few hundred thousand billions of red angels, with now and then a curiously complected diseased one. You see, they think we whites, and the occasional nigger, are Injuns that have been bleached out or blackened by some leprous disease or other—for some peculiarly rascally *sin,* mind you. It is a mighty sour pill for us all" (175). Stormfield finds some consolation in attending a particularly grand welcoming ceremony for a reformed barkeeper, which provides a rare chance to glimpse some of the biblical patriarchs. Here the published excerpt ends; the manuscript continues with a journey across the countless miles to another part of heaven, and then a quick visit to a miniature world for contrast. A final episode contains a creation story that would reappear in his "Letters to Earth."

Captain Stormfield has long been read as a satire of Phelps's supposedly more provincial representation of heaven, although in the minds of some critics, not much effort was needed to poke fun at "Phelps's Biedermeier paradise" (St. Armand Levi, 139). Twain includes none of the house-and-garden raptures that appear in *The Gates Ajar* and move to center stage in *Beyond the Gates,* though he also declines to make them objects of satire. One direct target is Phelps's pervasive sense of the immediacy of contact with dead. While Aunt Winifred consoles Mary in *The Gates Ajar* with the promise that her beloved Roy watches her every move, and while the dead in *The Gates Between* and *Beyond the Gates* move freely among the living when they wish, Twain places an impassable divide between living and dead: "I wish there were something in that miserable spiritualism, so we could send them word" (172), Sandy tells Stormfield. Yet they clearly can't, and by imagining a heaven where the dead learn to go about their eternal life rather than pine for loved ones still on earth, Twain attacks one of the principal appeals of consolation literature. The devastating story of the long-dead baby girl who, now a serious scholar, has little interest in meeting her uneducated mother, drives a deep wedge between the sentimental ideology that fueled the popular success of the *Gates* novels and the feminist undercurrent that provided much of their critical force. Yet the story of the thwarted mother-child reunion, for all its sentimental satire, nevertheless illustrates how much Twain borrowed from Phelps. Both writers reject a conventional heaven full of harp-playing angels in favor of one more analogous to earth, where people continue their education and activities according to their temperaments, free from the barriers of class and gender.[14]

Such borrowings, however, serve primarily to underscore the utterly different cultural functions of these two works. Phelps turned to heaven in order to shore up an ideology of white American triumphalism threatened by the carnage of civil war and the turmoil of industrialization; Twain, instead, turned to heaven in order to make that ideology fracture. One element in this process of devitalization has long been noted—the use of astronomical speeds and distances in order to dwarf any familiar human norms of scale. While living in Munich in 1878 through 1879, Twain took copious notes on Amédée Guilemin's *The Heavens* (1868), a book that popularized recent developments in astronomy, and much of that information made its way into *Stormfield*—from the captain's traveling speed, which he clocks at the speed of light by judging the time it takes him to get from the earth to the sun, to the distances between stars to the sheer number of stars, and planets that make up the universe (Baetzhold and McCullough 133). Twain is less concerned with the accuracy of the numbers than he is with their sheer immensity; he moves easily from millions to billions, and when he really wants to impress he simply invents new ones. The comet wins the race that opens the published text by dumping its cargo bound for Satan—all "eighteen hundred thousand billion quintillions of kazarks," a number big enough to stun even Stormfield, who finds out that a kazark is "exactly the bulk of *a hundred and sixty-nine worlds like ours!*" (150). The captain's ego is dealt a final blow when he arrives at the wrong gate to find that the geography that shaped his life does not apply in heaven. "San Francisco," "California," and the "United States" are meaningless terms to the clerk at the gate, who consults a map to find the earth:

He got a balloon and sailed up and up, in front of a map that was as big as Rhode Island. He went on up until he was out of sight, and by and by he came down and got something to eat; and went up again. To cut a long story short, he kept on doing this for a day or two, and finally came down and said he thought he had found that solar system, but it might be fly-specks. So he got a microscope and went back. It turned out better than he feared. He had rousted out our system, sure enough. He got me to describe our planet and its distance from our sun, and then he says to his chief—"Oh, I know the one he means, now, sir. It is on the map. It is called the Wart." (153)

The result of Twain's effort to represent accurately the earth's place in the heavens is a realism that mocks any sense of human reality, especially of the sort Phelps posed in the *Gates* novels and the ghost dancers described in their songs. Where these demarcated a heaven based on the scale of the parlor or teepee, a space that provides a comfortable measure for the versions of America found in both models of heaven, *Captain Stormfield* presents a heaven on a superhuman scale. The homely elements sprinkled throughout the text, such as Sandy McWilliams's cranberry farm, thus appear not as ordinary, naturalized elements of heaven that reify life on earth, but as mere devices, as self-evident props that serve to demystify their earthly counterparts. The pleasant, familiar landscape through which Stormfield wanders with his guide doesn't obscure the fact that on a map of the heavens, earth is but a flyspeck. This radically unsettling sense of scale drastically alters as well the meaning of ethnic identity. Much of Twain's satire is directed against the implicit whiteness of heavens like Phelps's—his accommodates not only blacks, Indians (American and Asian), Mexicans, Arabs, and Jews, but seven-headed, blue-skinned, one-legged extraterrestrials as well. Such a polyglot mixture deals a heavy blow to the ideology of Anglo-Saxon superiority that imagined the heavenly mansion as the White House.

Yet despite the genial multicultural gathering depicted in the opening chapters of the manuscript, the published chapters of *Captain Stormfield* don't include much interaction among ethnic groups. Though Stormfield hears of luminaries from other races and countries, he talks only to other white Americans in heaven, and from them he learns that most people stick with their own kind. *"What a man mostly misses, in heaven, is company—* company of his own sort and color and language" (175), Sandy tells Stormfield when advising him where to settle. Sandy's advice is hardly a ringing endorsement of multicultural harmony, but neither is it an endorsement of white supremacy. As Twain puts earth in a universal perspective, he places whites in their proper global perspective, as a minority race that has no inherent title over its neighbors. Nor, indeed, can it claim the exceptional cultural heritage claimed in the ideology of Anglo-Saxon superiority. England, says Sandy, "is not so very much better than this [American] end of the heavenly domain. As long as you run across Englishmen born this side of three hundred years ago, you are all right, but the minute you get back of Elizabeth's time the language begins to fog up, and the further back you go the foggier it gets. . . . Back of [that] time the English are simply foreigners, nothing more, nothing less" (176). The white privilege that drenches Phelps's version of heaven begins to evaporate in Twain's, and we are left not with a sense of a deeply rooted civilization overwhelmed by hordes of dark foreigners, as the rhetoric of white supremacy would have imagined, but instead with a sense that the roots of European-American civilization are not so deep after all. For Twain, people stick with their own kind out of the simple need to communicate, rather than the dynamics of racial pride, cultural entitlement, or nationalist yearnings that shaped turn-of-the century geopolitics. While such a stance does not repudiate racial division, it does work to undercut the ideology of racial superiority then building towards its zenith.

The cosmic scale and radical multiculturalism of *Captain Stormfield* build on a strategy Twain had been developing throughout his late writings. Susan Gillman has connected such works as *Following the Equator,* "Three Thousand Years Among the Microbes," and *The Mysterious Stranger* through what she terms the "racial occult," in which Twain, like his contemporaries Pauline Hopkins and W. E. B. DuBois, applied the New Psychology idea of divided consciousness to the question of race. Twain's late writings, argues Gillman, "invoke and adapt the notion of spirit communication and disembodied space-and-time travel, made newly respectable at this time by the investigation of psychical researchers, as a means of revisiting the old terrain of U.S. slavery and linking it to the newer global imperialism, the worldwide nationalism, nativism, and racism of the late 1890s" (194). By using race as an occult presence in such work, Twain opens a window on "the cultural unconscious of the late nineteenth-century world of empire" (208).[15] Though Gillman does not mention *Captain Stormfield,* the text clearly uses spiritualist categories in order to explore race; the long composition of the work, too, indicates that the racial occult had been an important category for Twain long before the 1890s. And while "occult" might at first glance seem an odd term to apply to such a vigorous burlesque, it nevertheless captures the unease— or better, dis-ease—surrounding whiteness in the text. White Americans are not simply minority inhabitants of heaven in *Captain Stormfield;* they are themselves made to partake of the malignant otherness that white supremacy had consigned to nonwhites on earth. They are, in the eyes of the Goobran tourists, merely "curiously complected, diseased" (175) Indians, former inhabitants of a world that, when finally distinguished from a flyspeck, is known as "the Wart" (153). The anxieties of whiteness—on earth projected upon the racialized bodies of immigrant, colonized, and fomerly enslaved others and stabilized in such purified, imaginary utopias as Phelps's *Gates* novels—won't be displaced in *Captain Stormfield's* heaven. There, the limits of race in fashioning identity are everywhere apparent.

Twain submits the category "Indian" to almost as much scrutiny as the category "white." There is no direct evidence that *Captain Stormfield* emerged in reaction to the Ghost Dance in the same manner it grew from *The Gates Ajar.* However, the text represents an important development in Twain's attitude toward Native Americans, and especially their role in European-American ideology; the extent of such development has been largely ignored by critics.[16] The Indian presence in heaven in fact marks how far Twain had come from his days as a reporter in the Nevada Territory. There, despite his contrarian sympathies for the Chinese immigrants who labored under intense discrimination, Twain happily participated in the general maligning of the Paiute and Ute peoples who had proven remarkably cooperative during white settlement. In one article he portrayed the Indian as a "filthy, naked scurvy vagabond" whose demise at the hands of the army was more than justified, despite the "wail of humanitarian sympathy" from the East (cited in Budd 45). *Roughing It,* written after Twain had been well ensconced in the polite eastern circles from which such wailing emanated, still only managed an oblique critique of Indian hating. He describes the "Goshoot Indians" of the Great Basin as "small, lean, 'scrawny' creatures; in complexion a dull black like the ordinary American negro; their faces and hands bearing dirt which they had been accumulating for months, years, and even generations, according to the age of the proprietor; a silent, sneaking, treacherous looking race; taking note of everything, covertly, like all the other 'Noble Red Men' that we (do not) read about, and betraying no sign in their countenances; indolent, everlastingly patient and tireless, like all other Indians; prideless beggars" (166–67). The passage continues, its invectives barely tempered by the tepid plea for sympathy that ends the chapter.

By the time he drafted *Captain Stormfield,* Twain's quarrel with James Fenimore Cooper had cooled, though some Indian-hating rhetoric survives in Sandy McWilliams's words to Stormfield. When advising the captain on where to settle in heaven, he says, "You see what the Jersey district of heaven is for whites; well, the California district is a thousand times worse. It swarms with a mean kind of leather-headed mud-colored angels—Digger Injuns, mainly—and your nearest neighbor is likely to be a million miles away" (175). Yet Sandy's account is countered to some degree by Stormfield's fond reunion at heaven's gate with the Pai Ute he knew from his own California days, a "mighty good fellow" and a member of the tribe to which the so-called "Diggers" also belonged. Stormfield himself remembers his funeral, "which consisted of him being burnt and the other Injuns gauming their faces with his ashes and howling like wild-cats" (156).

Unremarked by Twain is that among these Diggers and Paiutes the Ghost Dance of 1890 began—nor does he mention the earlier Ghost Dance of 1870, which proved especially long lived among the California tribes. Twain left no record of his reactions to either of these movements, yet *Captain Stormfield* remains remarkably open to both. Indians do, in fact, reassemble in heaven in all their strength and glory to resume their rightful place in an American landscape; while whites are neither burned, buried, nor forced across the ocean, they scarcely need to be, so small and scattered are their number. Twain, moreover, pays the brown-skinned angels the unusual respect of privacy. Indians, in heaven, are left alone to live as they wish. According to Twain's depictions in *Captain Stormfield,* the ghost dancers got their visions of heaven right—the patterns of traditional Indian culture continued unchanged. Yet while the great majority of Indians are free to live in heaven as if whites never existed, Twain also presents an alternative, for as in the *New York Times*'s account of Wovoka's vision, among the "heap of Indians" in heaven is one "dressed in white man's clothes." The Paiute clerk, like Wovoka himself, sends his heavenly message to people of all races, a symbol of the crosscultural promise of heaven. While *Captain Stormfield* is almost unique in turn-of-the-century European-American fiction in imagining a world in which Indian culture remains untouched by whites, it is careful too to offer, in the person of the Paiute clerk, a counter to the monolithic cultural traditionalism of the Ghost Dance.

In addition to undermining conventional racial identities, Twain is also intent on fracturing the formal unities so important in work like Phelps's. *Captain Stormfield,* in fact, might be read as an example of aesthetic devitalization. Many readers of the text have commented on its fragmented nature, and most have traced the story's rough form to Twain's difficulty in completing the text to his satisfaction. For a writer whose efforts to bring works like *Huckleberry Finn* to a tidy conclusion usually caused more problems than they solved, Twain's decision to publish *Captain Stormfield* as a fragmentary extract has been seen by at least one critic as an aesthetic improvement.[17] Yet the story remains, in the words of another critic, "outlandish," full of the disruptive wildness that lurks beneath the surface of even Twain's most conventional work and that, in his late works, emerges as an "anti-story configuration" (Michelson 220–22). The formal disruptions of *Captain Stormfield*— the abrupt beginning, repeated inversions, outlandish inventions, absurd realism, and unlocatable premise (who, after all, is telling the tale?)—do more than chart and resolve Twain's personal "metaphysical dislocations" (Michelson 222). If, as Richard Ohmann has argued, the formal structures of the fiction that appeared in popular magazines like *Harper's* at the turn of the century played an important role in iterating bourgeois ideology, then Twain's antistory works against that ideology, and indeed uncovers the workings of ideology itself, exposing and widening the ideological fissures that Phelps's heaven (and Wovoka's) sought to close. *Captain Stormfield,* with its hybridity, inversions, and playful deformulation of conventional aesthetics, shares with postcolonial fiction everything but cultural marginality. Located at the very center of metropolitan literary production, the text illustrates how an aesthetics of devitalization can work to subvert a dominant culture from within.

While the *Gates* novels and the Ghost Dance project structurally similar versions of heaven from the two margins of America's continental empire, heavens fashioned out of idealized similacra of earthly reality, *Captain Stormfield's* heaven resists such cultural navel gazing. By borrowing from both representations, Twain constructs a heaven that foregrounds its own determination, revels in the free play to be found in the discursive spaces between Wovoka's and Phelps's visions of the afterlife. Twain, marked by the biases inherent in his location at an imperial metropole, may not fully comprehend the cultural positions of a Paiute prophet or, for that matter, a spiritual feminist. Nevertheless, *Captain Stormfield* illustrates that although the distances between these heavens and the cultures that gave them birth may seem, at times, light-years across, they can be encompassed in the pages of a single book.

Spirits in the Contact Zone

Spiritualism and Local Color Writing

ॐ The Ghost Dance, the *Gates* novels, and *Captain Stormfield's Visit to Heaven* illustrate the spectrum of cultural forms that featured spiritualism. They also represent three elements that some authors used toward the end of the nineteenth century, creating one of the most prominent literary discourses of the era. Drawing on ethnography, sentimental fiction, and the magazine tale, local color writing, or regionalism, filled the pages of an increasingly national magazine press, powerfully shaping mainstream American attitudes about culture and identity.[1] Perhaps more importantly, these magazines welcomed for the first time writers from a variety of cultural positions, making local color writing a significant cross-cultural discourse at a time when white America was increasingly committed to Anglo-Saxon superiority. Spiritualism is a common, though neglected, feature of local color writing, and by examining stories by three writers, Sarah Orne Jewett, Charles Chesnutt, and María Cristina Mena, we can see how regionalists used spiritualism in their efforts to redraw the boundaries of American identity.

By the end of the nineteenth century, European-American spiritualism as a quasi-religious movement no longer had the broad appeal among white Americans that it had enjoyed during the antebellum era. Despite an upsurge in interest after the Civil War, the movement soon fell victim to celebrity mediums whose efforts to popularize spiritualism backfired amidst embarrassing revelations of fraud and outlandish behavior. The so-called "full spirit materializations" of Katie King; the scandals that swirled around spiritualist, socialist, feminist, and free-love advocate Victoria Woodhull; and the deathbed confession of Margaret Fox that she and her sister had faked spirit rappings by snapping their toe joints all combined by century's end to reduce the ranks of professed spiritualists to a small core of true believers. Newer movements like Christian Science and theosophy began translating the elements that helped constitute European-American spiritualism—European folkways, evangelical Christianity, pseudoscience, radical politics, and occult learning—into popular European-American movements.[2]

Two developments, however, did keep broad spiritualist issues at the center of American cultural life, and one in particular brought spiritualism's cross-cultural nature to the fore. First, the emerging discipline of psychology took a strong interest in spiritualist phenomena. In England and then in the United States, the Society for Psychical Research systematically examined mediums and various occult phenomena in order to classify them under the terms worked out by William James, Sigmund Freud, and other proponents of the New Psychology. Not surprisingly, researchers proved skeptical about the spiritual origins of rappings and trance speaking.[3]

A second development, the rise of ethnology as a scientific discipline, foregrounded the different cultural meanings of spiritualism. Though amateur anthropologists had been collecting folklore for generations, not until the end of the nineteenth century did such practices became professionalized under the auspices of the Bureau of Ethnology in Washington and in newly formed academic departments in universities. European-American ethnologists ranked distinct cultures according to an evolutionary hierarchy that invariably placed their own at the top; they also tried to describe other cultures before they vanished in the inexorable march of "progress." Since non-Christian spiritual beliefs received a great deal of ethnographic scrutiny, European-American spiritualist events like the Salem Witchcraft Trials and the Rochester Rappings increasingly appeared in the context of spiritualist beliefs rooted in very different cultures.[4] Thus even while ethnography reified notions of Anglo-Saxon cultural superiority, it extended the meaning of "spiritualism" far beyond the rituals and ideology adhered to by the Fox sisters and their followers.

As a scientific discourse that reinforced a racist ideology at a time when the United States emerged as an imperial power, ethnology proved broadly popular. Moreover, efforts to quantify the "primitive" cultures of newly acquired territories like the Philippines and Hawaii meshed with descriptions of the "primitive" beliefs of blacks and Indians in the United States itself. Legal segregation of blacks and whites, forced Indian assimilation, and imperial acquisition all depended upon a racist ideology of cultural evolution. As mainstream European-American culture continued to define itself against cultural others, ethnography became a staple of the national magazines. It helped inaugurate mass culture in America at the turn of the century and, consequently, helped normalize a nationalist, capitalist ideology.[5]

In this respect, ethnology was linked to another emerging popular discourse, regionalism. Regionalists offered portraits of localized, pre-modern communities saturated with traditional folk beliefs. While these writers sought artistic rather than scientific truths, both ethnologists and regionalists claimed some expertise on a marginalized culture, which they offered up to a metropolitan audience. Most regionalists described white, rural American communities, which offered a softer contrast to their largely white, urban readership than most ethnographies did. Nevertheless, like the more exoticized ethnographies about racialized, "primitive" others, local color portraits were a foil for an emerging national readership that defined itself in terms of Anglo-Saxon modernity. Indeed, ethnography and regionalism were often indistinguishable. For example, the Uncle Remus tales of Joel Chandler Harris, devoured by general readers and scholars alike in the 1880s, preserved a rich variety of African-American folklore while offering white readers a taste of how it might feel to own a plantation in the New South staffed by deferential and entertaining African Americans.

Yet in terms of power, the history of ethnography and regionalist fiction is not completely one-sided. Since both depended upon detailed, intimate knowledge of cultures peripheral to mainstream European-American life, and hence not always accessible to the educated elite who typically became writers, a number of writers of color were able to trade their insider's knowledge for access to national magazines. Thus, in the very pages of magazines that presented ethnographies designed to reify European-American cultural superiority, autoethnographies appeared. In such works, to borrow Mary Louise Pratt's formulation, "colonized subjects undertake to represent themselves in ways that *engage with* the colonizer's own terms. If ethnographic texts are a means by which Europeans represent to themselves their (usually subjugated) others, then autoethnographic texts are those the others construct in response to or in dialogue with those metropolitan representations" (7). Since regionalism became both a primary means by which metropolitan magazines represented others and a principal means by which those others represented themselves, the literary form became increasingly heterogeneous and overdetermined. Texts that worked to reinforce a dominant ideology were joined by texts (and subtexts) that worked to counter their ideological force. Thus the magazines which published them can be understood, to borrow again from Pratt, as "contact zones," "space[s] in which peoples geographically and historically separated come into contact with each other and establish ongoing relations, usually involving conditions of coercion, radical inequality, and intractable conflict" (6).

National magazines, of course, were published, edited, and overwhelmingly written and read by whites, and thus removed from the physical frontier of cultural contact. Yet as the space in which ethnographic and autoethnographic texts collided, these magazines did form a discursive frontier, a crucial site of cross-cultural negotiation. In this respect, the national magazines at the turn of the century were not nearly so monolithic in their ideology or cultural meaning as critics like Richard Ohmann and Richard Brodhead suggest. Though these magazines helped shape a capitalist, racist, nationalistic, imperialistic, and sexist U.S. cultural identity, they provided as well a means of opposing this metropolitan cultural hegemony for authors attempting to undercut ethnographic representations and pry apart rigid ethnic identities.[6]

Spiritualism played a vital role in this process, for while it had failed in its bid to become a central part of European-American culture, it nevertheless continued to possess an oppositional force and a cross-cultural appeal almost unique in this era. Spiritualism offered an epistemology very much at odds with the scientific rationalism of the professional-managerial class. By 1900, most spiritualists portrayed their movement as a viable alternative to mainstream science, a stance aided by organizations like the Society for Psychical Research. Yet spiritualism also fit alongside the folklore and ghost stories that were an integral part of the local color landscape. Hence writers of color, seeking to make their own cultures recognizable to an audience trained to see non-European cultures as demonstrably inferior, found their respective spiritualist traditions a useful means of establishing common ground in the mainstream press.

To illustrate, I will examine short stories published by three turn-of-the-century writers that use spiritualism to bridge the gap between peripheral and mainstream U.S. cultures. The first, Sarah Orne Jewett's "The Foreigner," appeared in the *Atlantic Monthly* in 1900. While Jewett referenced spiritualism throughout her work, "The Foreigner" explicitly uses spiritualism to test the limits of regionalism's cultural tolerance. Charles Chesnutt published "Sis' Becky's Pickaninny" in his collection *The Conjure Woman* a year earlier. Written in the wake of Joel Chandler Harris's tremendous vogue, the story carefully deploys a subtext of European-American spiritualism in order to counter the ethnographic distance created by conjure. Finally, María Cristina Mena, like Chesnutt, turns an ethnographic gaze upon European-American culture. While her early works made Mexican spiritualism familiar to an American audience, her late story "The Sorcerer and General Bisco" (1915) unleashes spiritualism's revolutionary potential in the pages of the mainstream periodical press. My goal is to show how each story illustrates spiritualism's ability to complicate the cultural hierarchies integral to white American identity in that era. Taken together, I will argue, they chart the range of cultural critique permitted in the mainstream press.

Jewett's Local Color Spiritualism

While spiritualism had declined in white America by the end of the nineteenth century, it nevertheless remained a strong cultural presence and a neglected undercurrent in the work of a number of prominent regionalists. Sarah Orne Jewett, perhaps the most successful New England local color writer, made particular use of it. Unlike many of the women writers upon whom she modeled her career, most notably Harriet Beecher Stowe and Elizabeth Stuart Phelps, little evidence directly ties Jewett to the séance table. Her interest in the occult, however, is well known. Marjorie Pryse has analyzed Jewett's feminist modulations of the ghost story tradition, and Elizabeth Ammons has argued that witchcraft serves as a master trope in Jewett's effort to fashion an "occult sisterhood" through her fiction.

While Jewett came of age long after the Rochester Rappings, she nevertheless shared many of its values. Josephine Donovan notes Swedenborgianism's deep influence on Jewett; Paula Blanchard cites Jewett's belief that her dead father remained present in her life: "It is all one life that we are living together—I am here and Father is there—the two worlds are one world after all" (121). Moreover, her local color writing, like spiritualism, cohered around domestic values rather than rational-scientific ones. In Jewett's regionalism, as in spiritualism, the home, especially the parlor, structures a community around familial ties maintained by women. The séance table, with a medium (usually female) at its head and a gathering of friends and relatives seeking communion with loved ones beyond the grave, mirrors the ritualized visits orchestrated by Mrs. Todd in the many stories Jewett set in Dunnet Landing. In both, social ties are strengthened by rehearsing stories that link the living and dead members of a local community. Mrs. Todd's knowledge of herbal medicine recalls both spiritualism's deep folk roots and the homeopathic medicine embraced by reformers who also explored the possibilities of spirit communication. Jewett's feminism, too, has much in common with European-American spiritualism. While a number of the most radical women's rights activists were spiritualists, spiritualists more typically extended women's social mobility by nominally adhering to traditional gender norms. Jewett's local color writing followed suit. Thus just as early female mediums were able to work as lecturers, ministers, and healers at a time when women were widely excluded from the podium, the pulpit, and the professions, so Jewett's women live virtually unconstrained by their gender. Moreover, Jewett, like most spiritualists, countered gender norms by celebrating the active abilities of "passive" women and the more "feminine" qualities of men. Many features of European-American spiritualism, of course, do not appear in the Dunnet Landing stories—the efforts to portray spirit communication as scientific investigation, for one, and the linking of spiritualism to a wider program of radical social reform, for another. In this sense, Jewett's feminist utopia has more in common with the spiritualist heaven of Elizabeth Stuart Phelps's works than with the radical, worldly spiritualism exemplified by Victoria Woodhull. Yet the spiritualism that informs Jewett's regionalism is a powerful cultural force.

A typical example of Jewett's local color spiritualism is "Miss Tempy's Watchers" (1887). Mrs. Crowe and Miss Binson, old schoolmates from different levels of the town's social strata, keep a vigil in the home of their recently deceased mutual friend, Temperance Dent, and under the felt presence of their friend's spirit, the two women heal the social rifts that had divided them over the course of years. While the women don't pull out a planchette or huddle over a rapping table, they scarcely need to. Miss Tempy's spirit infuses her house, bringing her friends together after her death more effectively than she could in life. "The watchers could not rid their minds of the feeling that they were being watched themselves" (243). Later, Miss Binson says, "I feel as if the air was full of her, kind of. I can sense things, now and then, that she seems to say. Now I was never one to take up with no nonsense of sperits and such, but I declare I felt as if she told me just now to put some more wood into the stove" (248). As the two watchers nod to sleep before dawn, the story's spirit almost materializes—"Perhaps Tempy herself stood near, and saw her own life and its surroundings with new understanding. Perhaps she was the only watcher" (253). Jewett carefully positions Miss Tempy's spirit between the ghost story and the séance—while her watchers don't consciously summon her, neither do they feel haunted by her presence. The story draws not so much on the pseudoscience of the Rochester Rappings or the Society for Psychical Research as it does on warmly remembered folklore set in the context of a pre-modern community. Jewett's spiritualism thus conveys her particular local color ideology: female centered rather than male centered; traditional and ritualistic rather than modern and standardized; intuitive rather than rational; communal rather than individualistic; rooted in a rich cultural heritage rather than in scientific progress.

Yet as a number of recent critics have pointed out, this vision also fits within the racial ideology taking shape in that era. Amy Kaplan insists that local color writing like Jewett's was part of the larger postbellum project of national reunification organized around a white, Anglo-Saxon heritage. Sandra Zagarell argues that Jewett's *Country of the Pointed Firs* (1896) in particular roots its powerful sense of community in a shared northern European culture, while Elizabeth Ammons notes that Dunnet Landing defines itself, on the one hand, against the material traces of empire and, on the other, through "protofascist" rituals like the Bowden family reunion that celebrate white ethnic pride (1994). While Jewett does not actively define the world of "Miss Tempy's Watchers" against the ethnic others located at the edges of the "civilized" world and in the burgeoning cities of the United States, much local color fiction, and much of Jewett's own work, did. Jewett's spiritualism, like her feminism, prided itself on its Anglo-Saxon (and in the case of Dunnet Landing, Anglo-Norman) pedigree. "Miss Tempy's Watchers" confines itself to a white cast and a white tradition. While Miss Binson may never have dabbled at the séance table, she willingly participates in the far older European practice of the deathwatch. By choosing a folk ritual over a pseudo-scientific experiment as the vehicle for her spiritualism, Jewett changes its resonance. In the local color spiritualism of "Miss Tempy's Watchers," deeply rooted in New England soil, Jewett carefully preserved an integral part of a distinctly European cultural heritage.

The antiscientific bias of Jewett's spiritualism grows more apparent in *The Country of the Pointed Firs,* where, in the chapter titled "The Waiting Place," Captain Littlepage relates a narrative he heard from the sole survivor of a scientific expedition to the far North. Weeks of travel brought the group beyond the pack ice to clear seas, and thence to a shadowy town full of ghosts, "all blowing gray figures that would pass along alone, or sometimes gathered in companies as if they were watching" (25). The men guess that the town is a "waiting place" for spirits moving on to the next world, made visible by the unusual conditions of light and the magnetic currents near the North Pole. Only one makes it back, and when Littlepage himself tries to interest the scientific community in organizing another expedition, no one believes him. Jewett ruthlessly undercuts the importance of Littlepage's scientific spiritualism, and with it the discourses of geography and ethnography so characteristic of the turn of the century. Littlepage's travels to the far corners of the world have, ultimately, left him "pathetic," staring at the margins of a school-house map in "bewilderment." Travel and science may secure his fortune and acquaint him with the customs of ports around the world, but they won't offer the rich solace provided by the communal rites like the funeral he has just attended. Jewett argues, ultimately, that science fails to provide a stable ground for European-American identity, offering only elusive, shadowy fig-ures upon which to ground the self. Jewett's attention quickly turns from Captain Littlepage's tales of discovery to Mrs. Todd's domestic rituals, from the ghostly margins of the known world to the folklore and customs at the fountainhead of America's Anglo-Saxon heritage.

Yet while Jewett clearly finds no use for scientific spiritualism, her story "The Foreigner" uses local color spiritualism to test Dunnet Landing's abil-ity to incorporate a figure from its margins. The foreigner is the long-deceased Mrs. Captain Tolland, of French birth and widowed by "a Por-tugee, or somethin'," rescued from destitution in Jamaica by Captain Tolland and brought back to Dunnet Landing as his wife. When her husband returns to sea, she finds herself friendless but for the kindness of Mrs. Todd and her mother; when Captain Tolland dies at sea, his wife follows him to the grave soon after. The story centers on the townspeople's reaction to the foreigner. Most are cold: the captain's sister extends her grudge against her brother to his new wife, and Mrs. Tolland herself secures the enmity of other towns-women when she out-sings a pair of locals at a church social. After that, she remains excluded from the tightly knit community. In Mrs. Todd's words, "she come a foreigner and she went a foreigner, and never was but a stranger among our folks" (170).

In the figure of Mrs. Tolland, Jewett comes as close as she ever does to confronting the issues of immigration and American identity in her work. In fact, a number of signifiers—Mrs. Tolland's poverty, her marriage to a "Por-tugee, or somethin'," her talent for music and dance, her free emotions, her Catholicism—link the sea captain's wife to the southern European immi-grants whose entry into the United States at the end of the nineteenth century so alarmed mainstream America. Several critics have argued that Mrs. Tol-land, with her conspicuously dark skin and her Jamaican origins, may be a creole.[7] By bringing a character so marked by otherness into the world of Dunnet Landing, Jewett, these critics argue, interrogates the racial ideology so central to her earlier work. Zagarell suggests that in "The Foreigner," Jewett highlights the limits of the Dunnet Landing community. Ammons, however, argues that this late gesture of tolerance, while laudable, "is not all that much" (1994, 97). For Mitzi Schrag, the sense of loss that pervades the story points to costs of racism for those who practice it—in turning their backs on the foreigner, the white women of Dunnet Landing not only turn on their communal ideals but also miss out on Mrs. Tolland's valuable knowledge. These critics disagree on exactly how, and how seriously, Jewett critiques her own earlier work. One way to measure Jewett's rethinking of race is to focus on another element that distinguishes this story from *Country of the Pointed Firs:* in "The Foreigner" Jewett tests her local color community by bringing it into contact with an "other world" at once ethnic and spiritualist.

While Jewett conspicuously rejected Littlepage's scientific spiritualism, in "The Foreigner" she draws heavily on the sentimental spiritualism so central to "Miss Tempy's Watchers." When Mrs. Tolland refers to Mrs. Todd's mother as "an angel," she summons an ideology intimately familiar to Jewett's readers. Indeed, the story is unusual in Jewett's corpus in drawing on an explicitly Christian sensibility more typical of early local colorists like Stowe, though some of the pronouncements in the story ("there might be roads leading up to New Jerusalem from various points" [175]) are certainly consonant with spiritualist theology. In the circular nature of the story, told and retold with greater depth until it reaches its climax, Jewett may invoke both the female discourse that shapes all the Dunnet Landing stories and the spiritualist paradigm of concentric spheres.[8] The death of Mrs. Tolland's children and two husbands certainly aligns her with the countless women (and men) who sought solace for their own griefs at the séance table, and, like many of them, she is not disappointed.

During her last illness, to the strains of spectral music emanating from the guitar hung by a ribbon next to an open window, a spirit appears. Mrs. Todd, watching over the deathbed, sees "a woman's dark face looking right at us; 'twan't but an instant I could see. . . . I saw very plain while I could see; 'twas a pleasant enough face, shaped somethin' like Mis' Tolland's, and a kind of expectin' look" (185-86). The spirit, while frightening at first to Mrs. Todd, comforts Mrs. Tolland, who says twice, "You saw her, didn't you? . . . 'tis my mother." Mrs. Todd responds, as Mrs. Tolland finally slips away, *"Yes, dear, I did; you ain't never goin' to feel strange and lonesome no more"* (186). Jewett's italics serve to underscore the doubled meaning of the apparition—Mrs. Tolland's welcome into heaven secures her integration into American society. By the story's end, the twice-widowed, doubly estranged foreigner belongs to the American sentimental spiritualist tradition.

Mrs. Todd's assertion that "the doors stand wide open" (186) echoes not only the title of Elizabeth Stuart Phelps's *The Gates Ajar* but also, perhaps, a liberal attitude toward immigration. Along with Phelps's novel, Jewett may have had in mind a poem published in 1892 by Thomas Bailey Aldrich in the *Atlantic Monthly,* which he edited from 1881 to 1890. "Unguarded Gates" heralds his work with the Immigration Restriction League; it includes lines like "Wide open and unguarded stand our gates / And through them presses a wild motley throng" (cited in Zagarell 41). As Jewett reassessed the exclusionary practices of Dunnet Landing, she may have reassessed the racial attitudes of her own literary community. Quite possibly, Jewett's reference signals her shift from Aldrich's xenophobia to Phelps's more ecumenical spiritualism. Like Phelps, Jewett imagines a heaven that is matrifocal and domestic, pervaded by a sense of community meant to serve as a utopian foil for a fractured American society. Unlike her, Jewett explicitly integrates a foreigner into her vision of the afterlife.

Thus Jewett uses spiritualism to question the racial attitudes she had helped construct in her earlier work. Spiritualism at the end of "The Foreigner" is an ideology of radical inclusion, welcoming all into a network of familial harmony where markers of racial difference dissolve. The dark face of Mrs. Tolland's mother figures both her otherness and her sameness, for it quickly fades into an apotheosis of sentimental communion. Indeed, Jewett calls attention to this racial marker only to erase it. Jewett implicitly critiques the racial exclusion of *Country of the Pointed Firs* by making the spiritualist community at the end of "The Foreigner" both tightly woven *and* racially mixed. The credo that ends the story, "we've got to join both worlds together" (187), is spiritualist *and* anti-racist. Mrs. Todd's own rapid transition from terror at the ghost to empathetic embrace is a synecdoche of her own relationship to Mrs. Tolland. Spiritualism draws the foreign into the web of the familiar—and thereby enriches the familiar world. Mrs. Todd gains wisdom from Mrs. Tolland's death as she gains a greater knowledge of herbs from the foreigner's very different cultural heritage. For a rare moment in her local color world, Jewett recognizes that Mrs. Todd's world does not have "pure" cultural roots. So Jewett's spiritualism problematizes the local color ideology that formed the bedrock of Dunnet Landing. If readers turned to Jewett's earlier stories for a profound sense of community structured around a shared northern European heritage, in "The Foreigner" they found that same sense of community shifted to a deracialized "other world."

Yet the story also marks the limits of cultural difference in Jewett's writing. Mrs. Tolland, despite the southern European and African register of many of her traits, is, after all, French by birth, a fact that tempers her exoticism as, similarly, her skill in making omelets and keeping house tempers her exotic delight in song and dance. Moreover, she marries into town society, settling not into an immigrant ghetto but into a respectable old house; her former name, a potent signifier of cultural difference for most immigrants, has been long forgotten. Her Catholicism, threatening to many of the locals, is carefully circumscribed—the priest who attends her deathbed simply appears from nowhere one day, as if Jewett were reluctant even to mention the thriving French Canadian communities then swelling the population of New England. Finally, the spiritualist episode that ends the story carries, in its deracializing thrust, the mark of cultural sameness rather than difference. It bears no trace of Mrs. Tolland's deeply held Catholicism, nor of the rich creole spirituality of the Caribbean; Jewett erases any distinct cultural referents in this universalized mother-child reunion. The price for Mrs. Tolland's assimilation into heaven, as into the world of Dunnet Landing, is her cultural identity. While Jewett uses spiritualism in "The Foreigner" to begin to address issues of race and immigration, she proves unable to integrate cultural difference into her local color universe.

Chesnutt's Trickster Spiritualism

While spiritualism for Jewett fits ultimately within an assimilationist framework, some writers of color found spiritualism a useful means of more effectively challenging racism. For Charles Chesnutt, regionalism proved an invaluable means of projecting an African-American voice at a time when his more stridently antiracist work proved unpublishable. Spiritualism is an important, if long overlooked, part of his strategy. The period between 1887, when Chesnutt published "The Goophered Grapevine," and 1899, when Houghton Mifflin brought out *The Conjure Woman,* marked the nadir in the status of African Americans in post–Civil War history, an era of retrenchment from the activist policies of Reconstruction. Chesnutt's subtlety in negotiating this bleak cultural scene has long been noted. Houston Baker explores the fluidity with which Chesnutt masters the form of that most racist regionalist genre, the plantation narrative, while subverting it, slipping in notes of dissonance and difference that enable him to preserve "a deep-rooted African sound" within a cultural form (local color fiction) that found its way into the drawing rooms of white middle-class America (49). As he frankly indicated in a journal entry written on May 29, 1880, Chesnutt crafted his stories to earn "social recognition and equality . . . to accustom the public mind to the idea; and while amusing them, to lead them on, imperceptibly, unconsciously step by step to the desired state of feeling" (140). While spiritualism helped Jew-ett stretch the borders of her local color community, it helped Chesnutt ne-gotiate the slippery terrain between the vogue for stories of the old plantation and the degraded civil status of African Americans.

Chesnutt's conjure has been read variously as an anthropological artifact, a site of deconstructive free play, a strategy of trickster subversion, and even a means of literary passing.[9] It has not been examined, however, in the way that many of the stories' first readers undoubtedly read it, as an addition to the discourse of spiritualism. Spiritualism was a logical referent for Chesnutt. Its roots were tangled inextricably in the same soil that nurtured both aboli-tionism and the women's rights movement; it had a long history of resistance to dominant cultural practice; and it had a powerful presence in the bour-geois, largely female audience for whom Chesnutt wrote. Chesnutt engages this discourse in order to accustom the public mind to the idea of a Negro equality that was relentlessly attacked in the pages of the popular press. Pub-lishing mainly in the *Atlantic Monthly,* Chesnutt, like Jewett, wrote for a large audience that was well established and long familiar with the literary conven-tions of the day. By tapping into the often radical tradition of spiritualism, he found one more means of critiquing the plantation tradition while still ap-pearing to speak from within it.

Like Jewett, Chesnutt left no record of his views on the Rochester Rap-pings and their aftermath. He did, however, express in his journal a far more skeptical attitude toward the folk spiritualism so cherished by Jewett:

Well! uneducated people are the most bigoted, superstitious, hardest-headed people in the world! Those folks downstairs believe in ghosts, luck, horseshoes, cloud signs and all other kinds of nonsense, and all the argument in the world couldn't get it out of them. It is useless to argue with such persons. All the eloquence of Demosthenes, the logic of Plato, the demonstrations of the most lerned [*sic*] men in the world, couldn't convince them of the falsity, the absurdity, the utter impossibility and un-reasonableness of such things. (81)

Chesnutt wrote this while struggling to gain an education in his late teens. As he began his writing career, he evidently came to believe it was better to exploit such "unreasonable" conviction than to root it out. A number of his unpublished poems carefully engage spiritualist conventions, as other ap-prentice poems engage sentimental and dialect forms in an effort to find the best voice in which to couch his antiracist agenda. A poem written in his jour-nal in 1882 about the death of a son has two alternate endings, both vaguely spiritualist: "what he may be in another sphere, / Only an angel's voice can tell" (174), and "I will dry my tears, for I have no fear / But that death was to him the birth / Into a higher and broader sphere" (179). Chesnutt's lack of investment in the poem's content is palpable; he comments that the poem is "defective" in its formal construction and wonders how to strengthen the argument. The sentimental spiritualism here is merely a vehicle for practicing his verbal craft. Another poem from the same period uses the afterlife to satirize segregation: "And some intellects philosophic, / Have thought that even in Heaven, / A sort of kitchen department / To colored folks will be given" (178). Both of these poems show Chesnutt to be an opportunistic spiritualist, happy to deploy European-American spiritualist notions of the afterlife when it suits his purpose, happy to abandon them when they don't.

In conjure, however, Chesnutt found a theme that mingled a variety of popular discourses, including spiritualism, that he could marshal in his effort to lead his audience to his "desired state of feeling." In his conjure stories, which center on the relationship between John, a white northern businessman recently transplanted in North Carolina, Annie, his wife, and Julius, a former slave that he employs, Chesnutt highlights those affinities between conjure and European-American spiritualism that would most effectively unsettle the assumptions and prejudices of his readers. One is the rather playful antiscientism that crops up whenever John offers a pat explanation for one of Julius's stories. An example appears in "The Conjurer's Revenge," when Julius answers Annie's contention that the tale appeared to be only so much nonsense:

Dey's so many things a body knows is lies, dat dey ain' no use guine roun' findin' fault wid tales dat mought des ez well be so ez not. F' instance, dey's a young nigger gwine ter school in town, en he come out heah de yuther day en 'lowed dat de sun stood still en de yeath turnt roun' eve'y day on a kinder axeltree. . . . [E]f a man can't b'lieve what he sees, I can't see no use to libbin'—mought's well die en be whar we can't see nuffin. . . . Hit's monstrous quare. But dis is a quare worl', anyway yer kin fix it. (1899, 128–29)

Whether Chesnutt was a flat-earther remains undocumented; he clearly shares with Jewett, however, a contempt for smug rationalism and a desire to counter it with a willingness to entertain what appears irrational, occult, and abnormal. Chesnutt makes what seemed most familiar in the world, from the rotation of the earth to American social norms, "monstrous quare." This passage performs an act of decentering that serves as an apt figure for the mech-

anism of the entire book. Rather than coming down on the side of Coperni-
cus or Ptolemy, Chesnutt unsettles both systems, showing that the world of
the slave quarters didn't revolve around the axis that the slaveholding class
thought it did. Uncle Julius's universe has two centers, the great house that
officially structured plantation life and the conjurer's cabin on the edge of
town, around which "all de darkies fum Rockfish ter Beaver Creek" revolved
in an orbit of fear and respect largely unnoticed by their owners. Between
both worlds stands Julius, and from his stance neither one can have the last
word. Within that renewed sense of strangeness Chesnutt hoped to work his
transformation of racial attitudes in America.[10]

The conjure stories also echo the bitter opposition of most spiritualists to
the medical establishment. Spiritualist healers went so far as to establish their
own journals and medical schools (enrolling a preponderance of women students) in the late nineteenth century (Braude 142–51). Their emphasis on
both psychic and herbal healing is analogous to the practices of Aunt Peggy.
In "The Goophered Grape-Vine," her intimate knowledge of herbs and roots
holds the power of life and death over the unfortunate slave Henry, who
feasted on the scuppernongs she had conjured. Her conjure certainly con-
founds the learning of the licensed physicians that attended the ailing Henry.
Aunt Peggy's command of both herbal and spiritual lore aligns her as well
with Jewett's Mrs. Todd. Both preserve traditional medical knowledge in rural
outposts far from metropolitan centers; both disregard a medical establishment actively engaged in standardizing the practice of medicine according to
scientific norms; and both are deeply rooted in both their local communities
and the natural world that surrounds them. Moreover, their knowledge of the
natural world extends seamlessly into the spiritual world. Limned in the col-
ors of benign witchcraft, Aunt Peggy and Mrs. Todd draw on a folk occultism
that was a common feature of local color literature. Ghosts and herbs, scoffed
at by a metropolitan medical elite, were taken seriously by a broad strata of
the reading public and by those writers who sought to reach them.

Yet for all the affinity between spiritualism and Chesnutt's conjure stories,
Chesnutt's local color spiritualism, unlike Jewett's, has a distinctly African
heritage. Conjure's African origins have long been noted, and Chesnutt himself published an article, "Superstitions and Folklore of the South" (1901),
that captures his ambivalent interest in conjure. Based on his own memories
of his childhood in North Carolina and some recent interviews with "a half
dozen old women and a genuine 'conjure doctor,'" Chesnutt's article relies
on the general model of cultural evolution developed in the nineteenth century. "Relics of ancestral barbarism remain among all peoples," Chesnutt

notes, "but advanced civilization has at least shaken off the more obvious ab-
surdities of superstition" (372). Unlike the highly figurative ambiguity characteristic of his conjure stories, Chesnutt the ethnographer often adopts a
condescending, even scathing, tone toward conjure in his article. One woman
who describes being goophered "very obviously had sprained her ankle"
(374), and Chesnutt describes a conjure doctor as "a shrewd, hard sinner, and
a palpable fraud" (373).

Yet while skeptical of the specifics of conjure, Chesnutt clearly respects
its roots:

It probably grew, in the first place, out of African fetichism [*sic*], which was brought
from the dark continent along with the dark people. Certain features, too, suggest a
distant affinity with Voodooism, or snake worship, a cult which seems to have been
indigenous to tropical America. These beliefs, which in their place of origin had all
the sanctions of religion and custom, become in the shadow of the white man's civilization, a pale reflection of their former selves. In time, too, they were mingled and
confused with the witchcraft and ghost lore of the white man, and the tricks and delu-
sions of the Indian conjurer. In the old plantation days they flourished vigorously,
though discouraged by the "great house," and their potency was well established
among the blacks and poorer whites. (371)

Chesnutt's ambivalence about African spiritualism is evident. Anxious to assert his own credentials as a member of modern society, Chesnutt distances
himself from the intercultural nexus of spiritualist beliefs that emerged in
America. Yet he nevertheless moves quickly from an ethnographic perspective that denigrates "African fetichism" along with its white and Indian
counterparts, to powerful longing for the customs of his dark ancestors. Now
a "pale reflection," Chesnutt implies that, free of the contaminating influence
of European and Indian culture, African spiritualism would rival the "white
man's civilization."

By highlighting conjure's fallen status in America, Chesnutt illustrates its
continuing importance to the African-American community. While spiritualism in white popular culture provided a means of subverting dominant society from the fringe, spiritualism in black culture, by recalling a proud African
heritage, provided a means of unifying a dispersed population and resisting
white domination. Conjure played an important part in a great many slave rebellions, and the conjure tales that inspired Chesnutt's stories almost always
center on opposition to cruel masters. Overseers are turned into animals at
night and ridden by vengeful conjurers; a master is hexed and dies with the

setting sun; a master's wife is made to feel each stroke of a lashing given to a slave; dogs pursuing a fugitive slave are hoodooed into barking at an empty tree.[11] Spiritualism in African-American culture had a far more radical tradition than it did among its white adherents, one full of a strong and often violent resistance to white domination.

Chesnutt carefully tempers conjure's radicalism in presenting his stories to a mainstream audience. Though *The Conjure Woman* is full of oblique and pointed resistance to slavery and the racism that survived it, his stories lack the open rebelliousness of many traditional conjure tales.[12] While conjure in its African-American context solidified black resistance to slavery, Chesnutt used it to bridge the cultural divide between the two races. In "Superstitions and Folklore of the South," Chesnutt further diminishes the ethnographic distance between his black subjects and his white audience by referencing a broader cross-cultural spiritualist context. Aunt Harriet "was a dreamer of dreams and a seer of visions" whose spiritualism happened to take an African cast. If Chesnutt patronizes her beliefs, he nevertheless makes it clear that "she is not the first person to hear spirit voices in his or her vagrant imaginings" (374). Yet while Chesnutt makes conjure both recognizable and nonthreatening to a white audience familiar with its own version of spiritualism, he embeds it firmly in an African-American past. Thus he offers his readers the possibility of understanding conjure without appropriating it as simply a variant of a more familiar European-American spiritualism.

To illustrate, I turn to one particular story, "Sis' Becky's Pickaninny," in order to trace the spiritualist resonances woven into the text, to shed light on the authorial position Chesnutt fashions, and to speculate further on how effectively the stories modulate local color norms to address the Negro Question. The story opens with the recurrence of Annie's poor health, a condition vaguely attributed to a harsh northern climate in the beginning of the volume, but whose return remains inexplicable. Annie sinks into the type of "settled melancholy, attended with vague forebodings of impending misfortune" (132) that would have been recognizable as a classic case of "nervousness" to a wide number of Chesnutt's readers.[13] A physician advises John to "keep up her spirits," and after fruitless recourse to the diversions favored by bourgeois society (novels, plantation songs, and letters), Julius arrives to offer his own variety of healing wisdom.

Julius's appearance a scant page after we hear the advice of "the best physician in the neighboring town" sets him (like Mrs. Todd) squarely in opposition to the medical establishment, while his proffering of his rabbit's foot places him firmly in the context of African folk practice. John clarifies the opposition with his comments on Julius's charm, in terms strikingly reminiscent of Chesnutt's own adolescent journal: "Your people will never rise in the world until they throw off these childish superstitions and learn to live by the light of reason and common sense" (135)—a comment that echoes both the program of racial uplift offered by Booker T. Washington and the scientific voice Chesnutt would adopt in "Superstitions." John understands the rabbit's foot through an analogy that connects the fortunes of the rabbit with those of the race who have fetishistic interest in its foot. Yet if John defines himself against an African-American folk tradition, Julius (and Chesnutt) quickly deconstructs the opposition: he, surprisingly, agrees with John's comments on the rabbit's foot, adding that "it has ter be de lef' hin' foot . . . er a grabe-ya'd rabbit, killt by a cross-eyed nigger on a da'k night in de full er de moon." Julius's response to John's binary reading (rabbit's foot equals black race) doesn't so much answer it as destroy its tidy framework. John's flustered reply, "They must be very rare and valuable," illustrates how effectively Julius unsettled him, and how poorly John understands the rabbit's foot's true value. Julius performs a typical trickster move, simultaneously mastering and deforming John's rhetoric, as Houston Baker argues. Julius also illustrates the formulation by Henry Louis Gates Jr. of the *homo rhetoricus Africanus,* the black speaker who can signify in two discursive universes at once (1988, 75). Julius inserts an excess of signification into his rabbit's foot that opens a space from which he can speak, a space between the scientific, material, rational, white discourse of the great house and the magical, spiritual, emotional, black discourse of the slave cabins. That the exchange takes place on the porch of John and Annie's house is not insignificant.

The deconstructive nature of the frame narrative is compounded within the story Julius tells. Transformations run amok, underscoring the perverse logic of slavery and subverting its cruel machinations. The story revolves around the exchange of Sis' Becky for a racehorse, a deal that doesn't include her young child, Moses. Separated, both mother and child grow ill, and it falls to Aunt Peggy to find a way to reunite them. After transforming Moses into a hummingbird and a mockingbird so he can fly and visit his mother, Aunt Peggy causes both Sis' Becky and the racehorse to turn sick enough that the plantation owners reverse their bargain. The story is a brutal critique of the materialistic logic of slavery, which insists on neatly assigning a price to people in a manner not unlike John's attempt to understand Julius's rabbit's foot in monetary terms. Countering that logic is the world of conjure—a world that, while not divorced from material concerns, balances them with the more powerful logic of community and healing. Aunt Peggy's conjure is classic tricksterism, subtly manipulating the terms of domination in order to enable a subordinate to survive. It is, to be sure, a tentative victory at best. Sis'

Becky is reunited with her child, but her husband remains in Virginia, and she has no guarantees that she won't again be made to suffer for the vicissitudes of the colonel's desire for horseflesh. The victory, though small, is nonetheless important.

Chesnutt's purpose in the 1890s, of course, was not to abolish slavery—it was to change the attitudes of his largely white readers about African Americans and their culture. By undercutting the smug rationalism of John and showing the power of conjure, Chesnutt opened a viable space for African-American spiritualism within the regionalist form.[14] Furthermore, I believe, by couching this story of resistance to slavery in spiritualist terms, he helped build empathy for blacks among his readers. Aunt Peggy performs what is in essence a spiritual healing of Sis' Becky and Moses. Both mother and child fall into a deep melancholy when they are separated—a melancholy that is indistinguishable from Annie's, and just as resistant to orthodox medicine. Moses's appearances before Sis' Becky bear a strong resemblance to the performances of mediums who reunited mothers with their dead children, and in the context of spiritualism, Becky's recovery—she "went 'bout her wuk wid mo' sperit" (148)—takes on an added resonance. The end of Becky's story, too, resonates powerfully with spiritualism. Moses grows up to earn both his and his mother's freedom, and once free he "tuk keer er Sis' Becky ez long ez dey bofe libbed" (158). In this fairy-tale ending with an African-American twist, freedom defines "happily ever after." And, in view of the constant troping of freedom with heaven in African-American Christian parlance, we are left with a mother and child reunited in a world analogous to the hereafter.

Annie's healing is wholly attributable to Julius's storytelling conjure. As mediums required sensitive listeners in order to summon the dead, Julius required an appropriate audience in order to work his magic, and Annie proved ideal. John watches her face express "in turn sympathy, indignation, pity and at the end lively satisfaction," and it is easy to imagine Chesnutt hoping to provoke a similar response in his own audience. Those reactions, the key to Annie's recovery, stand in stark contrast to the rational and materialistic values that characterize John's response to Julius's tales. Julia Farwell has argued that Chesnutt expands the simple survival goals of Brer Rabbit to include such communal interests as church and family, and I would add that this shift to communality is an essential part of both the African-American and European-American spiritualist discourses on which Chesnutt draws. Julius's conjure broadens the space within which persons of different races and traditions can live; it builds a multivoiced harmony far more complex than the hierarchical counterpoint of the plantation tradition. The spiritual healing in "Sis' Becky's Pickaninny" replicates the radical democracy of spiritualism. Those who respect its terms—Sis' Becky and Aunt Peggy, Annie and Uncle Julius—are connected in a chain of conjuration and healing in which no person has the last word, a relationship quite different from that of the strict hierarchy between doctor and patient. Julius heals Annie by inviting her into his world, allowing her to transgress the borders between white and black, science and folklore. Annie (and the white readers she figures) heals and prospers to the extent that Julius blurs the boundaries that define her world.

Figuring this transgressive move is Julius's rabbit's foot, a fetish of black spiritualism, a token of sympathy between Julius and Annie, a site of dissonance between Julius and John, a reminder of the appropriation of African-American culture by white fashion. Its varied signification figures the trickster tactics of Julius, but its shape and intimacy figure something else as well. If John's patriarchal certainty exemplifies Anglo-Saxon phallogocentrism, Julius' rabbit's foot represents a phallic power that is not confined to privileged males. At the end of "Sis Becky's Pickaninny," Julius is able, in a moment of intimacy, to pass the foot to Annie herself. A symbol of conjure, its power becomes as unfixed and transferable as spiritualism itself—the phallic "luck" that the rabbit's foot engenders in Julius can pass its potency to Annie as well. Chesnutt describes this scene of cultural miscegenation in sexualized undertones: Julius gives Annie the rabbit's foot when John has left the two alone on the porch, and he later finds it in the pocket of his wife's dress. Thus the potency of the rabbit's foot, like the potency of Chesnutt's spiritualism, grows as it crosses cultural boundaries. As the rabbit's foot links Annie and Julius, the handkerchief in which Annie wraps the foot provides a link to the head-handkerchief exchanged in the story. Black and white, story and frame pull together in a moment of transgression and transformation that signals far beyond the boundaries of the story itself. Chesnutt's trickster spiritualism fashions, in other words, a contact zone in which black and white norms of spirituality, economics, gender, and knowledge interact and recombine until neither black nor white is pure and neither wholly dominant.

Mena and Borderlands Spiritualism

For Chesnutt, crafting a strategy of literary access at the end of the nineteenth century, conjure provided a crucial vehicle in presenting a politically charged African-American spiritualism to a wide audience. For María Cristina Mena, shaping her representation of Mexican culture at the beginning of the twentieth century, spiritualism provided a means of grafting her sustained analysis of race and gender onto her increasingly radical politics. Like Jewett and Chesnutt, Mena used spiritualism in her local color fiction to critique metropolitan norms. Mena, however, went farther than her predecessors in using spiritualism to deconstruct Anglo-American categories of race, gender, science, and spirituality. As Mena's foothold in metropolitan literary culture grew more secure, her work grew more daring in its use of traditional Mexican spirituality to counter the rational, materialist, and ethnocentric channels of Anglo-American thought.

While Mena has long been dismissed for what at least two Chicano critics termed her "obsequious" portraits of Mexican life, more recent critical attention has focused on the means by which Mena drew on Mexican folk culture to undercut and transform her white readers' expectations.[15] Tiffany Ana Lopez insists that Mena's early stories be read in the context of the xenophobic essays on Mexican society that appeared alongside her work in *Century Magazine*—her Mexicans are not dangerous savages, but richly complicated characters with whom her readers can identify (26–27). Both Lopez and Amy Doherty trace Mena's increasing radicalism in her later stories, where Mena draws on such charged figures as La Malinche and Coatlicue in representing the Mexican Revolution to her American readers. Through such figures, Doherty argues, "Mena offers a vision of the Mexican woman as cultural mediator, translator and revolutionary" (xxxviii). Yet while Mena's use of Mexican oral tradition has gained deserved attention, it's important to keep in mind Mena's efforts to represent her cultural traditions in terms accessible to her Anglo audience. As Chesnutt rescued his conjure stories from the distancing effects of ethnography by weaving into them a European-American spiritualist resonance, Mena used spiritualism to draw her readers into a world whose sensibility grew increasingly revolutionary.

In Mena's first published story, "The Gold Vanity Set" (1913), Mexican spirituality offsets the figure of the New Woman widely celebrated (and more widely scorned) in the turn-of-the-century press. By 1913, when the story appeared in *American Magazine,* some of her features had been absorbed into the norms of middle- and upper-class American life, as epitomized by Mena herself, newly launched upon a writing career in New York. In the story, a New Woman, aptly named Miss Young, comes face to face with a paragon of traditional Mexican femininity, a young woman named Petra. When the American leaves behind her tour book and, folded within its pages, her gold vanity set, Petra, in moment straight out of Lacan, puts on the makeup held in the vanity set's gilded little boxes while gazing into the New Woman's mirror. And yet, "her concept of [the vanity set] was not simple like Miss Young's. Its practical idea became a mere nucleus in her mind for a fantasy dimly symbolic and religious" (5). Petra covers herself with makeup, rushes out into the stormy dusk, crowns herself with wildflowers, then returns to crouch before her husband. Deeply moved, Manuelo vows sobriety and better treatment of his young wife. When thunder strikes, both take it as a sign that the Virgin of Guadalupe has answered the vow, sanctifying the power of the gold vanity set. Mena weighs the modern American woman's "simple" gendering against the "symbolic and religious" fantasy of Petra, leaving no doubt that the humble Mexican's "ecstasy of devotion" holds more value than the crass consumption of the American tourist. Mena, in short, uses the spiritual immanence of the Virgin of Guadalupe to shift her readers' identification with a member of their own class to an identification with a Mexican peasant.

Yet while Mena makes Petra's cultural position understandable, she makes it problematic as well. First, while Mena joins the robust tradition of mockery that greeted white women's attempts to break out of traditional gender roles, she hardly offers an unequivocal endorsement of traditional femininity. What, after all, would her women readers make of the description of Petra turning to her husband after finding the vanity set? "She crept along the floor to him and he caught her under his arm, pulling his poncho over her head, and cuddled her to him with protecting caresses which she received with the trembling joy of a spaniel too seldom petted" (6). Such a passage points to the gender logic of the traditional culture within which Petra is so firmly rooted, a logic which Mena clearly does not endorse. Petra's spirituality opens a void between the American exemplar of the New Woman and the Mexican embodiment of traditional culture, and Mena's story positions her white, female readers in that abyss. Thus Mena, like Jewett and Chesnutt, uses the spirit world to undercut the norms of metropolitan identity.

In a later foray into Mexican spiritual traditions, Mena sharpened her critique of metropolitan norms. "The Birth of the God of War" presents a central Aztec tale in terms at once warmly familiar and deeply alien, forging a borderlands sensibility more aggressive than what we find in Chesnutt's conjure stories and ethnography. Unlike "The Gold Vanity Set," which makes Mexican folklore highly accesible to Anglo readers, Mena signals from the start that "The Birth of the God of War" belongs to a Mexican heritage sharply distinct from Anglo-American culture. She doesn't translate the term *cuentos,* and when she later refers to Aztec mythology, she quickly backs away: "It was not mythology to me; no, indeed" (64). Like Jewett and Chesnutt (at least in his fiction), Mena strongly identifies with the tradition she describes, thus evading the distancing gaze of ethnography. Yet "The Birth of the God of War" is a received story, not an original work of fiction. Neither local color nor "authentic" myth, the tale preserves a distinct Mexican voice located in the interstices of ethnography and regionalism. As in "The Gold Vanity Set," Mena alternately courts and spurns the expectations of Anglo-American readers, setting a tale about the bloodiest and (to Anglo tongues) most unpronounceable of Aztec deities, Huitzilopochtli, in the frame of a little girl's memories of her beloved grandmother. The tale signifies at once a proud and distinct culture ("our pristine ancestors") and a cross-cultural heritage, for once familiarized by the iconic grandmother and child, even the off-putting name of an alien god becomes manageable. By rendering his name "Weet-zee-lo-patchlee," Mena simultaneously grants her readers access to the oral dimension of the frame and highlights the distance between oral tradition and printed text. Translation thus emerges as a central problem in the story, constantly foregrounded by the grandmother's stilted diction and Spanish phrases that Mena insists she cannot accurately transcribe.

As Doherty argues, Mena's purpose grew from simply offering an "authentic" glimpse of Mexico to "revealing misconceptions, presenting legends and offering different versions of reality" (xxix). "The Birth of the God of War" is classic autoethnography, at once engaging and resisting metropolitan discourses in order to preserve a subjugated voice and to begin, at least, to transform the dominant culture. Her portrait of Mexican spiritualism accordingly reveals the fierce Aztec heritage that lies literally beneath the icons of Mexican Catholicism. The story begins with an animist invocation of the forest and ends with Huitzilopotchtli's immaculate conception and birth— throughout, Mena sketches a world where the spiritual and material are as intimately interconnected as anything imagined by Jewett or Chesnutt. Yet where those two writers used spiritualism to construct a vision of healing and harmony, Mena's Aztec spiritualism gives birth to a vengeful and bloody god, the "protector-genius of the Aztecs," whose allure easily survives the mama-grande's tepid Catholic moralizing. Thus spiritualism in "The Birth of the God of War" reaches back beyond the Spanish conquest to find a cultural heritage and spirit of resistance strong enough to combat metropolitan ideology. The grandmother's final words to the little girl, reminding her that the great cathedral in Mexico City was build on the foundation of Huitzilopotchli's temple, are addressed as well to Mena's tourist readers. Underneath the quaint memorials of Spanish Mexico lie the living memories of an Aztec past.

"The Birth of the God of War" not only marks Mena's shift to more overt politics in her fiction, but also teaches us how to read her final foray into Mexican spiritualism. "The Sorcerer and General Bisco" abandons the touristic mode of local color fiction for political allegory, and in Mena's fable of the Mexican Revolution, spiritualism emerges as a central battlefield.[16] As was true in the historic revolution, a corrupt establishment bent on modernizing Mexico for the benefit of a small elite battles a revolutionary movement rooted in the peasant class and its traditional Indian culture. Despite her upper-class background, Mena's sympathies were far more revolutionary than those of her typical American readers; thus, like Chesnutt, Mena used spiritualism to carry the political import of her fiction. The sorcerer of the title is Don Baltazar, whose ruthless exploitation of his hacienda aligns him with the worst of the landholding class, just as his interest in science aligns him with the forces of modernization emanating from north of the border. General Bisco, modeled, most likely, on Pancho Villa, is his opposite, a talented guerrilla leader who wears his peasant origins as a badge and uses his folk beliefs as a shield against the dangers of the modern world. Thus General Bisco's cutting of the telegraph wires to conceal the movement of his forces signifies both his military acumen and his resistance to an Anglo-American technocracy. He proves, however, no match for the wizardry of Don Baltazar. Well versed in the arts probed by the Society for Psychical Research, Baltazar hypnotizes the general and convinces him of his undying friendship. Between the two, Mena interposes Carmelita, the well-born young wife of Don Balthazar who has fled her treacherous husband with her lover. Her power, like Don Balthazar's, is figured through her spiritualist abilities— having plumbed some of her husband's secrets, she can see events taking place at a distance through the spiritual telegraph even when the mechanical one is cut.

Her power is rooted in far deeper soil than her husband's newfangled science. Though Carmelita claims before General Bisco that she learned what she knows of Don Baltazar's arts solely by spying upon him, she also invokes traditional Mexican Christianity, kissing a gold cross to rebut her husband's accusation of witchcraft and swearing her fidelity to the people in the name of the Virgin of Guadalupe. And like the Virgin of Guadalupe, Carmelita embodies a spiritual power that existed before the arrival of the first Catholic missionaries. As "The Birth of the God of War" teaches us to read the pre-Christian resonance of contemporary Mexican culture, so it helps us read the pre-Christian resonance of Carmelita's spiritualism. Like the Aztec priests taught their lore "by the forests, the waters, and the birds" (69), Carmelita gains strength from her flight to the forest, changing from a frightened fugitive and giddy, formulaic lover to something far more magical:

The way was full of difficulties, but not of terrors. Even when a large serpent reared at them obliquely with a strategic hiss as it spurted into the rustling mystery of a marsh, Carmelita laughed with sympathy, and then laughed at the transformation of her once fearful and fastidious self. Scratched and sunburned, soaked to the knees in black swamp-ooze, her dress torn, her bosom laboring from the exertion of the march, she wove a wreath of narcissus for her loosened hair, and when Aquiles showed fatigue she enticed him with snatches of song.

He looked at her with eyes reflecting the wonder of a miracle. That the mute and melancholy victim of his guardian's despotism should have been metamorphosed into this eager dryad! (98)

While the passage clearly registers a classical framework of Greek mythology and woodland lovers, Carmelita's transformation harks back as well to the Mexican spirituality of "The Gold Vanity Set" and, more powerfully, to the Aztec spiritualism of "The Birth of the God of War." Carmelita answers the mammagrande's impassioned entreaty, "Listen to the legend of the forest; listen to it as sung by the birds, the breezes, the waters!" (65). Carmelita's sympathetic laugh with the serpent signifies ("obliquely") her sudden contact with the animistic power of precontact Meso-American spirituality.

Gloria Anzaldúa notes that in "pre-Columbian America the most notable symbol was the serpent," citing the Olmec association of the serpent's mouth with the vagina, the most sacred and creative of places. She traces the evolution of the serpent goddess from Coatlicue, the "serpent skirt"—with her serpent's head, her necklace of human hearts, her skirt of twisted serpents, and her taloned feet—into Coatlalopeuh, "the one who has dominion over the serpents," or, in Anzaldúa's rendering, "the one who is at one with the beasts" (27, 29). The Spanish identified this last incarnation, which appeared before the Nahua Indian Juan Diego, or Cuautlaohuac, in 1531, with the Virgin of Guadalupe of western Spain. While Anzaldúa notes the Spanish effort to "desex Guadalupe, taking Coatlalopeuh, the serpent / sexuality out of her" (27), she insists the effort was never wholly successful. Mena certainly agrees. Although "The Birth of the God of War" carefully downplays Coatlicue's associations with the serpent, representing the goddess as a gentle and chaste analogue to the Virgin Mary, the story nevertheless summons the sexual powers that lay beneath the Catholic monuments of Mexico. In "The Sorcerer and General Bisco," these subconscious resonances finally surface. Once in the jungle, the virginal Carmelita taps into her sexuality—waist-deep in the fecund muck of the swamp, dress torn and breast heaving, Carmelita's knowing laugh with the serpent signifies her transformation into a modern Coatlicue.[17]

With her spiritual heritage comes what Anzaldúa calls *"la facultad"*: the nonrational, "primitive" ability to sense things invisible to the naked eye or to rational perception (38). Like Anzaldúa, Mena associates this ability with the full heritage of Guadalupe / Coatlalopeuh, a fruitful reunion of Mexico's Christian and pre-Christian heritage. Carmelita's spiritualism, moreover, manages to trump the more sterile parapsychology wielded by her husband. Out of touch with the people, with Mexican tradition, and with nature, Don Baltazar's spell over General Bisco is broken by his fear of a tarantula crawling over his library floor. Spiritualism in Mena's world, as in Jewett's and Chesnutt's, belongs not to the cold, masculine rationality of science, but to a woman-centered world of traditional religion; not to the modern universe centered in the American metropole, but to the world of the folk. In her rendering, Carmelita's revolutionary neo-Aztec spiritualism is a vital antidote to the lures of wealth and modernity that seduced so many of Mexico's political leaders. As an allegory of the Revolution of 1912, Carmelita's spiritualism helps General Bisco / Pancho Villa keep faith with the people.

Clearly a stand-in for Mena's own sympathies as she watched events unfold in Mexico, Carmelita embodies Mena's solution to the problem of remaining loyal to her Mexican heritage while enjoying a New Woman's liberated status. Carmelita's immersion in Mexican folk culture separates her from the New Woman pilloried earlier in Mena's work. She remains a figure of multiplicity, finding a very modern freedom through her recuperation of traditional female mythology. Versed in the arcane secrets of modern science, she draws a greater strength by tapping into folk wisdom. Thus she can mediate between—and master—both worlds, not merely translating between Don Baltazar and General Bisco, but ultimately shaping their interaction in the interests of the Mexican people. In shaping Carmelita, Mena may have reached back beyond the Mexican Revolution to an earlier figure, to the mystical Indian woman who joined Cortez on his path of conquest. Mena may imagine her heroine as an alternative La Malinche who casts her lot not with the rapacious Western invader who marshals technology and native superstition in the service of greed and plunder, but with her own people. Carmelita's spiritualism, similar to Don Baltazar's but rooted in a vastly different context, signals Mena's loyalty to her Mexican roots and her power to resist the forces— of modernity, of capitalism, of American hegemony—arrayed against them.

Mena's fiction, struggling to voice a folk Mexican sensibility in the heart of the American metropolis, exhibits the classic features of a text in the contact zone. As it had for Chesnutt, spiritualism for Mena provided a crucial element in her efforts to craft an oppositional discourse within a hegemonic literary form. Spiritualism was, for each writer, and for Jewett as well, inherently political. Jewett used sentimenal spiritualism to question the role of race in constructing a modern American sense of community. By drawing subtle connections between conjure and European-American spiritualism, Chesnutt both undermined the terms of white racism and established a common ground between black and white cultures. Mena drew on her Mexican spiritualist heritage to critique not only the arrogance of the New Woman but also the political force of Anglo-American culture. The political dimension of local color writing has attracted increasing attention in recent years, both for unprecedented access regionalism granted writers of color and for its tendency to confine those very groups to the margins of American society. Such contradictory social meanings are, of course, entirely typical of spaces where different cultures meet, negotiate, and clash along conflicting lines of interest and power. One strength of regionalism in this contest was its claim to authenticity. Magazines granted access to marginalized writers because of their purported accuracy as native informants in representing real people and societies to a mainstream, white American audience. Yet if realism was the determining ideology of local color writing, why did spiritualism play such an important role in so many stories?

One answer is that spiritualism provided a useful space in which writers could rehearse some of the ideological struggles contained in their genre. As folklore and quaint local custom (though no longer reputable science), ghost stories, conjure, and Mexican spirituality fit naturally into a regionalist landscape without being bound by realist conventions. Spiritualist episodes in these stories served as a fantasy space divorced from realist conventions, dream sequences in which issues repressed from the ordinary realm of local color writing could safely surface. Rather than proffering spiritualism as a scientific truth, regionalists used spiritualism to explore alternate sensibilities and complex psychological situations. Indeed, in the context of an increasingly rationalist and secular hegemonic ideology, spiritualism itself was oppositional, a powerful non-scientific realism that flourished at the margins of mainstream American culture. Especially for writers working under strict rules of literary access, as Chesnutt and Mena did, spiritualism allowed their oppositional voices to speak (spiritlike) through a veil.

Yet as my discussion of these writers shows, the social meaning of spiritualism in local color writing is hardly uniform. If local color is indeed a genre of the contact zone, in which ethnographic and autoethnographic texts engage in a politically charged dialogue, then the spiritualism that emerged in these texts can only be contradictory and overdetermined; in a word, dialogic. Compared to its earlier manifestations in American literature, spiritualism in magazine fiction at the turn of the century is far more self-reflexive in its deployment, far more elusive in its intent, and far more overdetermined in its meaning. Jewett, Chesnutt, and Mena all highlight spiritualism's folk roots, but in ways that range from sentimental conservatism in "The Foreigner" to cautious resistance in "Sis' Becky's Pickaninny" to thinly veiled radicalism in "The Sorcerer and General Bisco." Spiritualism's scientific plausibility, long an article of faith among adherents, receives various treatments: scorn (with Captain Littlepage), gentle mockery (via Uncle Julius), and deep distrust (of Don Balthazar). These writers instead insist on spiritualism's indeterminacy, clearly fictionalizing and carefully framing their most vivid spiritualist episodes. By suspending judgment about the veracity of spiritualism, these writers suspend any hegemonic certainty. And spiritualism's politics, reliably reformist in its heyday, become conservative and nativist (though feminist) in Jewett's hands, progressive in Chesnutt's, and revolutionary in Mena's. Spiritualism, long a coherent signifier in mainstream European-American culture, proved infinitely malleable in the world of local color fiction. Such was not the case with the mainstream American novel, where works by Henry James and William Dean Howells managed to confine spiritualism to a European-American context, and hence to a more coherent politics. In the magazines, however, where writers from an unprecedented array of cultural positions gained unprecedented access to print, spiritualism became as richly textured and as vigorously contested as the meaning of America itself.

Chapter 5

Spirit Nation

Spiritualism and National Ideology in Henry James's
The Bostonians *and Pauline Hopkins's* Of One Blood

In 1866, an unlikely friendship sprang up between two particularly celebrated American women. Cora Hatch, then in her twenties, was a successful medium and trance speaker who had been captivating audiences across the country with her golden curls and eloquent discourses on the New Revelation for over a decade. By the time Sojourner Truth met Hatch in Washington, she was close to seventy, having spent almost thirty years as a preacher and activist. Both spoke at the National Spiritualist Convention in Rochester in 1868.[1] Their styles on the platform reflected their vastly different personal histories. Hatch, born in Wisconsin and raised in European-American reformist circles, carefully couched her radical message in the ideals and trappings of white domestic femininity. Truth, who lived as a slave in New York until 1826, proudly drew on the vernacular cadences and culture that had carried her through her long years in bondage. Yet Hatch and Truth shared in spiritualism a system of beliefs well suited to both their medium and their message. Spiritualism offered not only a rationale for the equality of every individual soul, regardless of race or gender, but also a means of getting around the proscriptions facing women who entered public life. The spirits who spoke through Hatch and Sojourner when they mounted the platform or pulpit couldn't be dismissed as merely the voice of a pretty but poorly educated young woman or an entirely uneducated former slave. Instead, their words came from a place beyond the localized space of their own bodies, and their message offered a means of critiquing the very regimes of power that attempted to fix them according to gender and race.

As America struggled to fashion a national ideology that would hold the country together after the Civil War, spiritualists took an active role in shaping that identity, contributing, as they had before the war, to richly interwoven efforts to reform American society. They became increasingly important in efforts to theorize how such a national identity took shape. As the intertwined efforts of the New Psychology and the Society for Psychical Research suggest, the figure of the trance speaker was crucial to developing a new understanding of the self, a means of exploring how the apparently self-willed, sovereign subject was in fact haunted by a "hidden self" that was far less independent, spontaneous, and free than people had believed. Toward the end of the nineteenth century emerged a view of the human subject as indelibly marked, on the one hand, by the raw Darwinian forces of natural selection and, on the other, by the cultural forces mapped out by the emerging disciplines of psychology, anthropology, and sociology. As this emerging model of identity took shape in a culture obsessed with what it meant to be "American," a number of writers turned to spiritualism to explore the complicated psychology of national identity.

Cora Hatch and Sojourner Truth played important, if veiled, roles in this effort. Henry James attended one of Hatch's trance lectures in the early 1860s, and while he proved somewhat dismissive of her message, he was intrigued by her person. In *The Bostonians* (1886), James borrowed her youth, appearance, and style of performance in building the character of Verena Tarrant. While Sojourner Truth fails to appear in *Of One Blood* (1903), Hopkins scatters recognizable elements of her character throughout the novel, from Dianthe's career on stage to her visions of spirits to the strong vernacular voice of Aunt Hannah. Sojourner Truth's example of black womanhood was clearly important to Hopkins. In her series of articles entitled "Famous Women of the Negro Race" published in the *Colored American Magazine,* Truth is one of two women to merit an article to herself, (124 – 32). More problematic than the assignment of models for the heroines of these novels is the relationship between their authors. Despite their difference in age, their widely divergent economic, educational, and social status, their virtually unassimilable aesthetics, and their very different means of reaching a broad public, James and Hopkins, like Hatch and Truth, had some significant common ground. Their novels both take root in Boston's physical and intellectual terrain; both center on women who perform to public acclaim; both juxtapose strong-willed, unrepentant southerners and highly gifted, though emotionally frail, exemplars of American modernity.[2] Both use the entanglements that follow as an allegory of national politics.

Most importantly, both use spiritualism as the organizing device of their novels. They apply the term broadly—James with particular attention to trance speaking, fraudulent mediums, and the rich nexus of spiritualism's al-

lied reform movements; Hopkins with special emphasis on psychical research, spirit visitations, and a mythic African spiritualism strongly resonant
with theosophy. Yet despite their differing representations of the movement,
for James and Hopkins (as for Hatch and Truth), spiritualism proves a powerful tool for interrogating American culture and a potent figure for the different voices struggling to speak toward the end of the nineteenth century. In
both novels, the medium stands in for the subject spoken by American identity and serves as a mold for how identity itself takes shape. Thus spiritualism
in both novels is used as a means of critiquing specific American ideologies
and as a vehicle for examining ideology in general. The two writers, however,
differ in their understanding of spiritualism and the ideology it represents. Is
spiritualism (and ideology) a set of sincere but illusory beliefs that are ultimately determined by the material conditions of society? Or does spiritualism (and ideology) capture the elusive, complicated, and contradictory nature of an identity that has no clear access to an outside reality?[3]

In *The Bostonians,* James uses realism to critique Reconstruction, where
northern "radicals, and spirit-rappers, and roaring radicals" (3) sought to im-
pose a reformist ideology on the rest of the nation. The almost mesmeric
struggle between Olive Chancellor and Basil Ransom to possess Verena figures the struggle to shape the soul of the nation in the wake of Reconstruction. James uses this struggle to suggest that ideology is a kind of false consciousness that obscures the real conditions of existence (a stance that has, of
course, its own ideology). By turning a realist gaze on the trance-speaking
Verena Tarrant, James shows that "beneath" her spiritualism and feminism
is a naturalistic realm of reproductive forces.

Hopkins takes an opposite approach. If James strips national identity of
its mystification, "unmasking" spiritualism to reveal the raw natural forces
that create its effects, Hopkins radically literalizes spiritualism and the national ideology it represents, pushing spiritualism to extremes in order to
show that ideologies of identity (racial, regional, national, cultural, and sexual) are always interconnected, contingent, and tentative, with no stable ground
to anchor them. As the easily entranced, spirit-seeing, mixed-race Dianthe
figures the black female artist possessed by competing ideologies, Reuel's explorations of the "undiscovered country" yield not a "real" identity but a
labyrinthine strangeness. His journey to the African heartland offers a jarring
insight into an origin that is at once radically universal and uncannily personal. For Hopkins, the hidden self is not a stable ground of identity but an
incestuous maze of mirrors, a version of ideology that offers no access to any
outside reality. At an historical moment when race, gender, and class were in-

creasingly fixed by the sort of realist ideology James employs in *The Bostonians,* Hopkins uses spiritualism to contest the meaning of nation, identity, and reality itself. Hopkins and James, culture workers writing in an era of maturing capitalism, develop in their novels an increasingly sophisticated grasp of America's ideological mechanisms and a growing sense of how they might be critiqued.

The Bostonians: *Naturalizing Spiritualism*

By the time Henry James began composing *The Bostonians,* he had had a lifetime's experience with spiritualism, most of it negative. His father, subject to occasional visions, was perhaps the leading American advocate of Emanuel Swedenborg, the Swedish mystic whose explorations of the spiritual world provided much of the theoretical framework for American spiritualism (Edel 7–8). The elder Henry nevertheless proved an early critic of the movement, dismissing the spirits who appeared at the séance table as "so many vermin revealing themselves in the tumbledown walls of our old theological hostelry" (James Sr. 418). Among the many intellectuals, writers, editors, and reformers who made their way to the James household were many who took a deep interest in spiritualism, and in his lifelong omnivorous relationship to European and American culture, the younger Henry James attended his share of trance lectures and séances. He was twenty when he attended one of Cora Hatch's New York performances. In a letter to T. S. Perry, he compared this "congregation of the new dispensation" to the early Christians meeting in the Catacombs; the lecture, on "The Evidence of the Continued Existence of the Spirit after Death," he found "a string of such arrant platitudes, that after an hour of it, when there seemed no signs of a let-up we turned and fled" (1974, 45). Leon Edel later follows the now-mature James, living in Cambridge in 1870, as he "ventured into private meetings and seances, demonstrations of mesmerism, speeches by ardent young reformers or discourses by lady editors advocating new religions, listening attentively to their flow of ready-made oratory" (118).

While James never caught his brother William's intense enthusiasm for spiritualism and other psychic phenomena, he carefully followed William's efforts to use mediums and trance speakers to chart the unconscious. William always maintained a stronger belief in the possibility of spirit communication than in the validity of the mediums he actually studied, and remained a sympathetic, if unconvinced, investigator.[4] Henry dutifully respected his interest:

when William died in 1910, Henry remained in Cambridge for several months to see if his brother would succeed in contacting his family from beyond the grave, as he had promised to try. Henry, however, was hardly sympathetic to spiritual investigation, even in his grief—he greeted news of William's voice at a séance as "the most abject and impudent, the hollowest, vulgarest, and basest rubbish" (670). Yet if Henry found little evidence to convince him that most mediums were anything but frauds, he nevertheless held on to some elements of his father's spiritual beliefs. When the elder Henry James died in 1882 (as *The Bostonians* was taking shape), at his grave in Cambridge the younger Henry read William's most recent letter. He wrote to William that he was certain his father heard him, "somewhere out of the depths of the still bright air" (Edel 284–85).

The Bostonians conveys little of this guarded sympathy for spiritualist beliefs. The novel places spiritualism squarely in the febrile mix of northern reform movements, with Basil Ransom dismissing the guests gathering at the veteran reformer Miss Birdseye's house as "mediums, communists, vegetarians" (28). James's introduction of this Boston stalwart, read as a thinly veiled portrait of Elizabeth Peabody, generated some significant ill will when the novel began serialization in *Century Magazine* (Edel 313):

She belonged to the Short Skirts League, as a matter of course; for she belonged to any and every league that had been founded for almost any purpose whatever. This did not prevent her being a confused, entangled, inconsequent, discursive old woman, whose charity began at home and ended nowhere, and who knew less about her fellow creatures, if possible, after fifty years of humanitary zeal, than on the day she had gone into the field to testify against the iniquity of most arrangements. . . . She looked as if she had spent her life on platforms, in audiences, in conventions, in phalansteries, in seances. (23–24)

While James moderates his portrait of Miss Birdseye as the novel progressed, if anything he sharpens his critique of Verena's father, Selah Tarrant, a fraudulent medium who now makes his living as a mesmeric healer. A one-time pencil salesman and member of the "Cayuga community, where there were no wives, or husbands, or something of that sort," he became a successful medium, only to have his career ended "for reasons of which Mrs. Tarrant possessed her version," having herself helped a table rise or supplied a soft grasp in place of the recalcitrant spirit of a lost loved one (66). Selah carried from that episode a lingering terror of people who are "in earnest," for the "people he had ever seen who were most in earnest were a committee of gentlemen who had investigated the phenomena of 'spirit materialization' some ten years before, and had bent the fierce light of scientific method upon him" (148). He now pinned his hopes for success on his daughter, a beautiful young woman who, once placed "in report" with the invisible world by her father, proved a compelling speaker on the rights of women. Yet Verena herself placed little faith in her father's mesmerism, acceding to his mesmeric gestures merely to humor him; when she joins Olive Chancellor, she forgoes the last vestiges of trance in her speaking.

Remarkably for a writer who made frequent and powerful use of ghosts and other psychic phenomena throughout his fiction, James includes not a single occult occurrence in this novel about spiritualism. This may be due in part to the rather low fortunes of American spiritualism in the1870s and '80s. Attempts to build a national organization by the end of the 1860s had faltered due both to efforts to limit the influence of women on the part of male spiritualists and to deep-seated resistance to standardizing and codifying spiritualist doctrine or practice among believers. The ascension of the controversial Victoria Woodhull to the presidency of the American Association of Spiritualists further divided the movement. Despite (and partly because of) her attempts to weave together women's rights, spiritualism, and socialism into a coherent political force, these movements grew increasingly marginalized and fragmented just as the controversy over "spirit materializations" erupted. Ouija boards, tipping tables, spectral music, and invisible touches had supplemented the rappings along the spiritual telegraph since the 1850s; despite frequent investigations of the sort visited upon Selah Tarrant, mediums sought increasingly elaborate effects to draw audiences. Ann Braude notes a marked shift in the 1870s from trance speakers like Cora Hatch, who advocated a wide agenda of social reform (with special emphasis on the rights of women), to mediums who traveled the burgeoning circuit of spiritualist camp meetings, painting flowers blindfold, handling fire, channeling spirit voices, and, eventually, summoning fully embodied spirits. Camp meetings were held in scenic retreats all over the country and attracted thousands of visitors, but most came seeking entertainment rather than education. By the time Verena begins her career in the mid-1870s, trance speaking had largely been replaced by more sensational forms of mediumship.[5]

One of the most dramatic of these events was the materialization of a spirit named Katie King, summoned by the Philadelphia mediums Mr. and Mrs. Nelson Holmes. Robert Dale Owen, a prominent reformer and sympathetic investigator of spiritualist phenomena, endorsed the phenomenon in an article in the *Atlantic Monthly;* he learned she was a fraud too late to retract the article, and the magazine's editor, William Dean Howells, had to insert an embarrassing disclaimer (Braude 179-80). The episode didn't shake the faith of committed spiritualists, but it certainly deepened the distaste of skeptics, including Henry James. A longtime friend of Howells, he was living in New York when the scandal broke in 1875; his novel *Roderick Hudson* began its serialization in the *Atlantic* in the same issue as Owen's article.

By the time James began writing *The Bostonians* in 1883, spiritualism had not yet benefited from the renewed interest and publicity afforded by the Society for Psychical Research—a renewed attention that is certainly reflected in the increasing role of the occult in James's later writing. There were other reasons, though, for James to turn a skeptical eye on spiritualism. Having broken into print in the 1860s as an interpreter and as a critic of the French and English realist writers, James was just entering his own most realist period. *The Bostonians* and *The Princess Cassamassina* are generally cited as the two novels that adhere most closely to a naturalist aesthetic; in its rigorous attention to the details of setting and its effort to capture the character and tone of a particular locale, *The Bostonians* particularly has been seen as his strongest gesture toward that particularly American brand of realism, regionalism.[6] While James was never entirely comfortable with the farthest reaches of naturalism, finding the frank treatment of sexuality by writers like Flaubert and Zola distasteful, he absorbed the materialist bias of the movement, its tendency to read cultural phenomena through the prism of science, and its fascinated attention to the darker underside of civilization. In 1884 he went so far as to tour London's stark and forbidding Millbank Prison to gather material for *The Princess Cassamassina*. "You see," he wrote to a friend, "I am quite the Naturalist" (Edel 315). While James's credo of the novel ("The Art of Fiction" [1884]), leaves plenty of room for exploring the subtleties of human consciousness, the overall thrust of his piece is in the direction of realism, social history, and the raw stuff of life—an aesthetic that would have little interest in ghostly effects of the séance.

Instead, James took social history itself as his primary topic in *The Bostonians*. "I wished to write a very *American* tale, a tale characteristic of our social conditions," he wrote in his notebook as he began work on the novel. He chose to focus on "the situation of women," since it seemed to him the most pressing question of the age; it would also allow him to explore a Boston marriage, "one of those friendships between women which are so common in New England" (James 1987, 18-19). In framing the novel, James set as his subject not American spiritualism, but America itself, as it appeared in a region of the country he knew especially well. Having settled permanently in

England, James was ready to turn a critical eye on the country of his birth, and hence *The Bostonians* takes on a national scope. The women's movement, the relationship between Verena, Olive and Basil, the sharply sketched minor characters from across the social spectrum, the local color landscapes of Boston and New York—all serve as vehicles for James's effort to take stock of America in the years of Reconstruction.[7] Even the manner in which it saw print underscores this purpose: published serially in *Century Magazine*, a periodical explicitly founded to help unify the country after the Civil War, *The Bostonians* shared its pages with two other self-consciously "American" novels, *The Adventures of Huckleberry Finn* and *The Rise of Silas Lapham*. Indeed, the meaning of America, and the terms by which it could rebuild a coherent and durable identity after the trauma of civil war, would remain a cultural obsession for decades.

Yet if America is James's theme, why does spiritualism, of all the myriad movements available to his satiric pen, play such a central role in the novel? Clearly, fraudulent mediums and angelic trance speakers made for compelling reading, and clearly, too, spiritualism was a prominent landmark in the social conditions he wished to map, especially in the ongoing struggle for women's suffrage. I argue, however, that spiritualism was more than simply an extra layer of Balzacian detail in his portrait of American life. It occupies a central place in James's meditation on the struggle to rebuild a fractured American consciousness. The séance and the trance, for James, served as means to connect the spiritual and the material at the very moment when American culture was adapting to new social and economic conditions. *The Bostonians* covers the American scene at a time when a number of powerful forces converged to shake the foundations of American identity. The effort to reconstruct the southern states (and the entire nation) along entirely different racial lines, the revolution in gender norms begun at Seneca Falls, the unchallenged primacy of industrial capitalism, the rising tide of immigration, the absorption of the West into the national polity, and the emergence of the United States as an international power all contributed to the pervasive sense of profound change that marks all of James's American fiction. They provide a crucial (though oblique) context for James's novel, and James uses spiritualism to explore how such deep structural transformations of American social conditions are mediated through a uniquely American consciousness. Spiritualism, in short, is a primary tool James uses to map the transformation of American ideology in the years after the Civil War.

The national focus of *The Bostonians* is apparent from its first pages. When the Mississippi native and Civil War veteran Basil Ransom calls on his distant cousin Olive Chancellor at her Boston home, James brings together the two extremes of antebellum America. Basil, with his strong accent, exaggerated manners, and smoldering eyes, is the very embodiment of the South; his dinner at the home of an equally characteristic Bostonian then serves as kind of familial reconstruction. Olive lost her two brothers in the war, but her sentiment on sitting down with an unreconstructed Confederate veteran mirrors the dominant tone periodicals like *Century* took in shaping the legacy of the war: a recognition of mutual bereavement and an admiration for the heroism shown by soldiers of both sides (Gooder xxxvii). Basil's lingering memory of the war is one of bitter defeat, compared to Olive's grim triumphalism—he seems disinclined to admit, as Olive imagines he does, "that the North and South were a single, indivisible political organism" (James, 1984, 10)—but despite their inherent differences, the dinner goes off "brilliantly" (16), a small step forward in the long and delicate path toward national reconciliation. This strand in the novel reaches its climax in the early courtship of Verena and Basil, where this granddaughter of abolitionists and this veteran of southern battles tour Harvard's Memorial Hall. There Basil "forgot, for now, the whole question of sides and parties" (252) and surrendered to the noble solemnity of the place. The tone is very different from the first encounter between Olive and Basil, where despite their polite chatter, both were locked into competing ideologies and memories; James describes instead a genuine movement toward reconciliation. In his attempt to capture the unifying effect of the building, James elides the fact that Harvard southerners were excluded from the rolls of the dead. That Basil and Verena's relationship grows suddenly serious under the watchful gaze of these memorials to fallen soldiers underscores the political resonance of their union; they themselves realize that "there was no want of decency in lingering there for the purpose" (234).

James had initially conceived of Basil as hailing from the Far West, setting up an opposition between "old" America and its new territories. By shifting Basil's home to the South, James shifts the terms of his national allegory to focus more squarely on the aftermath of the Civil War. In turn, James has Verena Tarrant just returning from urban centers of the American West, cities such as St. Louis and Topeka, in order to complete the national credentials of the novel's central trio. By shifting around the geographical origins of Verena and Basil, James manages to cast the novel as the struggle between the South and North for the possession of the new America symbolized by the West. James is careful not to keep the terms of this allegory too strict—Verena also hails from lower-middle-class environs of Cambridge, and stands more broadly for the wide stratum of the American public who nurtured the many reform movements satirized in the novel. While she is the unapologetic granddaughter of abolitionists and the daughter of what Basil calls a "detested carpet-bagger" (53), the exact social position of this "attractive but ambiguous young person" (53) remains vague. Indeed, Olive, from her Beacon Street perch, sees Verena as part of "the miseries and mysteries of the People . . . a flower of the great Democracy" (104). That much of the action takes place in New York, by now firmly established as the economic and cultural capital of the country, further establishes the national scope of the unfolding conflict.

The conflict is indeed intense, and the fragile edifice of reconciliation gradually crumbles beneath increasingly violent clashes of competing interests and raw power. Yet while the book is haunted by southern battlefields, the conflict in *The Bostonians* is fought on the terrain of its characters' consciousness—the conflict is, in a word, ideological. Realism played a key part in this process. In sketching his two antagonists, James draws heavily on the naturalist credo that people's identities are determined wholly by the material conditions of their environments and thus consciousness flows directly from social position. Basil, in this construction, is as fully explainable though his Mississippi heritage as Olive is by the address of her home on Beacon Street; their appearances, their manners, their inflections, and their ideas embody their places of origin. From this perspective, the correlation between one's material origins and worldview are rather direct and fixed, and hence rather easily read from the outside. Spiritualism is, in the early pages of the book, a good example—Adeline's initial dismissal of "mediums, and spirit-rappers, and roaring radicals" quickly locates the movement within a narrow social stratum, and Basil picks up the thread of ideological analysis when he asks whether the evening at Miss Birdseye's will be "something very Bostonian" (17). For Basil, the nexus of racial beliefs is rooted firmly in the material conditions of New England; for Olive, speaking from within that perspective, "it isn't Boston—it's humanity" (18). Such a view illustrates the naturalizing effects of ideology, from Basil's unthinking dismissal of a reality so different from his own to Olive's unwavering belief that hers are universal truths frustrated by a world in the grip of false ideas.

Much of the novel elaborates this materialistic view of human consciousness, one quite consistent with the theory of ideology most fully elaborated by Karl Mannheim as the "sociology of knowledge." In Mannheim's view, Marx and his followers seized rather narrowly on class as the primary determinant of social thought, focusing solely on exposing the false consciousness of oppressive groups. The proper task for the sociologist of knowledge, according to Mannheim, is to analyze all the ideological positions in a given social situation in order to arrive at a total picture of a society's weltanschauung (49–55). Mannheim's conception of ideology neatly parallels James's own novelistic project. To the naturalist imperative to fully detail the material conditions of a given society, James adds a decided emphasis on exploring social consciousness. *The Bostonians,* in short, can be read as a sociology of American knowledge, carefully mapping the thoughts of characters occupying a wide range of social positions in postbellum society.

For James, spiritualism offers a powerful means of exploring how social position enters consciousness, one he elaborates during Verena's trance speech in Miss Birdseye's parlor. Basil neatly pins down Selah as "the detested carpet-bagger," then watches as Selah entrances his daughter. Basil's distaste comes from his quick conclusion that Verena, rather than tapping into the wisdom of spirits, "had been stuffed with this trash by her father" (57); he hardly feels the need to enter into a rigorous analysis of the Tarrants' class position in order to dismiss Verena's ideas as false consciousness. James then subjects his most ferocious critic of false consciousness to a similar ideological critique. He turns a spiritualist eye on Basil's own rather reactionary "queer heresies," noting that "he seemed at moments to be inhabited by some transmitted spirit of a robust but narrow ancestor, some broad-faced wig-wearer or sword-bearer, with a more primitive conception of manhood than our modern temperament appears to require" (181)—as sharp a summary as we have of southern planter ideology.

Once the spiritualist metaphor is firmly established, James continues to map the connections between ideology and self, noting how Verena, in her first private conversation with Basil, tends to "drop into oratory as a natural thing" (217), and then noting how Verena's views, once under Olive's tutelage, reflect more and more fully those of her patron. Other characters respond to Verena in ways entirely characteristic of their social position, from Mattias Pardon's sense of her as a journalistic gold mine to Henry Burrage's courting of Verena as a rare, aesthetic ornament. James reserves his most withering material critique of his characters' consciousness for the elder Tarrants. Mrs. Tarrant is the strongest example in the novel of a character who survives the vagaries of her social condition with the salve of false consciousness, clutching to her "own version" of the events that lead to the end of her husband's career as a medium and grasping at the chance to use her daughter's gifts to help her claw her way back to the social respectability she lost with her marriage. Selah himself salves whatever vestiges remain of his conscience by keeping the reality of his means just below the level of his consciousness. By never confessing his humbuggery "even in the privacy of domestic intercourse" (68), by never quite lifting the veil that shields his spiritualist and ideological machinations, he keeps his self intact.

Selah's refusal to admit the real conditions of his existence even in his own home signals one of James's key insights into the nature of ideology in postbellum America—the rooting of identity not in some interior space but in the public sphere. Public and private continually blur in the novel, with private revelations quickly finding their way into print and parlors often standing in for inner consciousness ("Mrs. Tarrant was delighted, as may be imagined, with her daughter's account of Miss Chancellor's interior" [92]). If spiritualism, with its belief in the ultimate primacy of an immaterial existence in a spiritual world, holds little appeal for James, his novel takes the idea of immaterial existence in print very seriously indeed. Selah, certainly, is far more interested in achieving immortality in print than he is in the spiritual world. "There had been a Spiritualist paper of old which he used to pervade; but he could not persuade himself that through this medium his personality had attracted general attention," he laments (96); lingering around newspaper printing rooms, he finds that "he would like to go in himself, bodily" (99). Publicity has become the primary battlefield of competing ideologies in James's vision of America—Mattias Pardon, the Tarrants, the Burrages, and even Basil and Olive themselves struggle to control a public sphere shaped by an increasingly omnipresent mass media.

James's realism, here, has left the world of the strictly material—by locating one key source of identity in the ubiquitous print culture that was fast becoming a defining element of American society, James hints at a model of consciousness that is far more diffuse, complex, and interconnected than an ideology of social position would suggest. James offers other complications in what might be termed his "study of naturalist consciousness." Many characters resist a simple correlation between ideology and social position. Olive Chancellor and her sister Adeline, for one example, diverge to a degree that can hardly be explained by Adeline's marriage and a number of years in Europe. Basil, for another, is on the one hand the very embodiment of the planter class of the antebellum South, his ideas springing from the very soil that nurtured his ancestors; on the other hand, he is marked from his introduction by a curious note of difference. "His discourse was pervaded by something sultry and vast, something almost African, in its rich, basking tone, something that suggested the teeming expanse of the cotton field" (3). Basil undercuts his racial purity the moment he opens his mouth, suggesting that he, like Verena, is possessed by something he can't quite acknowledge. Southern white elite culture doesn't occupy a fixed and coherent social position, but rather is itself mixed, if not in blood, than in something as subtle and pervasive as discourse. While James can hardly be accused of adopting Foucaultian language (more likely he draws here on the climate theory of culture to complicate the theories of racial typology still prevalent at the time), it is clear that James wants to complicate Basil's social position from the start, and to suggest that there is something "sultry and vast" in the reactionary southerner's speech of which he himself may not be aware.

Spiritualism becomes for James a means of exploring how ideology itself takes possession of a subject. Verena is crucial to the novel not because she neatly exemplifies how consciousness arises from an essential selfhood or from a certain social position, but rather because she appears to have no fixed subject position at all. She is, for James, the blank slate of ideology. When she speaks, James presents an image of discourse originating not in the individual soul, but from somewhere beyond:

She began incoherently, almost inaudibly, as if she were talking in a dream. Ransom could not understand her; he thought it very queer. . . . She proceeded slowly, cautiously, as if she were listening for the prompter, catching, one by one, certain phrases that were whispered to her a great distance off, behind the scenes of the world. Then memory, or inspiration, returned to her, and presently she was in possession of her part. She played it with extraordinary simplicity and grace. (55)

Verena's fascination comes not from Verena herself, but from her self playing a part. The charm, in other words, lies in the queerness of Verena's performance, in the space she pries open between her self and the ideas she speaks— or rather the ideas that "speak her." Verena repeatedly emphasizes that it isn't her speaking, but something impersonal, "some power outside" that flows through her (51).

Verena's performance opens up the space for ideological analysis. In this, James is in close sympathy with the practitioners of the New Psychology, particularly Gabriele Tarde, who used hypnotism to explore how the autonomous self was in fact imitative, and that what appears to the self as spontaneous, personal, and individual is in fact socially determined—an insight gleaned not only in clinical wards, but also in "seances and performance halls."[8] The "queerness" of this insight is crucial to James's portrait of Verena. In a novel conspicuously lacking in the occult effects so common in James's fiction, Verena is the character who most closely approximates the ghosts that haunt so much of his prose. Martha Banta has noted how James throughout his oeuvre uses the calculated eruption of the Other in his fictions of normal life to signify the visiting dead and that which is not contained within a particular character's being (141). Verena's speech summons something from beyond her, but it is clearly not the dead—what becomes visible through her is ideology itself.

Once ideology is firmly fixed in view, the novel attempts to lift its veil to gaze upon the reality that lies beneath. The first glimmer of this occurs in Memorial Hall, the scene of Basil and Verena's allegorical courtship, where the spell of national ideology begins to possess them both. Their relationship is not driven forward by their rather genial ideological banter; what pulls them together is Basil's request that their visit be kept a secret. Fully sworn to the integrity of her relationship to Olive and the larger struggle for women's rights it embodies, Verena at first demurs, saying "I tell her everything." Yet she blushes, and Basil stands quietly "tracing a figure on the mosaic pavement with his cane" (234). If Verena's words signify the ideology to which she's fully committed herself, Basil's figure gestures to something beyond, something not quite readable, but more *real* nonetheless.

The nature of that figure becomes more apparent in the next meeting between Basil and Verena, during the following summer in New York. There, Basil's description of Verena as an ideological puppet stops her short: "It isn't you, the least in the world, but an inflated little figure (very remarkable in its way, too), whom you have invented and set on its feet, pulling strings, behind it, to make it move and speak, while you try to efface yourself there" (325).[9] "Something" makes her stand and begin to move away (the ideology imposed by Olive), but she realizes that her "real self was there with him now," a realization begun by the timely appearance of a perambulator a few pages earlier. Though Verena doesn't articulate it, the naturalist forces of reproduction drive a wedge between her real self and the ideology she has so carefully cultivated, and James underscores this with the use of a spiritualist metaphor. Thinking of Olive, Verena muses, "What would be her state now, poor forsaken friend, if some of [the things he had said to her] had been borne to her in the voices of the air?" (326). In a distinctly naturalist sense, the voices do convey Basil's message, for Olive at that moment is sitting in Washington Square surrounded by the voices of children.

The conflict between feminist ideology and more "innate" female desires has at this point another hundred pages to play out in the novel, but the course of the conflict from here on is foreordained, with Verena torn between the ideological imperatives embodied in Olive and the naturalist forces she finds irresistible in Basil. We are shown Verena's determination as, locked in a cottage in Marmion, she develops her gift with a singlemindedness born of "her education, in the atmosphere of lecture rooms, of séances, her familiarity with the vocabulary of emotion, the mysteries of the spirit life" (366). Counterposed is the inexorable pull of her walks with Basil, notable not for any of his dated and provincial ideas but for his distinctly phallic presence: "[S]he felt his tall, watching figure, with the low horizon behind it, represented well the towering eminence he had in her mind—the fact that he was just now, to her vision, the most upright, the most incomparable object in the world" (371).

Spiritualism at this point in the novel has become a thoroughly ironized marker of materiality. Olive imagines Basil, for example, as "deputed by fate to exercise this spell" on Verena (370); "voices in the air" whisper to Basil to return to Marmion after a brief departure; the hotel in Marmion itself, with its poor service, is "an establishment conducted by invisible agencies" (333). The one sympathetic reference to spiritualism is the view from the dying Miss Birdseye's invalid chair—"the hazy shores on the other side of the water" (344) are a likely hint of the Summerland formerly limned by Mrs. Ada T. P. Foat. Yet this tender glimpse of a spiritualist afterlife merely signifies the reformer's confinement to an ideological haze, blind to the raw struggles going on about her. Caught between her beliefs and her irrepressible desires, Verena "had the sensation of being ground very small indeed" (371), a rare industrial metaphor in James. The starkest naturalist epiphany is reserved for Olive: "[S]he knew, again, how noble and beautiful her scheme had been, but how it had all rested on an illusion of which the very thought made her feel faint and sick. What was before her now was the reality, with the beautiful, indifferent, sky pouring down its complacent rays upon it" (395). James leaves Olive bereft not only of her great love but also of the ideology that had shaped her entire self; she stands before the world at this moment knowing herself to be a puppet of false consciousness, to be (to borrow Mrs. Tarrant's word) a humbug.

What is left after this Jamesian glimpse of the stark materiality that underlies ideology? One option is a world of Selah Tarrants, of cynics who trade in ideologies they know to be false, blithely uttering banalities as they pocket whatever gains they can wheedle out of those still in the grip of ideas. Peter Sloterdijk sees this stance as a defining feature of modern capitalism, a condition he calls "enlightened false consciousness," characterized by the endlessly ironic cynicism of a society that sees its deepest beliefs as mere rationalization (cited in Eagleton 1991, 39). Such a result is entirely consistent with the naturalist project, which relentlessly strips away the illusions of its characters by confronting them with the raw, natural forces that operate beneath the various familial, gendered, religious, and social pieties which only *seem* to govern people's lives. Certainly few characters survive *The Bostonians* with their ideals intact. Verena dreads her attraction to Basil as much as Olive does, while only the strained decorum of the deathbed keeps Miss Birdseye's frail beliefs from being rent by the storm going on around her. The characters whose worldviews best survive their contact with reality are those who, like Adeline or Doctor Prance, are essentially nihilists, or, like Basil, have beliefs reactionary enough as to come to essentially the same thing.

The great casualty, then, in James's allegory of national identity is the reformism that was a defining feature of Reconstruction; what remains is a world of impersonal natural forces underneath a veneer of progressive ideology. That this sounds a bit like unchecked capitalism should come as no surprise. James was even more reluctant to talk about money than he was to talk about sex, but here these two forces are omnipresent and interchangeable, driving James's bleak vision of a capitalist America in the grip of the raw forces of desire. While James's ideological critique of America in the Gilded Age has little to say about industrial exploitation and offers no insight at all into the consciousness of the working class, it offers a sharp account of how alienated the ideas and cultural practices of middle- and upper-class America are from forces that determine their existence. His is an ideological analysis divorced from any political agenda—a stance that has, nonetheless, certain politics. Such accounts of capitalism appear to be without ideology, in that they offer no comforting illusions to the people who make it work. This naturalist view, however, is hardly appropriate to understanding James himself, a highly successful purveyor of commodified culture publishing at the very epicenter of the American culture industry. James's naturalism ultimately naturalizes capitalism by offering no alternative to the unregulated flow of desire, a view that is one of capitalism's most potent ideologies. James sees enough to undercut reformism, but can offer nothing but a cynical quietism to replace it. Basil and Verena's tearful union before a ranting crowd thus symbolizes the dark future of the nation.

Yet if Verena falls silent at the crumbling of her feminist beliefs, Olive, ultimately, does not. Her rush to the platform of the Music Hall in the face of a hostile crowd, knowing that the woman who had embodied her hopes and dreams was firmly in the arms of a reactionary chauvinist, offers at least a hint of an alternative to a cynical quietism. Her actions are described in significantly doubled terms. She is, first, driven by the intensely naturalist motive of social status—the sarcastic gloating of Mrs. Farrinder, a well-established and jealous women's rights orator, "had been a lash" (433), but she is also filled "with sudden inspiration" (433), a phrase that signals, perhaps, the tentative reformation of her ideology. The renewed force of her feminist beliefs are barely apparent even to herself—she claims to want to confront the raw fury of the crowd "to be hissed and hooted and insulted" (434), to sacrifice herself, as James's reference to Hypatia suggests, on the burning embers of her ideals. Yet the very act of mounting the platform summons her ideology from beyond its grave. The process of performing an ideological action that she herself knows to be illusory makes it, through some miracle of praxis, real—a process verified by the respectful silence of the audience. She is, hence, at once the murdered philosopher and the "feminine firebrand of Paris revolutions" (433).

James presents in the figure of Olive's speech a more nuanced sense of ideology than the model of real base/false consciousness suggested by Basil's hollow victory. Olive's speech suggests instead the sense of ideology explicated by Slavoj Zizek, in which a subject may know she is following an illusion, but, in doing so, help to bring that illusion into being (1989, 28–30). Consciousness, though springing from mixed motives and tied to natural forces that it tries to repress, nevertheless has real effects rooted in social practice. Olive, by wittingly living out her ideology, helps bring it into being. She offers a possibility of truthfully speaking one's illusions; a sense of consciousness as woven into practice; a possibility of ideology functioning even when it can see its limits. And if such an insight offers a glimmer of hope for Olive, it does the same for the nation figured by the Music Hall audience, which is not quite the howling naturalistic mass it at first appears to be. James suggests that in the presence of ideology, it too can be transformed (if only tentatively) into "the great public" (1886, 434).

We never hear Olive's speech, however, for the narrator turns away just as the audience falls silent, an act typical of this curious authorial perspective that peers effortlessly into characters' minds but pulls back from from key scenes. This narrative voice may suggest James's own reservations about naturalism and its access to truth. By adopting a narrator who is clearly omniscient but who refuses to see everything, James may be suggesting the limits of naturalist insight. Naturalism may give us glimpses of the real, but it stops short of any final truth—as James himself can point to the limits of the ideologies swirling in the mainstreams of American culture, but leaves them, finally, partially intact.

Of One Blood: *Spiritualism and the Hidden Ideological Self*

Pauline Elizabeth Hopkins wrote her fourth and final novel, *Of One Blood; Or, the Hidden Self*, from 1902 to 1903, almost a generation after James's most detailed exploration of the intersections between spiritualism and national consciousness. Those issues at the center of *The Bostonians* took on an added urgency in Hopkins's time. The Society for Psychical Research was at its highwater mark in England and America, and William James's use of spiritualism to explain his conception of the unconscious reached a wide audience. The juncture of spiritualism and New Psychology also began to take an overtly political turn with W. E. B. Du Bois's use of double consciousness to map the tortured dynamics of African-American racial psychology. This emerging model of the self took shape in a period of brutal racial division, sharply contested notions of gender, massive immigration, and abruptly realized imperial ambitions; in such a context, national identity was both a deep obsession and an intractable problem. Spiritualism, for Hopkins, is a means of weaving together these often contradictory cultural strands into an ambitious and problematic novel that struggles mightily to map the ragged ideological terrain of American society at the beginning the twentieth century.

One strategy she uses is an aggressive intertextuality. While her novel contains no explicit references to *The Bostonians,* Hopkins firmly roots her work in spiritualist literature. Cynthia Schrager notes her veiled quotation from William James's essay "The Hidden Self," which serves as the novel's leitmotif (184); Hopkins also includes a number of specific or oblique references to William Dean Howells's *The Undiscovered Country* (448) and Hawthorne's own explorations of the occult (477). Eric Sundquist argues that Du Bois, too, inhabits *Of One Blood* in the many references Hopkins makes to "the veil" (572–74). In her portrait of mesmerism as a means of sexual control, Hopkins draws on a long line of darkly eroticized mesmeric relationships that came into being before Hawthorne's *Blithedale Romance;* the theme had recently seen a hugely popular incarnation in George du Maurier's *Trilby* (1894). By explicitly summoning her literary forebears in the body of her text, Hopkins not only places her novel squarely within a coherent tradition of literary spiritualism but also casts her work as a commentary on that tradition.

Indeed, her novel is in many ways a revision of James's own spiritualist work, a *Bostonians* with difference. Hopkins opens her novel in the very same low-rent neighborhood of Cambridge that Basil glimpses from Olive's dining-room window, as if to turn her authorial gaze back on the cultural privilege from which James writes. Reuel Briggs, poor, talented, and misunderstood, comes north (to Harvard) to make a name for himself, eking out a scant living by tutoring the dissolute sons of the wealthy and contributing articles (on pyschical research) to national periodicals—characteristics he shares with Basil Ransom. He competes for the charms of a beautiful but malleable performer, Dianthe, with his social opposite, Aubrey Livingston, in what becomes a contest of magnetic will rife with political overtones.

These parallels, of course, pale in comparison to the vast differences in plot, structure, and tone between the two novels. Indeed, the parallels between Verena Tarrant and Hopkins herself—both lived in the same area of Cambridge[10]; both became celebrated and politically engaged performers—underscore the racial divide that separated the world that white reformer James satirized and the segregated black society that Hopkins inhabited. Born in Portland, Maine, to a former slave and a New Hampshire native, she grew up in Boston, where as a schoolgirl she won a prize for an essay on temperance. In 1879, at the age of twenty, she wrote and starred in a play about the Underground Railroad, launching a career as a popular local singer, actress, and speaker that would last for twelve years. We don't know whether James became aware of this young and captivating black woman during his months in Cambridge in (1882–1883), but by then Hopkins was firmly enmeshed in a social milieu about which James remained almost entirely ignorant. By 1900, she would become the most influential "lady editor" in African-American print culture, helping to organize, run, and fill the pages of one of the first national general interest periodicals aimed at a black audience, the *Colored American Magazine.* Her role in shaping editorial policy became increasingly public until, like Verena, she was silenced by the patriarchal and political will of a powerful man—in her case, Booker T. Washington, who gained control of the magazine in 1904 and forced Hopkins out soon after, apparently displeased by her increasingly radical politics.[11]

Hopkins, despite her detailed knowledge of elite white society, was never welcomed into its ranks as Verena Tarrant is; the "mint of money" that dangled before Verena's career never materialized for Hopkins herself. And while for Verena and Olive, the great—the only—question of the day is the liberation of women, for Hopkins, every question of reform was indelibly marked by race. Clearly, these two novels, like these two writers, enter into a strained and uneven dialogue. The relationship between them is not that of, for example *The Bostonians* and *The Blithedale Romance,* where James self-consciously revises Hawthorne's masterly text. Placing *Of One Blood* and

The Bostonians in dialogue reveals, instead, their dialogic relationship, high-lighting the different voices, fissures, and lacunae inherent in their authors' different social positions.

Min Song terms this process of placing writers with different themes, aesthetics, and cultural contexts side by side as "interrogative switching," arguing that such a juxtaposition reveals a great deal about the artistic choices, cultural positions, and literary receptions of such texts. Indeed, Hopkins's novel doesn't so much respond to *The Bostonians* as it shadows it, adding a texture and resonance to James's characters, situations, and insights not apparent when read in isolation. The novel of manners, the international theme, the question of style, the social satire, the engagement with realism, the narrative voice, the exploration of consciousness—all the elements of James's aesthetic appear in sharper relief when viewed next to *Of One Blood*. Similarly, *The Bostonians* raises sharp questions of Hopkins's novel, some of which concern her elite cultural perspective, the nature of her engagement with mainstream culture, the role of working-class characters in her work, and the function of her style. How does James's realist analysis of gender shape our understanding of Dianthe? What does James's expatriate perspective share with Hopkins's international frame of reference? How does James's account of elite culture (and its lower-class counterpart) differ from that of Hopkins? How does James's silent adoption of race theory shed light on Hopkins's own complications of racial identity? And most importantly for this study, how does spiritualism help both authors explore how such concerns determine and disrupt the workings of the self? These texts, in a word, haunt each other, adding to our critical perspective a doubled voice that materializes at unexpected and highly charged moments. They may not cohere into an explicit commentary or a crisp ideological critique, but they add richness to our understanding of both texts, making visible the shadows that lie between.

Certainly, *Of One Blood* shares with *The Bostonians* a clear national allegory. The *Colored American Magazine* was founded to help bring African-Americans the full rights of citizenship (Carby xxxii), and the novels Hopkins published during her tenure at the magazine steadily worked their way through the various arenas of American cultural life: the club movement that defined late-nineteenth-century civil society in *Contending Forces*, Washington high society in *Hagar's Daughter*, the mythology of civil war in *Winona*. In each setting, Hopkins had her authorial eye firmly on national norms of racial identity, class privilege, and historical memory.[12] *Of One Blood* extends the national scope of her earlier novels, placing Reuel in the intellectual center of American life, tracing the historical provenance of her characters far beyond the antebellum society that served as the starting point of her earlier novels, and placing their actions in first a national and then an international context. Spiritualism plays a key role in this extension—as Cynthia Schrager has noted, Reuel couches his enthusiasm for psychic investigation in the very words of the prospectus for the *Colored American Magazine,* as a means of "unveiling the vast scheme of compensation and retribution carried about in the vast recesses of the human soul" (448). To underscore the connection, Reuel makes his comment just as he and Aubrey are off to the Tremont Temple to hear the Fisk University singers, introduced with a brief history of postbellum African-American education. Reuel may dodge Aubrey's posing of "the Negro problem," but the apparition of Dianthe's face before the dogged investigator of spiritualist phenomenon signals that mysticism will be the key to the national politics of race.

Hopkins was not the first to make this connection. Du Bois's *The Souls of Black Folks* was published as *Of One Blood* was being serialized, and she almost certainly read the earlier version of the famous first chapter when it appeared in *Scribner's Magazine* in 1890 (Sundquist 570). There, Du Bois develops the connections between the New Psychology and race consciousness, articulating his theory of racial double consciousness and using as his primary metaphor the veil. For Du Bois, the racial politics of the Jim Crow era profoundly influenced consciousness itself (for whites and for blacks), and so Hopkins joined in a sustained movement to help fashion a "New Negro" by reshaping black consciousness. Jennie Kassanoff places Hopkins within the intense struggle in the African-American community to help redefine race. The debate took place in the context of a mainstream discourse of Social Darwinism and racial determinism that sought to define racial identity in scientific and genetic terms—the same ideological framework in which literary realism flourished. While African Americans in general fought for a more culturalist conception of race, there were sharp divisions in their tactics (165). Advocates of manual training and economic improvement, grouped under the leadership of Booker T. Washington, sought to combat this ideology on its own ground, arguing that changing the material conditions of African Americans would surely transform white prejudice.[13] This "realist" strategy for fighting racism was opposed by culturalists like Du Bois, who sought to intervene directly in the realm of cultural production, challenging the racist assumptions of mainstream culture and locating racial identity not in science and the body, but in history and cultural practice.[14] And for a model of how social forces took shape in the human mind, they turned to the New Psychology, with its paradigm of the self shaped by forces beyond consciousness.

If, as their culturalist stance suggested, these forces were social and historical in nature, then the most effective way to help construct a New Negro identity was to transform the cultural forces that shaped racial identity. While the culturalists hardly ignored the material structures of racial oppression (indeed, engaging them far more directly than Washington preferred), they directed at least as much attention to the culture of racism that structured American society and American consciousness. The New Negro project, then, was not to unmask a false racial ideology but to counter the dominant culture's hegemonic force. This Gramscian approach locates revolutionary struggle in the myriad conflicting strands of ideology that run through any society and that may be woven together to win the support of oppressed classes. The task of anyone hoping to transform an unjust society is to untangle and reshape the cultural nexus that supports the existing social structure.

Thus Du Bois, in *The Souls of Black Folks,* followed his exposition on African-American psychology with long chapters on history and sociology; and thus Hopkins chose to struggle against racist ideology from the masthead of the *Colored American Magazine*—an ideological apparatus that could be turned against the state. There, she occupied the position of an organic intellectual (to borrow again from Gramsci), aligning herself with an emergent social class, theorizing its relationship to the dominant culture, and shaping, out of the range of intellectual and cultural practices available at the beginning of the twentieth century, a new and coherent identity that would enable her African-American readers to transform their social position. Hopkins, of course, is hardly an exemplar of Marxist social critique: she has little to say about capitalism per se, and while she is often sympathetic to working-class characters, she spends far more time initiating her audience into the mysteries of bourgeois culture than she does adopting a proletarian perspective. Yet unlike Henry James's fiction—that of a traditional intellectual rooted in a dominant class whose art tended (usually) to defend its privilege against all comers—Hopkins's work claims bourgeois cultural status for African Americans, and thus is nothing short of revolutionary.

Spiritualism is a powerful example of Hopkins's counterhegemonic practice. On the one hand, Hopkin firmly embeds spiritualism within the dominant culture and its scientific knowledge. Hopkins presents spiritualism not, as James does, as one of many reform movements characteristic of a specific American group, but as the leading edge of transatlantic science. Spiritualism here thus belongs to the world of psychical research and the broader concerns of psychology, medicine, and chemistry. While frowned on by his professors, Reuel's interest in spiritualism is maligned not as the disreputable fellow traveler of abolitionism and women's rights, as it is in James's novel, but rather as one of those overlooked corners of scientific inquiry that so often transform the entire field. Hopkins casts Reuel as the rising star of a new science whose success is apparently independent of his racial background but whose African heritage conveys a strong ideological message: that a race marginalized by science can master that very discourse. Reuel, in short, is an exemplar of racial progress and assimilation, a star among the "talented tenth," a key contributor to human knowledge, the George Washington Carver of psychical research. Hopkins thus makes use of one of the disciplinary mechanisms—science—that helped structure racism in America. Although we don't know how seriously Hopkins took spirits and trances in her private life, for such realist writers as Mark Twain, Frank Norris, and Hamlin Garland psychical research was very much a science, however much it assumed symbolic or satiric treatment in their fiction.[15] While Reuel's investigations into the "unclassified residuum" quickly assume a symbolic dimension in Hopkins's novel, they are presented first and foremost as real scientific advances.

Yet why is his field of expertise spiritualist phenomena? One answer is that the focus on research into the occult undercuts the Darwinian materialism that underlies most of the era's scientific theorizing about race, just as Hopkins's recurrent use of mixed-race characters problematized the rigid racial classifications of the day. Another is that her focus on the controversial terrain of psychology allows her to yoke science to the study of consciousness. Thus, Hopkins can authenticate her culturalist explorations of black consciousness by appealing to science without being tied to the naturalism so important to *The Bostonians*. Reuel's research into spiritualist phenomena becomes an important tool in constructing the New Negro.

This shift from the science of consciousness to the construction of racial identity occurs abruptly. The first half of the novel builds toward Reuel's triumphant revival of Dianthe after a train wreck leaves her in a state of suspended animation, which other doctors mistake as death. While his theory "smacks of the supernatural . . . charlatanism, or dreams of lunacy," in the words of the chief surgeon, Reuel agrees to a "practical demonstration" (469). His encounter with the scientific method is far happier than was Selah Tarrant's, and with the stunning validation of Reuel's scientific discoveries, "fame and fortune awaited him" (472). Yet, Reuel's success is thwarted by his friend Aubrey's revelation of his racial secret. When his only option for gainful employment and, with it, marriage to Dianthe is to take the position of doctor to an archeological expedition, Reuel sails off to confront his African heritage and the uncharted regions of his racial self. Spiritualism quickly becomes central to this journey—the key feature of the lost city of Telessar is its mastery of psychic phenomena of the sort Reuel himself was just beginning to rediscover. The fact that Reuel and Ai share the same vocabulary and understanding is a sign, for Hopkins, of both the universalism of science and the tenacity of African cultural heritage. The fact that Reuel's gifts for psychical research are passed down from a long line of female "voodoo doctors" (603), as Hopkins describes Reuel's grandmother, signifies that, in the mind of the New Negro, an au courant mastery of European-American science can coexist with a fully acknowledged African heritage. The spectral appearances of Mira, who reveals, at key moments, the machinations of Aubrey's plan to seize Dianthe for his own, force the two heroes (and the reader) to address the legacy of American slavery even as Reuel comes to the heart of his African self. Spiritualism, then, stands for three of the major cultural strands Hopkins weaves together in her effort to fashion a new African-American identity: a rich African heritage, a sharp critique of America's racist history, and a firm command of European-American cultural capital.

Yet if there is a certain elegance to this reading of Hopkins's cultural allegory, it is clearly belied by the novel itself, which is anything but neat. *The Bostonians* has an aesthetic and ideological tightness that only at rare moments begins to break down; the novel's realist framework, though it occasionally groans and creaks, generally holds firm. *Of One Blood,* from the standpoint of a Jamesian aesthetic, is a mess. Rather than read this as a sign of Hopkins's artistic failure, a number of readers had seen it as symptomatic of the novel's attempt to synthesize competing strands of cultural discourse. Elizabeth Ammons suggests that all of Hopkins's novels revel in a Bakhtinian play characteristic of any revolutionary discourse (1996). Dana Luciano argues that the formal unruliness of *Of One Blood* results from Hopkins's exploration of the historical trauma of slavery—in her view, the extremes of melodrama narrate the melancholia inherent in American race relations. In this sense, the structure of *Of One Blood,* rather than abandoning the conventions of realism, might be seen as a realistic projection of the unconscious. The rigid authority of naturalism, relentlessly stripping away the illusions of its characters until they confront the raw ground of truth, is hardly suited to capturing the hesitations and erasures, the sudden projections and insistent hauntings, that characterize the mind as described by the New Psy-

chology, in which patient study reveals no solid ground, but only hidden
chambers and unknowable depths that reveal the self as a stranger to itself.
Hopkins adds politics and history to the subterranean forces that structure
identity, but they offer no solid foundation for her portrait of American culture. Spiritualism in Hopkins's novel thus tracks the workings of the political
unconscious as it shapes the identity of the New Negro. For rather than offer
an analysis of the ideology of race from some material perch in a "real" world
supposedly outside of ideology, *Of One Blood* offers a glimpse of the immaterial workings of ideology itself, endlessly shaping and fracturing and re-
combining the elements of consciousness in a ghostly dance with the real.

   One sign of Hopkins's turn to the unconscious is the overdetermination
of one of the terms used to describe its workings. The veil is the dominant
metaphor of *The Souls of Black Folks,* a rich and sharp symbol of the doubled
nature of African-American consciousness and a sign of its difference from its
white American counterpart. Cynthia Schrager argues that Hopkins substitutes for Du Bois's model of doubleness a rhetoric of surface and depth, of a
hidden African self that structures the American ego. Hopkins's use of the
veil suggests a less stable opposition—as the novel progresses, it becomes increasingly difficult to discern what is surface and what lies beneath. If the veil
suggests the line between the signifier and the signified, then it becomes, in
Hopkins's use, a slippery line indeed.[16] When Reuel contemplates suicide,
the veil is the barrier between life and death (442); when Aubrey admits that
he knows of Reuel's African blood, the "dark veil" stands for the racial secret
of passing (483); when Dianthe lies poisoned, Hopkins lowers the veil of genteel discretion, hinting at (by covering) her sexual abuse (612). Early in the
novel, Reuel hopes that his studies of mysticism will lead to the "unveiling of
the vast scheme of compensation and retribution of every soul" (448)—a sign
of spiritualist revelation that carries with it the strong political overtones of
Reconstruction politics. The most charged and elusive mention of the veil
(and the only place where it is capitalized) occurs when Dianthe, recovering
from the train accident, speaks in a trance: "I see much clearly, and much
dimly, of the powers and influences behind the Veil, but I cannot name them"
(475). If "the Veil" represents the barriers of consciousness, it is impossible
to determine who speaks from behind it. Dianthe's identity has begun to blur.
Though fresh from a tour with a mesmerist, the voice can hardly be that of
her former employer; the voice speaks of a future when Dianthe will be
healed, suggesting that the voice is not Dianthe's own. We learn later that the
most likely candidate is Dianthe's mother, Mira, who will appear to both
Reuel and Dianthe, but at this moment we are certain only that Dianthe has
become a cipher, a mask through which forces beyond the veil can speak.

More unsettling still, this moment of mediumship marks the beginning of Aubrey's erotic interest in Dianthe. For Aubrey, like Basil Ransom, the brief erasure of identity that comes with trance speaking proves irresistible; though while Basil begins the slow process of refashioning Verena in his own ideological image, Aubrey succumbs to the slippage of his shadowy self. Seeing her jolt awake as she speaks with a stranger's voice, he "feel[s] the glamour of her presence and ethereal beauty like a man poring over a poem that he has unexpectedly stumbled upon, losing himself in it, until it becomes part of himself" (475). The loss of self visible in this spiritualist moment triggers his erotic response—a moment that suggests not the rigid norms of romantic love but the strange depths from which attraction springs. The moment grows increasingly strange in retrospect, for as Hopkins reveals that the voice speaking through Dianthe is Mira's, we gradually recognize that Aubrey has fallen in love with both his sister and his mother. Hopkins thus offers an uncanny glimpse of the Freudian dynamics of attraction. By framing familial conflict and psychological inheritance within the allegory of nation, she suggests how the most intimate functions of the self are shaped by the combined forces of history and the unconscious; she lays bare, in this moment, the workings of ideology. As the mesmeric control of Aubrey's father over Mira was an occult manifestation of the political relationship between a master and his female slave, Aubrey's own power over Dianthe suggests the continuing power of racial ideology in postbellum America, triggered in this case by Aubrey's manipulation of his victim's racial secret.

Spiritualism, ghosts, and mesmerism in this context belong not to the newest discoveries of Western science but to the world of a hidden self repressed by America's racist ideology. If for Henry James spiritualism is a facade beyond which lurk the real forces of desire, for Hopkins spiritualism signals a beyond that resists understanding. Reuel's science, after all, can't summon or explain the apparition of Dianthe that appears before he goes to her concert and again before the train wreck; they lie beyond the horizon of the explainable, as Dianthe's "dual mesmeric trance" (471) undercuts Reuel's authoritative certainty in reanimating his ghostly lover. The doubled trance is one of many points in the novel where Hopkins layers her narrative, pulling the rug out from under smug scientism that is spiritualism's other register. Who has Dianthe in her dual trance? The mesmeric doctress? Aubrey? Mira? Reuel himself? Or has Dianthe herself entranced Reuel, having, as Elizabeth Ammons notes (1992, 82), reanimated him by her ghostly appearance? If so, the two are locked in an echo chamber, North and South, science and art, white and black, male and female signifying back and forth in a "mesmeric sublime" that leaves the reader dizzy, with no ground or outside point of reference. The dual trance casts them (and us) into a free-floating world of spirits, of ideology, that offers no stable point of reference. Spiritualism here is the contact point between multiple ideologies, where frames of reference and codes of explanation blur and erupt.

This uncanny excess erupts again when Dianthe regains her ability to sing after Reuel has departed for Africa: her "unearthly" appearance signals the return of the spiritual. Her song ("Go Down Moses") is joined by "a weird contralto, veiled, as it were, rising and falling upon every wave of the great soprano, and reaching the ear as from some strange distance" (501–2). Appearing at the moment when Aubrey has begun his bid for sexual control, spiritualism signifies Dianthe's resistance, a struggle that involves far more than just these two. If Aubrey summons, metaphorically, the spirit of his father in exercising his mesmeric arts, Dianthe here is joined by the voice of her mother (the most likely source of the contralto), the slaves who first sang the spiritual, and the countless voices of the African diaspora whose heritage the song conveys. The song is personal, familial, political, and cultural at once; in drawing on ideologies resistant to Aubrey's mesmeric power, it recalls as well Mira's own resistance to Aubrey's father. Once mesmerized, she prophecizes the outbreak of war and its deadly consequences—a case of mesmerism gone awry. While racial politics and ideology allow the Livingstons (father and son) to dominate Mira and her daughter, such political and ideological control is neither pure nor complete; other ideological positions remain hidden even in the most abject self, offering the chance to resist.

The multiplicity of the hidden ideological self is the key to Hopkins's strategy for resisting racial hegemony. While a character like Jim Titus, the faithful servant of the Livingstons, knows his place all too well in American society, the ones whose places are ambiguous are most capable of evading its ideological constraints. Thus the mixed-race characters central to Hopkins's literary imagination are "mixed" in more than just blood: they carry as well a mixed unconscious that includes the mixed currents of American ideology. Dianthe's and Reuel's mixed-race status, the secret complication of their identity, makes them vulnerable to someone who, like Aubrey, is in the know, but it also enables them to move seamlessly among different ideological neighborhoods, from the humble cabins of former slaves to the grandest parlors of Cambridge. And yet these characters, lacking a stable race, lack a stable identity as well. The scene where Aubrey reveals to Reuel, over an intimate dinner, that he knows Reuel's racial secret, is famously ambiguous. Aubrey reaches across the table, grabs Reuel's hand, and whispers a sentence that makes Reuel blush, before assuring him that "the secret is safe with me"

(480). Written in the language of a homosexual tryst, the passage is suggestive rather than revealing, casting Reuel's African heritage (and, in narrative retrospect, Aubrey's) as tentative, elusive, and ungrounded. Aubrey may claim to know for sure the truth of Reuel's identity, but Hopkins's novel doesn't—the "hail" of ideology speaks here with a fractured voice.

The announcement of Reuel's secret frames Reuel's subsequent journey to Africa as something other than a return to a pure racial and cultural heritage. Most commentators read the journey to the lost Ethiopian city of Telessar as a firm endorsement of Pan-African values.[17] Hopkins's representation of Africa fits uneasily, however, into the opposition between white and black that structured both the imperial conquest of Africa and the growing resistance to it by people of African heritage. There is, for example, the problem of Hopkins's own anxieties about Africa that crop up throughout the expedition narrative, from her description of Tripoli as a place of "Orient charm" (509) to Charlie's dismissal (from the standpoint of his "healthy American organization") of the undeveloped African hinterland: "Here there was no future" (526). On traveling up the Nile, Hopkins mediates on the fallen heirs of Egyptian culture, saying, "This is the people whose posterity has been denied a rank among the human race, and has been degraded into a species of talking baboons!" (538). While Hopkins frames this meditation with the perspective of a white archeologist, Dr. Stone, and is careful to assign blame to imperialist ideology, the venom of the passage bleeds through. Hopkins's ambivalence about Africa is most apparent in her descriptions of the inhabitants of Telessar, who "ranged in complexion from a creamy tint to purest ebony" (545). While Ethiopia, as Eric Sundquist notes, may stand in African-American discourse for Africa in general, in Hopkins's formulation it deconstructs racial difference itself. This lost origin of Western culture in the center of Africa, filled with people of every color dressed in vaguely Greek garments, is not the answer to Reuel's racial identity but the question itself. The city of his origin is a city of racial indeterminacy.

And it is a city of spiritualism. Hopkins describes Telessar in the cadences used by people like James's Ada T. P. Foat to capture the ethereal beauties of Summerland. Telessar is a "city beautiful" set in a deep valley framed by waterfalls and filled with fertile fields and vineyards (550). Though Hopkins, unlike Elizabeth Stuart Phelps, doesn't guide us through the intricacies of heavenly urban planning, she makes it clear that her description borrows as much from English literature as it does from African explorers: a long citation from Milton completes her portrait of this Anglo-African Eden. Yet Telessar's provenance is not so much the afterlife as the inner life, the world of the unconscious. Luciano argues that this dream-city is in fact a symptom of the melancholia that pervades the novel, a counterprojection of America's dimly recognized racial trauma and, hence, "a perpetuated ideal, a horizon of possibility that must be continually reinvented" (156). Yet while Luciano is certainly right to situate Telessar within the formations of the unconscious, she is too quick to dismiss its utopian function; for as a space fashioned in direct opposition to America's rigid racial hierarchy, standing at the fountainhead of Western and African culture, it is surely the ideal self toward which Hopkins's New Negro ideology yearns.

It is, however, a sublime utopia, one that eludes identity even as it helps to fix it, one whose signs point beyond what is knowable. Luciano notes that the city's written language is unknown to Reuel, suggesting that it is "the lost language of the prelapsarian, monolingual (and monogenist) past" (171). Reading the signs at the gate to the city aren't enough even for so avid a student as Reuel; to enter into the mysteries of this world, he must lose consciousness. Many of the mysteries of the city revolve around spiritualist knowledge, but while some elements remain accessible to Reuel's Harvard-trained mind, many more recede into the esoteric realm of the occult. Though some of Ai's commentary on the city's spiritualist knowledge is couched in the democratic and accessible tones of European-American spiritualism ("There are always angels near!" he exclaims [573]), more remains inaccessible, the provenance of a secret priesthood. Ai marks a theosophical turn in Hopkins's spiritualism, a shift from the psychic discourse of rationality to one of occult wisdom preserved in the jealously guarded traditions of priests, one that remains, to the reader, unknowable. The spiritualist credo offered by Ai is not, after all, entirely comforting: "To us who are so blessed and singled out by the Trinity there is a sense of the supernatural always near us—others whom we cannot see, but whose influence is strong upon us" (573). The nature of those others and the outlines of the destiny toward which they work may, we hope, be good, but they show our familiar selves to be confined in the (spirit) hands of forces beyond our control.

Hopkins, in short, has ignored Charlie Vance's advice to the good Professor Stone: "Don't touch upon the origin of the Negro; you will find yourself in a labyrinth" (521). The revelations of the lost city are nothing if not labyrinthine—Reuel finds in his new identity and new wife, the bronze Venus, Candace, not so much a new identity as a confused echo of his earlier one, a supplement that estranges rather than completes what has come before. So too for Dianthe, who in her wandering through the "mazes of unfamiliar forest paths" (603) stumbles across the cabin of the old conjure woman (Reuel's grandmother) and the secret to the incestuous nature of her current life. Such revelations are more than America's bitter fruit of slavery and the poisonous racist ideologies that followed; they are more, too, than the eruptions of melancholia that such a social history is bound to induce. By pushing her exploration of racial and cultural ideologies to their breaking point, by taking her novel into the labyrinth of racial identity, Hopkins points to undifferentiated terrain of the Lacanian "real," from which all ideology, all identity, is formed. Spiritualism is the primary vehicle for this unconscious excess, this field where identities warp and double and reappear without warning and with uncanny effect. That Aubrey, Dianthe, and Reuel fall dead or silent by the novel's end is an entirely understandable effect of such a glimpse behind the veil.

Does it necessarily figure Hopkins's own fall into silence as well? By the time she finished *Of One Blood,* she may well have understood that her own future with the *Colored American Magazine* would soon come to an end; Reuel's retreat to Africa may, on the one hand, suggest her own frustration at finding her own voice proscribed. Or it may, as Schrager suggests, signal Hopkins's growing pessimism about the reformist possibilities of literature, despite (or perhaps because of) the increasingly strident tone and theme of her novels. Reuel's silence may also be a symptom of how difficult it was for Hopkins to put together the pieces of a national black identity. As Dianthe's rape and murder suggest the failure of bourgeois norms of domesticity in a racist society, Reuel's frustrated career hints at the limits of the capitalist work ethic. In addition, Reuel's deferral to Ai's insight and mystical powers during his return to America points to the difficulty of applying a genuine Pan-African sensibility to an American context. Finally, I would argue, Hopkins's dissatisfying ending illustrates the dangers of looking beyond a politics of identity. Rather than fashion a coherent New Negro ideology by mixing the norms of mainstream America with a Pan-African world view, *Of One Blood* opts to undermine the very terms of racial and cultural identity itself, returning to a point of mythic origin where structures of racial and cultural difference collapse, a world where the stable moorings of identity sink into the quicksand of the real.

Yet while such an approach may not offer a stable ground from which to launch a coherent program of social protest, it would be a mistake to underestimate the power of Hopkins's critique. Her work points to the lack of closure in American racial ideology at the beginning of the twentieth century, and any effort to pry open the gaps and fissures of such an oppressive regime are valuable enough.

Conclusion

The Poetics and Politics of Spiritualism

While the Rochester Rappings were a nineteenth-century phenomenon, angels, ghosts, spirits, and devils of every color and creed haunted the American cultural landscape long before and long after the Fox sisters began their ghostly communion. Spiritualism in America has always served as a vehicle for a rich, complicated, and often treacherous cultural exchange, and it has remained an important site of cultural crossing into the twentieth century. Early in the century, European Americans turned in ever-greater numbers to non-Western forms of spiritualism, while Americans of color continued to find spiritualism an effective means of access to mainstream culture. Theosophy, for example, brought a rich (though often highly mediated) Asian-Indian heritage to an elite group of European Americans, who grafted it onto Rosicrucian and other occult European traditions.[1] The rise of Boasian anthropology in the same era signaled a growing mainstream appreciation for non-Western cultures. Whereas Harriet Jacobs and Charles Chesnutt could present conjure only in the most guarded terms to their white readers, writers of color like Zora Neale Hurston could (with the blessing of Franz Boas himself) fully celebrate African-American spiritualism before a white audience. Autoethnographies such as Hurston's *Of Mules and Men* (1935), to say nothing of *Black Elk Speaks* (1932), emerged, of course, in the context of primitivism and patronage. Yet the difference between *Of Mules and Men* and Chesnutt's "Superstitions and Folklore of the Old South" (1901) or the difference between *Black Elk Speaks* and *Copway's American Indian* (1851) bespeaks a fundamental shift in the cross-cultural dynamics of spiritualism in America. European-American spiritualists were ready as never before to learn from (and, often, appropriate) cultures that had long been ruthlessly marginalized, while writers from marginalized cultures were free as never before to celebrate their heritage openly. The terms of access and equity, it seems, had changed.

Or had they? We are now in the midst of a spiritualist movement as widespread and dynamic as its nineteenth-century predecessor. The panoply of spiritual leaders and sects loosely gathered under the heading "New Age," the now-ubiquitous "angelmania," and the increasing appearance of ghosts and other occult phenomena in popular books and films mark at once how little and how much spiritualism in America has changed.[2] Like the ultraist reformers who first opened their homes to the Fox sisters, many practitioners of New Age religions are veterans of social reform movements focused on improving the status of blacks and women. The two spiritualist movements share an evolutionary ideology, the hope of heralding a new phase in human and cosmic consciousness, one that unites religion and science. The Rochester Rappings attracted at least as much criticism and derision as the New Age movement does now, though the direction of that criticism is slightly different—if anything, the New Age movement has been more roundly mocked from the left than was nineteenth-century spiritualism. Contemporary American spiritualism, like its predecessor, offers adherents the opportunity to rechannel their frustrated reformist energy into spiritual pursuits. And like its earlier manifestation, it has diverse cultural roots, it eschews any kind of formal institutional structure, and it happily exploits the media and merchandising techniques of capitalist society as it spreads into the cultural mainstream.[3]

The differences between the nineteenth-century spiritualist and the New Age movements, however, are instructive. The New Age movement, for one, emerged at a greater distance from the high point of social reform. While nineteenth-century spiritualism spread alongside the abolitionist and women's rights movements, contemporary spiritualism began to flourish only in the 1980s and 1990s, in the midst of a conservative retrenchment following the reformist zeal of the late 1960s. This difference in timing suggests that the New Age movement is not a part of but a reaction to an era of intense social reform. Equally important is the different cultural context of New Age thought. Schooled in the ethnic pride movements of the 1960s and often loosely informed by relativist rather than evolutionary anthropology, New Age practitioners typically eschew the Christian framework of their nineteenth-century predecessors and turn to non-Western spirituality for inspiration. Many draw on Buddhist and Hindu traditions, many others on Native American and other pre-modern spiritual practices. While nineteenth-century spiritualists occasionally contacted Indian chiefs and vaguely "oriental" spirits, most of their contact with the spirit world was confined to a close circle of friends and family (and the European ancestors they shared). New Agers, by contrast, typically reject inherited Western traditions in their search for spiritual fulfillment, turning instead toward non-Western religions, wholly original revelations, or a "global shamanism" (Brown 30), all utterly alien to the movement's nineteenth-century predecessor.

The phrase "global shamanism" seems to promise a new, rigorously crosscultural spiritualist paradigm. Many critics, however, have argued that New Age movements misrepresent, misuse, and exploit the cultures and peoples from whom they seek to learn.[4] While some Native Americans and other people of color have found comfortable niches within New Age movements, it remains overwhelmingly white. At the same time, many writers from marginalized cultural positions have turned to spiritualism in their own work, drawing on spiritualist traditions kept alive in many U.S. cultures and subcultures. Tony Kushner's *Angels in America* (1989), Leslie Marmon Silko's *Almanac of the Dead* (1991), Maxine Hong Kingston's *Woman Warrior* (1976), Toni Morrison's *Beloved* (1987), and Cristina García's *Dreaming in Cuban* (1992) are all works that powerfully engage spiritualism from a wide variety of cultural perspectives, none of which could be considered New Age.[5] Spiritualism also has become a favorite Hollywood device. Films and television programs have given starring roles to spirits who typically, in the past, were consigned to bit parts as Gothic monsters or holiday props.

In all of these ways, spiritualism saturates contemporary American culture, but its import seems even more elusive and contradictory than its predecessor's a century and a half ago. Michael Brown argues in his study of channeling that New Age spiritualism offers a salve for people overcome by the "fragmentation of the self" in postmodern America (12), a means of preserving radical individualism and subverting traditional identity categories. Kathleen Brogan suggests that the resurgence of ghost and spirits in ethnic literature especially is an effort to confront "partially erased cultural history" (2). Mark Edmundson argues instead that the culture's fascination with spiritualism (a term he stretches to include Foucaultian notions of power) is symptomatic of the decline of a viable political left.

How are we to read this spiritualist renaissance in America? Does contemporary spiritualism retreat from history, or engage with it? While a full account of recent spiritualist phenomena is far beyond the scope of this study, my exploration of earlier manifestations offers some guidelines for how to read this current outbreak of ghost, spirits, and angels in America.

The Pueblo Revolt illustrates the sheer range of positions spiritualists can occupy in a contact zone, from the mestizo informants, to Otermín's army who carefully adapted Pueblo spiritualism in Catholic terms, to the "coyotes" who drew on both Indian and Spanish spiritualism in order to straddle the colonial divide, to the separatism of both Popé and Otermín, whose insistence on mutually exclusive, culturally pure spiritualisms structured the very terms of the revolt. Such a range certainly captures the variety of political positions occupied by spiritualists today. The Salem Witchraft Trials illustrated a similar range of spiritualist positions while underscoring the political effects of a contact spiritualism. Tituba, by drawing on a rich Carribean spiritualist heritage in her testimony before her Puritan judges, inserted an uncanny difference into the trials that helped transform them into a lethal outbreak of colonial paranoia. Tituba in Salem and Spanish-speaking Pueblos like Pedro Naranjo prefigure a cross-cultural spiritualist practice that would appear throughout American history, one that borrows from the different cultures their speakers inhabit and signifies in each.

In Rochester in the middle of the nineteenth century, Harriet Jacobs exemplified a slightly different cross-cultural spiritualism. Writing to win her white audience to the antislavery cause, Jacobs carefully referenced European-American spiritualism in order to familiarize her harrowing story. For Jacobs, as it did for many later writers of color, spiritualism provided a crucial bridge to a mainstream audience, one that carried radical resonance important to her cause. Yet Jacobs used spiritualism's cross-cultural dimension to help preserve a distinct African-American identity, weaving into her autobiography an African spiritualism that preserves an irreducible difference even as it signifies across cultural lines.

Such delicate negotiation between shared belief and cultural difference was equally apparent as spiritualism spread through the burgeoning print culture of nineteenth-century America. Spiritualism provided a target for the disembodied, rationalist, white male elite who controlled the national magazine press, helping this elite fashion a public sphere partly in opposition to a marginalized European-American spiritualism—a dynamic similar to that operating today. Periodicals like the *Cherokee Advocate* and the *Anglo-African Magazine,* serving subordinated cultures, entered the public sphere by adopting a rationalist, skeptical tone toward spiritualism. That writers of color today feel more comfortable drawing on spiritualism may signal, on the one hand, a greater mainstream tolerance for non-European spiritualist beliefs; on the other, a sometimes misguided assumption on the part of mainstream readers that the spiritualism in such works is "merely" literary. How effectively such works contribute now, as then, to a truly harmonious national culture remains open to debate.

These conflicts also shaped three postbellum efforts to imagine the afterlife. Elizabeth Stuart Phelps's *Gates* novels, the Ghost Dance of 1890, and Mark Twain's *Extract from Captain Stormfield's Visit to Heaven* construct versions of the afterlife that help mark out the cultural divisions of the era. Yet each bears as well the markings of a common imperialist infrastructure. Both the Ghost Dance and the *Gates* novels help revitalize cultures under stress by turning to a heaven that crystallizes their respective ideals. Though these two heavens come from opposite sides of the European-American effort to build a continental empire, both repress cultural difference. They also form interesting parallels to contemporary visions of the afterlife. Those from the mainstream, such as the television series *Touched by an Angel,* help revitalize a bourgeois culture through a highly circumscribed accommodation of racial difference. Those emanating from a Native American perspective, like Louise Erdrich's *Tracks* (1988), often reference the Ghost Dance and serve a similar revitalizing function. Twain critiques white imperialism by bringing these two versions of heaven together, drawing on the uncanny intersection of white and Indian notions of the afterlife in order to unsettle imperialist ideology. A contemporary, though less cross-cultural, analogue might be found in the film *Dogma* (1999), which combines ethnic working-class Catholic spiritualism and an anarchic sensibility to launch a frenzied assault on contemporary bourgeois norms.

While ethnography and local color fiction also contributed to imperialist ideology at the turn into the twentieth century, writers from a number of cultural perspectives used spiritualism to extend the borders of the local color universe. In her early work, Sarah Orne Jewett used European-American traditions of ghosts and spirits to underscore the cultural homogeneity of places like Dunnet Landing; her late story "The Foreigner," however, illustrates how a more cross-cultural spiritualist perspective undercuts an ideology of racial exclusion. For such writers of color as Charles Chesnutt and María Cristina Mena, spiritualism provided a means of both accessing and critiquing mainstream culture. While Chesnutt weaves a spiritualist resonance into his conjure tales in order to make African-American culture more familiar to a white audience, Mena quickly turns local color spiritualism into a radical critique of Anglo-American hegemony. Their model has proven durable, for writers from across America's many cultures have continued to use ghosts, angels, and spirits to unearth injustices long repressed and to broaden the ethnic borders that define this country.

Finally, spiritualism served for at least two writers as a means of analyzing and critiquing the very workings of the national ideology that emerged at the end of the nineteenth century. In *The Bostonians,* Henry James uses spiritualism to mount a realist assault on the ideals that structured postbellum America. Trance speaking, from this perspective, was not so much a vehicle for social reform as a veneer of false consciousness; for James, the medium figured the ideology masking the naturalist forces that really shaped American society. While James satirized spiritualism in an effort to stand outside of ideology, for Pauline Hopkins spiritualism is a means of exploring the hidden regions of the self and mapping the shifting currents of ideology that swirl in the unconscious. Rather than offer a firm ground for identity, the ghosts, visions, and trances that unsettle the narrative world of *Of One Blood* reveal that the meaning of America is as transient, unsettled, and elusive as the spirits that so persistently haunt its shores.

Two critical imperatives have shaped this study. The first is to read cross-culturally. Spiritualism is at once universal and culturally specific, and in the United States particularly, it offers a rich opportunity to explore how the many cultures that make up this nation intersect. While it has long helped distinct communities preserve their identity, the shared belief in an accessible spirit world offers an important common ground for spiritualists of every culture and creed. Each culture, of course, shapes its spirit world in its own image; each ghost and angel bears the marks of a specific history. Any synchronic study of contemporary spiritualist movements must therefore begin diachronically, with a clear sense of how a given culture's spiritualism fits within a specific history and heritage. Yet while monocultural studies of spiritualism certainly have value, to read spiritualism through only one cultural perspective is to downplay the cultural conflict and contact that make up every people's history.

To study distinct spiritualist traditions in tandem is not to endorse a fuzzy multicultural relativism. Cultural contact in this country often occurred in a context of brutal and sometimes genocidal coercion, with profound and often indelible effects on both the subordinant and the dominant culture. Multiculturalism at its worst places distinct cultural traditions side by side with no attempt to read the dynamics of their interaction; a cross-cultural methodology brings those dynamics to the fore. While there are certainly traditions, movements, and texts best understood within a single cultural framework, by focusing on moments when different cultures do in fact intersect we highlight the history of exploitation, subordination, communication, and cross-fertilization that has shaped America's richly varied and sharply contested traditions. Thus alongside this imperative to read cross-culturally is a related one: to set spiritualist movements in their material context. Since all spiritualists know that the other world is intimately tied to this one, they use

the spirit world to identify and resolve conflicts and crises here on earth. Political context does not, of course, preclude the psychodynamics that shape
every dream and vision; nor does it dictate the terms of a given spirit world—
spiritualist visions have rich cultural roots independent of whatever historical forces bring them to flower. But to leave aside the material context of a
spiritualist movement is to miss its cultural meaning.

These two imperatives suggest the key features of cross-cultural spiritualism: it is heterogeneous, overdetermined, and uncanny. No spiritualism—no
cultural form—is purely homogeneous, especially in a country with so rich a
heritage of cultural interaction as that of the United States. Even the typically
cited examples of (white) literary spiritualism I've not been able to discuss in
this study—including Charles Brockton Brown's gothic musings, Edgar
Allan Poe's supernatural fiction and poetry, Nathaniel Hawthorne's *Blithedale Romance* (1852), and Emily Dickinson's many poetic interrogations of
the afterlife—though typically read from a single cultural perspective, bear
the marks of centuries of cultural contact. While the spiritualist examples I've
focused on in this study highlight this cross-cultural legacy, every example of
spiritualism bears its trace.

Thus every spiritualist movement is richly overdetermined, signifying in a
variety of cultural fields and meaning many things at once. Always located at
the juncture between this world and the next, and often at the juncture of different cultures as well, spiritualists operate in a liminal space where meanings
multiply and ordinary certainties erode. Not surprisingly, tricksters and
hucksters flourish in such circles. Indeed, mainstream cries of hucksterism
are reactions as much to the liminal nature of spiritualist discourse as to the
misdeeds of fraudulent mediums. Spirits haunt whatever house holds them,
providing a discursive excess that resists formal closure. Such excess makes
spiritualism, especially in its most vigorously cross-cultural manifestations,
uncanny. Spirits, ghosts, and angels are typically ciphers that carry powerful
traces of otherness. Their voices can speak things long repressed, and spiritualism attracts intense resistance because it often voices a political unconscious. It often voices as well a conscious politics, carefully deployed where a
more overt voice might be silenced. These politics are as heterogeneous and
multivoiced as spiritualism itself.

This study has several implications for understanding American literature
and culture. One is that it moves spirituality to center stage in cultural, and especially cross-cultural, studies. While religion often suffers given the materi-

alist bias of the academy, my own account of spiritualism stresses, first, the central importance of religious beliefs in a wide variety of contexts and, second, the close connections between spiritual and material concerns. Far from being a sideline to more pressing political issues or a remote superstructure ultimately determined by an economic base, spiritualism, like religion in general, has been a crucial means of framing and negotiating material imperatives. By focusing on spiritualism, with its myriad manifestations across a wide range of cultures, I've attempted as well to show how broadly conceived a category like religion can—and should—be. Spiritualism read as an exotic religion practiced by an eccentric fringe of white radicals and hucksters is little more than an amusing footnote to the main currents of nineteenth-century American culture. As a belief system that cuts across cultural boundaries and draws on diverse folk traditions, varied philosophical sources, emerging scientific knowledge, and broad coalitions, spiritualism, like religion in general, becomes an almost ubiquitous medium of cultural fashioning. Spiritualism thus becomes a crucial perspective from which to interpret a wide variety of movements and texts.

As I've tried to show, such interpretation is best done not by isolating spiritualist manifestations, but by looking for links, junctures, and conflicts between peoples and texts. Any effort to grapple with such a multifarious phenomenon as spiritualism, and, indeed, with America's diverse heritage, must focus on places where these cultures intersect. Thus I've looked for spiritualist texts from a variety of cultural perspectives that converge around a significant date (the late seventeenth century), a shared social context (Jacobs and others in Rochester, James and Hopkins in Boston), a common medium (magazines at the middle and end of the nineteenth century), or a similar theme (heaven). Such conjunctions bring each respective culture into sharp focus while enabling us to trace the terms and stakes of their interaction. By placing texts together, terms and phenomena like spiritualism gain a resonance and richness they wouldn't have in a monocultural context. Such a methodology couldn't, of course, replace studies that focus on texts and movements from a single cultural perspective. What I hope I've shown is the importance of supplementing such studies with a cross-cultural critical practice.

Such a practice helps illuminate and interrogate not just our understanding of nineteenth-century American culture, but our own assumptions and biases as well. As writers from various perspectives and traditions used spiritualism to question, problematize, and broaden mainstream attitudes, a cross-cultural criticism focusing on a broad and resonant phenomenon like spiritualism forces us to attend to distinct cultures and to negotiate the borderlands of different critical methodologies. Anthropology and religious studies, race studies and critical multiculturalism, folklore and feminism, utopian studies and the public sphere, postcolonialism and poststructuralism: these are some of the approaches that inform this study. As different contexts suggest different critical approaches, so a varied critical methodology helps avoid the blind spots of any given one. Studying spiritualism, finally, helps interrogate more personal biases as well. Though not part of reality for most academics, ghosts, angels, and spirits are very real, and often very intimate, members of the universe for people from a great variety of cultures and perspectives. While sustained and serious attention to spiritualism may not bring most scholars to share their views, it may help us better understand what we do not know.

Notes

Introduction

1. The two best histories of American spiritualism in recent years, Howard Kerr's *Mediums, and Spirit Rappers, and Roaring Radicals* and Anne Braude's *Radical Spirits*, use this as their starting date; Kerr summarily opens his survey of the movement by asserting "Spiritualism in America began in 1848." Frank Podmore, writing what remains the most authoritative account, *Modern Spiritualism*, in 1902, treats both the date of 1848 and the term "spiritualism" as problematic.

2. Braude's and Kerr's studies stand in contrast to E. M. Lewis's *Ecstatic Religion* (1989), a sociological study that places European and American spiritualism in the context of world religions. Other recent studies use the same word to describe movements in places as diverse as Zimbabwe (David Lan, *Guns and Rain: Guerillas and Spirit Mediums in Zimbabwe*) and Thailand (Rosalind Morris, *In the Place of Origins: Modernity and its Mediums in Northern Thailand*). Other recent studies explore how European-American Spiritualism merged with local spiritualist traditions in places like Iceland (William Swatos Jr. and Loftur Reimar Gissurarson, *Modernity and Mediumship in Icelandic Spiritualism*) and Brazil (Diana DeG. Brown, *Umbanda: Religion and Politics in Urban Brazil*). Spiritualism is but one of a variety of names for religious practices that facilitate contact with a spirit world—spirit possession and shamanism are two that signifiy closely related phenomena. Less important than terminology is the cultural and historical matrix in which these practices take shape. Nevertheless, terminology is a good index of a study's parameter. Podmore speaks of Modern Spiritualism to signify the recent and coherent nature of his subject. Lewis uses the same term to mean roughly the same thing, but leaves "modern" in lowercase; modern Spiritualism in his usage is subsumed under the broader terms of "shamanism" and "spirit possession." Kerr leaves "spiritualism" unrestricted by "modern" and lowercased despite the narrow parameters of his study, while Braude and Carroll prefer to treat "Spiritualism" as a proper noun. This usage

seems most appropriate when signifying a narrow nineteenth-century European-American context for spiritualism; my usage is meant to highlight the broader cultural parameters of my study.

3. Information about this battleground is best preserved in the official Spanish documents about the Pueblo Revolt collected by Charles Hackett. The collection is a stunning source for analyzing the ends of rhetoric, in which the Spanish governor, the friars who acted as his scribes and ideologues, and the Indians who appeared before them sought to shape the narrative of the revolt to serve their own ends. The documents taken together portray the effort of Spanish colonial discourse to grapple with a world shaped by a harsh desert environment, the Indian inhabitants who sought to reclaim it, and the Spanish who sought to write themselves within it.

4. A thorough bibliography of the Salem Witchcraft Trials is beyond the scope of this study, and it may be that the sheer volume of material has encouraged most scholars to limit their studies to either one aspect of the trials or, at most, to the context of colonial New England. Elaine Breslaw's *Tituba, Reluctant Witch of Salem* is an example of an extended study of one actor in the trials; Richard Godbeer's *The Devil's Dominion* is an example of the widest range of studies, examining magic and religion across colonial New England. Paul Boyer and Stephen Nissenbaum spurred a shift away from the spiritualist dimensions of the witchcraft trials and toward localized material analyses with *Salem Possessed,* published in 1974, a trend Carol Karlsen expanded to include a material feminist analysis in *The Devil in the Shape of a Woman.* Peter Charles Hoffer, in *The Devil's Disciples,* examines events in Salem in the context of an Atlantic Rim economy and an evolving English colonial discourse, without reference to later American spiritualist episodes. Bernhard Rosenthal's *Salem Story* is rare among recent studies in its diachronic orientation, but while it offers a thorough and insightful ideological analysis of the Salem Witchcraft Trials throughout American literature, he makes no reference to the trials' role in later formulations of spiritualism.

5. Frank Podmore's *Modern Spiritualism* is an example from early in this century, while Howard Kerr and Charles L. Crow's *The Occult in America* is a more recent effort to study nineteenth-century spiritualism in the context of colonial witchcraft.

6. Tituba's cross-cultural spiritualism stands in marked contrast to that of two other slaves in Salem. A decade earlier, a man named Wonn accused a woman of witchcraft; the accusation had her employing traditional European signifiers of witchcraft, including spooked horses, a black cat, and spectral pinches (Boyer and Nissenbaum, 158). These claims were too consonant with the prevailing norms of witchcraft discourse to spark any hysteria. The testimony of Candy, another slave from the West Indies who testified later in the inquiry, was *too* marked by difference. Transported to Salem in 1692, Candy demonstrated to the investigators creole magic. She showed how cheese, grass, and cloth dolls were used in casting spells, and she burned one of the dolls to the apparent discomfort of the girls who claimed to be bewitched. Her more clearly African spiritualism did not register in the legal discourse, despite the best effort of the bewitched women. Wonn's testimony might be considered, then,

an assimilated spiritualism; Candy's a multicultural spiritualism coextensive, but not imbricated, with Puritan spiritualism.

7. In their one-volume collection of primary documents, *Salem-Village Witch-craft,* Boyer and Nissenbaum include an excerpt from Calef, but none from *Wonders of the Invisible World.* Mather's account is, of course, widely anthologized, but it is usually read as a literary document that offers insight into Puritan ideology, rather than as an historical source. Rosenthal is typical of moderns scholars in his heavy reliance upon Calef's account for data and his use of *Wonders* for ideological analysis.

8. In the wake of 1692, accounts were clearly cast in the "was it real?" mode exemplified by the accounts written by Mather and Calef. Such historical give and take has followed Salem historiography down to the present. Chadwick Hansen is rare among modern historians in taking evidence of witchcraft seriously, arguing that even if no one actually rode brooms through the skies of Massachusetts, some of the accused probably thought of themselves as witches. Bernhard Rosenthal has taken the more popular skeptical stance in his careful reading of the evidence; his account, grounded in the belief that "it remains possible to separate to a large degree these forces of myth and history that compete to claim the past" (9), is directed substantially against Hansen's thesis, and self-consciously aligned with the counterthesis of outright fraud on the part of the accusers, traceable back at least to Calef.

9. Chapters 1 and 2 of this study will explore more fully spiritualism's trajectory in mid-nineteenth century literary culture. Two of the most influential early texts to advocate spiritualism were John Worth Edmonds and George T. Dexter, *Spiritualism* (1853) and Robert Dale Owen, *Footfalls on the Boundary of Another World* (1860); two early debunkings were E. W. Cabron's *Modern Spiritualism: Its Facts and Fanaticisms* (1855) and Benjamin Hatch's *Spiritualist Iniquities Unmasked* (1859). A number of nineteenth-century magazine accounts withheld judgment while offering learned summaries on Swedenborgian philosophy and Middle Eastern mysticism. A good example of such a response appeared in the *North American Review* 80, 1855 (April), entitled "Modern Necromancy." Since Podmore's *Modern Spiritualism,* defenses of spiritualism, from Sir Arthur Conan Doyle's *History of Spiritualism* (1926) to *Zolar's Book of the Spirits* (1987), have come from avowed partisans.

10. Barrow's *Independent Spirits* (1986) promises a sustained analysis of spiritualism within the dynamic of class conflict, but devolves into episodic biographies of spiritualists whose working-class credentials he brandishes, then drops. More helpful is his formulation of spiritualism as a "democratic epistemology," joining with folk culture to form a cosmology that is not at all dependent on the ideological apparatuses of the British state. In *The Other World* (1985), Oppenheim traces spiritualism though progressive, though generally elite, intellectual and social circles. Owen's *The Darkened Room* (1990) and Sword's *Ghostwriting Modernism* (2002), the most theoretically au courant of the recent English accounts, frame spiritualism in poststructuralist terms. Owen's analysis centers on the gendered valence of spiritualism, measuring how spiritualist discourse offered Victorian women a strategy for maneuverability and resistance that did not, ultimately, do much to transform the categories

of gender it managed to evade. Sword, treating a number of male and female modernist and postmodernist writers, sees spiritualism primarily as a metaphor for poetic influence and textual indeterminacy.

11.   Much of this discussion owes a debt to Paula Gunn Allen's seminal essay on multiculturalism, "Border Studies: The Intersection of Gender and Color" (1995). She offers a classic articulation of the need to address different cultures: "It is not merely biculturality that forms the foundation of our lives' work in their multiplicity, aesthetic largeness, and wide-ranging potential; rather it is multiculturality, multilinguality and dizzying class-crossing" (34). She also exemplifies some of the pitfalls, articulating what is often an unspoken corollary of multicultural critical practice in its earlier phase.

> We know this: in the void reside the keepers of women. Women of color are willing and well equipped to approach the still, dark center of the heart of the gynocosmos where nothing at all exists and whence, paradoxically, all must emerge. Other writers, strangers to the source of meaning, have talked about that mysterious, foreboding place, the dark heart of creation, but it is we—perhaps because we are nothing ourselves—who stalk the void and dance the dervish of significance that is born through our parted lips and legs. (34–35)

In her effort to undercut the totalizing, exclusionary rhetoric of conservative ideology, she posits a counterhegemonic discourse that is equally totalizing, shifting the void from the borders between cultures to the center of a "gynocosmos" that is almost solely the provenance of women of color.

Allen's totalizing multiculturalism leads her to another difficulty: "To be sure, it may seem that elements of Western literary practice are discernible in work by women of color. But the similarities are likely to be more apparent than actual" (37). She then cites *The Tale of Genji* as a non-Western ur-form for writings by women of color, as well as for the "preexisting poetic forms" found in every culture.

Chapter 1: Around Rochester

1.   The most thorough account of Harriet Jacobs's life is still her *Incidents in the Life of a Slave Girl* and Jean Fagan Yellin's biographical notes to her edition of the book. Nancy Hewitt has written a biographical essay on Amy Post, and Anne Braude gives a thorough sketch of the Post circle in *Radical Spirits: Spiritualism and Women's Rights in Nineteenth-Century America*.

2.   One modest exception is Anne Bradford Warner, who speculates briefly on the influence Post's spiritualism had on Jacobs in "Carnival Laughter: Resistance in *Incidents.*" Caroline Sorioso's article, "'There is Might in Each': Conceptions of the Self in Harriet Jacobs' *Incidents*" argues that nineteenth-century spiritualism helped counter an incipient scientific essentialism, but doesn't discuss Jacobs's relation to

spiritualism in any more specific terms. Anne Braude makes no mention of Jacobs when discussing the origins of spiritualism in the Post household; nor does Yellin make any mention of spiritualism when discussing Jacobs's year in Rochester.

3. The fullest account of occult and folk epistemology in the eighteenth century is Herbert Leventhal's *In the Shadow of the Enlightenment.* For a brief summary that stresses the legacy of witchcraft in New England, see Richard Godbeer's epilogue to his *Devil's Dominion.*

4. Donald Hall's *Worlds of Wonder, Days of Judgement* traces the intellectual currents surrounding the evolution of Unitarian and other post-Calvinist religious beliefs. Whitney Cross's *The Burned-Over District* is still the most authoritative account of religious revivalism in upstate New York. For an excellent account of the survival of localized folk beliefs, see John Brooke's *The Refiner's Fire,* which follows the migration of occultism from Rhode Island and the Blackstone Valley to upstate New York on the heels of the families who would make up the core of the early Mormon converts.

5. Howard Kerr offers a cogent summary of spiritualism in *Mediums, and Spirit-Rappers, and Roaring Radicals* before tracing its trajectory through nineteenth-century literature. Anne Braude's survey of spiritualism and women's rights is the most comprehensive modern history.

6. Cora Hatch proved a potent cultural figure for the evolving role of women, at least in the eyes of a number of male writers. Howard Kerr argues that Hatch was the model for a number of writers who subjected spiritualism and women's rights to withering satire throughout the century, from T. S. Arthur in *The Angel and the Demon* (1858) to Henry James in *The Bostonians* (1886).

7. Douglass's views on spiritualism in general and the Rochester Rappings specifically remain obscure. His biographers make no mention of the subject, and his own published writings make virtually no direct mention of the phenomenon. The *North Star* makes a few scant notices of spiritualist activity, publishing a detailed but somewhat skeptical account of the exhibition at Corinthian Hall in Rochester on November 23, 1849. Douglass showed little enthusiasm for a movement that entranced so many of his abolitionist colleagues and friends. Such an attitude may have indicated a politely restrained skepticism, or perhaps interest checked by his disciplined focus on his primary goal of abolition. For a thorough account of the personal and professional complexities of Douglass's Rochester years, see McFeeley (146–82).

8. Hewitt describes Douglass's reconciliation with the Posts in the late 1850s (190). Douglass attracted the warm attention of other members of the Post circle. In his biography of Douglass, William McFeeley quotes a letter in which Margaret Fox writes to Amy Post, "Frederick is as fine looking as Ever. I think he is the finest looking gentleman I have seen since I have been in Cincinnati" (163). Further details about the relationship between Fox and Douglass remain undocumented.

9. Willis's social climbing and literary sophistication made him for at least one recent critic, Gabrielle Foreman, the very avatar of the confidence man (86–87).

10. This episode is followed by the story of Luke, a slave subject to "the strangest

freaks of despotism" by his master. Clearly, the Fugitive Slave Law brought with it associations of the worst horrors of slavery to Jacobs; the juxtaposition of her confinement in the Willis household and the story of Luke may hint at a coercive sexual relationship between Willis and herself.

11. Jacobs's letter is reprinted in *The Black Abolitionist Papers* (1985), volume 3, edited by Peter Ripley. Barbara Goldsmith devotes a chapter in her cultural biography of Victoria Woodhall, *Other Powers* (1998), to the domestic miseries that drove Horace and Mary Greeley to the séance table. Jacobs might well have entered print by writing about the Fox sisters, whom she knew as well as anyone from her time with the Posts in New York City.

12. See, for example, Andrew Jackson Davis's description of death on page 162 of *The Great Harmonia* (1852), an influential text that combined Swedenborgian and spiritualist thought. Elizabeth Stuart Phelps included a butterfly on the cover of *The Gates Ajar* (1868)—an image by then instantly recognizable as a spiritualist emblem.

13. See, for example, page 11 of J. B. Ferguson's *Spirit Communion: A Record of Communications from the Spirit-Spheres* (1854).

14. For a wide-ranging account of tricksterism in its American context, see Ammons and White-Parks, *Tricksterism in Turn-of-the-Century American Literature* (1994).

15. Yellin describes the garret as both war room and "aberrant alter ego of the angel in the house" (xxix–xxxi). On the loophole as womb, see Mills (117); on the loophole as a gloss on Foucault, see Burnham.

16. By proposing an African antecedent for the snake imagery in *Incidents,* I don't by any means wish to discredit a more Freudian interpretation that might read the snake as a figure for Dr. Flint's patriarchal and sexual domination.

17. Warner presents a compelling reading of the Johnkannaus section of *Incidents* as an example of folk resistance along the lines of Bahktin's theorization of the carnival in early modern Europe; such a reading, however, underemphasizes the cross-cultural nature of the chapter.

Chapter 2: Public Spirits

1. Frank Luther Mott's *History of American Magazines* (1938) is still the most thorough source on nineteenth-century magazines, though a more recent collection, Kenneth M. Price and Susan Belasco Smith's *Periodical Literature in Nineteenth-Century America,* offers useful case studies in addition to a helpful overview. Ronald Zboray's *A Fictive People* gives a careful analysis of publishing in general, with an emphasis on books and their distribution.

2. Smith and Price briefly sketch the postwar transformation of periodicals into advertisement-driven vehicles. In *Selling Culture,* Richard Ohman gives more careful analysis of this trend as it unfolded at the turn of the century.

3. Recent commentators on Habermas continue to overlook the role the public sphere played in fashioning national identity in an age of imperialism. Though a number of scholars whose articles are collected in Craig Calhoun's *Habermas and the Public Sphere* (1992) carefully redress Habermas's inattention to issues of gender, and though Habermas himself revises his rather glib dismissal of plebeian public discourse, only Mary Ryan's article even raises the issue of ethnic identity, and then only as a complement to her analysis of gender in the American public sphere.

4. For a useful sketch of the evolving editorial differences between *Harper's* and *Putnam's,* see Sheila Post-Lauria's "Magazine Practice and Melville's Israel Potter" (1995).

5. Such is the opinion of William McLoughlin, who details the efforts of the Cherokee to reconstruct their society in Indian Territory in *After the Trail of Tears* (1993).

6. In *Radical Spirits* (1989) Anne Braude details the central role child mortality played in the growth of spiritualism.

7. Nina Baym's *Women's Fiction* (1978) was one of the earliest, and is still one of the most thorough, accounts of sentimental fiction.

8. The many incarnations of the Ghost Dance illustrate this phenomena—such movements served to shore up traditional tribal culture in the face of white colonialism.

Chapter 3: The Politics of Heaven

1. This anxiety is more evident in the articles used to delimit the "New Indian messiah" of the title, described alternately as "a Christ," "this Christ," and, in a brief moment of spiritual and articular solidarity, "the Christ."

2. I begin with Ghost Dance for several reasons. Although the Ghost Dance is generally understood as a singular movement in the early 1890s, there were in fact numerous Ghost Dance movements throughout the history of European colonization. Thus, while the Ghost Dance of 1890 occurred a generation after Phelps published *The Gates Ajar,* its immediate predecessor, the Ghost Dance of 1870, was contemporaneous with that novel. More importantly, I want to prioritize what has been traditionally marginalized, and hence use the Ghost Dance to frame my discussion of Phelps. Whites have long sought to understand Indian spirituality from a European-American perspective; much can be gained by reversing the process.

3. In this respect, Native American beliefs were far closer to European-American spiritualism than either was to traditional Christianity. Both were predicated upon the immediate presence of spirits in the world, both developed rituals that provided regular contact with these spirits, both favored direct contact with spirits over an earlier revelation, and both organized themselves around a decentered "priesthood" of men and women who possessed an unusual, though not unique, ability to contact the spirit world. I have been unable, however, to locate any evidence of direct influence

between the two. White spiritualists who contacted Indian spirits proved more interested in the political injustice Indians faced than in a shared spiritual sensibility, while Indians who commented on spiritualist phenomena among whites tended not to take them seriously.

4. It has proven remarkably difficult to untangle the threads of Indian and white religious influence in even the most "authentic" Native American spiritual texts of the period. See Albert Furtwangler's *Answering Chief Seattle* (1997) and Julian Rice's *Black Elk's Story* (1991) for recent studies that grapple with two of the most famous texts.

5. It did not, however, entirely die out. The Ghost Dance remained a powerful presence in a number of tribes long after Wounded Knee, and Wovoka is still revered as a powerful holy man among the Pauites and among the broader population of Native Americans. Alice Beck Kehoe (1989) describes a community in Saskatechwan that still adhered to his teachings in the 1960s.

6. Mooney's *The Ghost Dance Religion and Wounded Knee* (1896) is one of the first scholarly accounts of the Ghost Dance, and remains the most authoritative. Recent studies have been content either to update Mooney for a contemporary audience, like Alice Kehoe's *The Ghost Dance: Ethnohistory and Revitalization* (1989), or situate Mooney's account among the ideological battles of turn-of-the-century America, like Michael Elliot's "Ethnography, Reform and the Problem of the Real: James Mooney's *Ghost Dance Religion*" (1998). More accounts of the Ghost Dance have focused on specific tribes, such as William McLoughlin's *The Cherokee Ghost Dance* (1984). My summary of the Ghost Dance draws largely on Mooney. For an account that places Mooney in the context of contemporary anthropology, see L. G. Moses's *The Indian Man: A Biography of James Mooney* (1984).

7. For a useful overview of nineteenth-century Christianity, see Sydney E. A. Ahlstrom, *A Religious History of the American People* (1972).

8. Stanley French provides a good introduction to the rural cemetery movement in "The Cemetery as Cultural Institution," in *Death in America* (1975), ed. David Stannard. Bertrand St. Armand Levi discusses the broader cultural context of the Mount Auburn School in *Emily Dickinson in her Culture* (1984).

9. See David Reynolds's *Faith in Fiction* (1981) and Bertrand St. Armand Levi's *Emily Dickinson in her Culture* for this view of Phelps's work.

10. The *Gates* novels have often been read through a utopian lens, most recently by Carol Kessler (1983). Such a perspective is less common in studies of the Ghost Dance, though B. C. Mohrbacher's "The Whole World is Coming" (1997) is an exception.

11. The extent to which Wovoka's vision was influenced by Christianity has been a matter of continuous debate. The earliest white commentators speculated that Wovoka had spent time among the Christianized Indians of the Pacific Northwest, especially among the Indian Shakers of Puget Sound; others pointed to the Mormon endowment robes as a source for the ghost shirts worn by some of the Plains tribes. Other commentators, beginning notably with Mooney, stressed the continuity of the

Ghost Dance with native traditions, and one recent text, Garold D. Barney's *Mormons, Indians and the Ghost Dance of 1890,* explores the cultural borrowings of the Ghost Dance. Most recent scholars of the Ghost Dance and of Indian religions in general, however, have argued that such parsing of native and white strands of influence is a rather unfruitful enterprise, given the multivocality and flexibility of most Indian religions—despite their myriad differences, native traditions were transmitted orally and hence continually evolved to incorporate the changing social and economic context facing the each generation. While the Ghost Dance, with its apocalyptic overtones, its monotheism, and, perhaps, its handful of Mormon-derived paraphernalia may have borrowed from European-American religions, it remained rooted in a distinctly Indian sensibility.

12. The totalizing undercurrent of Ghost Dance ideology attracted the attention of at least one contemporary writer. Sherman Alexie's short story "Distances," in *The Lone Ranger and Tonto Fistfight in Heaven,* imagines the Ghost Dance as a dystopia of Indian traditionalism run amok.

13. For a detailed discussion of the composition of *Captain Stormfield,* see Howard Baetzhold and Joseph B. McCullough's introduction to *The Bible According to Mark Twain.*

14. Robert Rees pointed out Twain's debt to Phelps in Rees's article *"Captain Stormfield's Visit to Heaven* and *The Gates Ajar"* (1970). Both Twain and Phelps, following the trend of nineteenth-century liberal Christianity, also dismiss traditional Protestant ideas of hell. In his very last piece of writing, "Etiquette for the Afterlife," Twain brutally satirizes the Presbyterian theology of damnation he learned in childhood. While Phelps confines the souls of the spiritually lost to the earthly sphere, they have every hope of advancement; Stormfield's heaven, it seems, is ample enough to include the sinful.

15. Gillman draws on the work of several other recent critics, including Thomas J. Otten, "Pauline Hopkins and the Hidden Self of Race," *ELH* 59 (1992): 227–56; Eric J. Sundquist, *To Wake the Nations: Race in the Making of American Literature;* and Bruce Dickson Jr., "W. E. B. DuBois and the Idea of Double Consciousness," *American Literature* 64 (1992): 299–309.

16. David L. Newquist makes no mention of *Captain Stormfield* in "Mark Twain among the Indians" (1994). Louis J. Budd, in *Mark Twain: Social Philosopher* (1962), briefly mentions *Captain Stormfield* in noting Twain's gradual drift away from racism.

17. Everett Emerson, *The Authentic Mark Twain* (1984), p. 113.

Chapter 4: Spirits in the Contact Zone

1. Elizabeth Ammons and Valerie Rohy are only the most recent scholars to alternate the terms "regionalism" and "local color" (*American Local Color Writing, 1880–1920*). In *Cultures of Letters: Scenes of Reading and Writing in Nineteenth Cen-*

tury America (1993), Richard Brodhead prefers "regionalism," though "local color" appears synonymously. Josephine Donovan uses "local-color" in *New England Local Color Literature: A Women's Tradition* (1983), though she also uses "regionalism" in her essay "Breaking the Sentence: Local-Color Literature and Subjugated Knowledges" in *The (Other) American Traditions* (1993), ed. Joyce Warren. Judith Fetterley and Marjorie Pryse have been most insistent about a distinction between the terms, beginning with their *American Woman Regionalists, 1850–1910* (1992). Since there is as yet no consensus about their definition, I use them both.

2. Anne Braude traces spiritualism's history to the end of the nineteenth century. For a detailed cultural biography of Victoria Woodhull, see Barbara Goldsmith's *Other Powers: The Age of Suffrage, Spiritualism and the Scandalous Victoria Woodhull* (1998).

3. Michael Kenney's *The Passion of Ansel Bourne* (1986) explores the role spiritualist research played in the New Psychology. Frank Podmore's *Modern Spiritualism* (1902) is a contemporary history of spiritualism that grew out of the Society for Psychical Research. While the New Psychology did not explicitly engage issues of cultural difference in its exploration of spiritualist phenomena, this new discipline did prove useful to at least two African-American writers, W. E. B. Du Bois and Pauline Hopkins. Both drew on its scientific epistemology and its model of divided consciousness in their efforts to represent an African-American sensibility. For more specific accounts of the role the occult and the New Psychology played in the work of W. E. B. Du Bois and Pauline Hopkins, see Cynthia Schrager, "Both Sides of the Veil: Race, Science and Mysticism in W. E. B. Du Bois," and Susan Gillman, "Pauline Hopkins and the Occult: African-American Revisions of Nineteenth-Century Sciences," respectively.

4. A cogent account of the rise of ethnology in the United States appears in *The Indian Man: A Biography of James Mooney*, by L. G. Moses (1984). Mooney's *The Ghost Dance Religion and Wounded Knee* (1896) is perhaps the preeminent example of an ethnography that examines spiritualism in a cross-cultural context. Edward Tylor's *Primitive Culture* (1871), a founding text of British anthropology, also discusses Victorian Spiritualism in conjunction with spiritualist religions from around the world.

5. For a comprehensive survey and analysis of the ideological function of popular magazines at the end of the nineteenth century, see Richard Ohmann, *Selling Culture* (1996). Richard Brodhead's *Cultures of Letters* (1993) focuses more narrowly on the literature that appeared in those magazines, and considers as well the opportunity these magazines afforded to cultural outsiders.

6. Other recent scholarship focuses on the oppositional function of turn-of-the-century fiction. Elizabeth Ammons and Annette White-Parks's *Tricksterism in Turn-of-the-Century American Literature*, for example, is a collection of essays on a number of writers of color who worked within and against metropolitan norms. Tiffany

Ann Lopez's essay (1994) on María Christina Mena influenced my own discussion of Mena, below.

7. Sandra Zagerell notes the racial marking of Mrs. Tolland and hints she may be of "mixed race." Mitzi Schrag (1999) argues that Jewett self-consciously constructs the foreigner as, in Toni Morrison's term, an "Africanist persona" (191).

8. Numerous critics, including Josephine Donovan (1983), Marjorie Pryse (1984), Judith Fetterley (1992), and Sarah Sherman (1989), have developed this argument about female circularity. The most detailed study of the Dunnet Landing stories is Elizabeth Ammons' "Going in Circles: The Female Geography of *Country of the Pointed Firs*" (1983). For a careful application of this thesis to "The Foreigner," see Marjorie Pryse's "Women at Sea: Feminist Realism in Sarah Orne Jewett's 'The Foreigner'" (1984).

9. For these four ways of reading Chesnutt's conjure, see Eric Sundquist, *To Wake the Nations* (1993); Houston Baker, *Modernism and the Harlem Renaissance* (1987); Julie Farwell, "Goophering Around" (1994); and Robert Nowatzki, "Passing in a White Genre" (1995), respectively.

10. Chesnutt used the tactic elsewhere—in one place spoofing the myth of George Washington and the cherry tree by claiming to have found its source in ancient Egyptian hieroglyphics; in another place turning the Negro question, including the laws that defined the color line, on its head by examining the question "What is a White Man?" (Keller 94–95; 131–32). In Chesnutt's assessment, attempts to fix boundaries between the races proved more unnatural than anything young scholars learned in school.

11. The most detailed account of conjure and other African-American folk beliefs remains Harry Middleton Hyatt's multivolume *Hoodoo-Conjuration-Witchcraft-Rootwork* (1970). A very useful shorter work is Lawrence Levine's *Black Culture and Black Consciousness* (1977). For a more detailed account of Chesnutt's own adaptations of African-American folklore, see Robert Hemenway's "The Function of Folklore in Charles Chesnutt's *The Conjure Woman*" (1973).

12. The material in Chesnutt's "Superstitions and Folklore of the South" (1973) is even further removed from a political context. His principal informant, Aunt Harriet, relates stories that deal principally with grudges and lovers' quarrels within a closely knit black community.

13. The identification of ill health of Annie's variety with leisured white women, and its pairing with Sis' Becky's depression when separated from her child, encourages some speculation that her ill health might be tied to a miscarriage. Such events were as unmentionable in polite literature as they were common at the time, and such an explanation might shed some light on Annie and John's conspicuous lack of children.

14. In this context, Judith Fetterly and Marjorie Pryse's distinction between local color and regionalism is relevant. In *American Women Regionalists* (1992), they de-

fine local color as primarily ethnographic in nature, with metropolitan narrators re- cording (and marginalizing) local folk traditions; they define regionalism as a type of autoethnography that actively deforms metropolitan norms. While such a distinction is highly problematic in connection to Chesnutt, it usefully describes his transforma- tion of plantation fiction.

15. The word "obsequious" appears in both Raymond Paredes's *Three Ameri- can Literatures* (50) and Tatum's *Chicano Literature* (33).

16. Most recent criticism on Mena, including that by Lopez and by Doherty, dis- cuss this story in the context of the Mexican Revolution. Whether Mena intended a specific allegory for identifiable historical figures remains conjecture.

17. Lopez also argues that Mena aligns Carmelita with the traditional Mexican figures La Malinche and La Llorona and the Aztec deities who inform them, though her reading emphasizes their trickster heritage and sexual power. Neither Lopez nor Doherty, who follows Lopez closely, discusses the spiritualist context of the story.

Chapter 5: Spirit Nation

1. Truth and Hatch's friendship can be traced in their letters to their mutual friend Amy Post; see Braude, p. 48. Truth lived briefly with the Post family in Rochester in the early 1850s, the same period Harriet Jacobs joined that remarkable household. For a thorough account of Truth's somewhat ambiguous relationship to the spiritualist movement, see Carleton Maybee, *Sojourner Truth* (1993):240–43.

2. Reuel, the hero of Hopkins's novel, proves to be the southerner Aubrey's brother as well as classmate at Harvard. Yet Reuel seems to have no home beyond his shabby Cambridge rooms, and he is not distinguished by any of the regional mark- ers Hopkins uses to identify Aubrey. Like Olive Chancellor, anxious to ditch her in- herited claim to Beacon Street in an effort to stake her claim to the leading edges of reform, Reuel makes his home into an outpost of modernity. Such a stance is very consistent with the typical opposition posed by regionalist writers between an Ameri- can backwater and the modern world.

3. The debate over the nature of ideology is long and complicated, and I have chosen to focus on only two of the many formulations of the concept. The definition of ideology as false consciousness is usually associated with an early, "vulgar" strain of Marxism, but it is only one of the definitions offered by Karl Marx himself, whose writings on ideology in *The German Ideology* (1845–46), *A Contribution to the Cri- tique of Political Economy* (1859), and *Capital* (1867) are highly suggestive and often contradictory. The interpretation of ideology as a lived reality more loosely tied to an economic base is generally attributed to such later theorists as Antonio Gramsci, Louis Althusser, and Roland Barthes, though such a definition is also evident in Marx's work. Two excellent recent surveys of the ongoing debates about the nature

of ideology are Terry Eagleton, *Ideology: An Introduction* (1991), and David Hawkes, *Ideology* (1996).

4. For a collection of William James's many writings on spiritualism, see *William James on Psychical Research* (1960).

5. Braude 173–76. Braude also notes that many trance speakers, like Verena, transferred their allegiance from an increasingly apolitical spiritualist movement to the campaign for women's suffrage (192–94).

6. See, for example, Sarah Blair's essay "Realism, Culture and the Place of the Literary: Henry James and *The Bostonians*" (1998). For a sustained discussion of James's engagement with naturalism, see Millicent Bell's *Meaning in Henry James* (1991).

7. In the past decade a number of scholars have focused on James's role in fashioning a national identity, beginning with Kenneth W. Warren in *Black and White Strangers* (1993). The most extensive, Sarah Blair's *Henry James and the Writing of Race and Nation* (1996), places James's work in the context of ongoing debates about racial identity and the nature of American culture, arguing that his international focus and sustained exploration of the connections between high and low culture "unmoor[s] racial and national affect from the project of cultural mastery" (10). Min Song devotes a chapter of his dissertation, "The Height of Presumption: Henry James in the Age of Nation-Building" (1998), to *The Bostonians,* noting especially how orientalism figures into its national allegory.

8. I am indebted here to David Zimmerman's cogent summary of mesmerism and the New Psychology in "Frank Norris, Market Panic, and the Mesmeric Sublime" (200):78–80.

9. The connection between Basil's figure of speech and the manufactured effect of the séance table and spiritualist exhibition are striking; the female medium herself was also frequently described as a passive figure "spoken" by other voices.

10. The Cambridgeport area was developed in the period after the Civil War as inexpensive housing in what was then an emerging industrial area of the growing city; it housed a significant middle-class black population. For good overviews of what little biographical information we have about Pauline Hopkins, see Hazel Carby's introduction to the *The Magazine Novels of Pauline Hopkins* (1988) and Nellie McKay's introduction to *The Unruly Voice* (1996). Both draw heavily on Dorothy B. Porter's entry on Hopkins in the *Dictionary of American Negro Biography* (1982).

11. For a cogent discussion of Hopkins's tenure at the magazine, see Nellie McKay.

12. For a discussion of Hopkins's use of regionalism to frame a national allegory in *Contending Forces,* see Sawaya (1997); Ammons discusses the revisions of national mythology in "Winona, Bakhtin and Hopkins in the Twenty-first Century" (1996).

13. This is not to say that the Washingtonian strategy of racial uplift wasn't also culturalist—as numerous critics noted, Washington's influence was most strongly felt not in the material conditions of the black poor but within the black and white pub-

lic sphere. The manual training offered at places like Fiske and Tuskeegee had little effect on black poverty, but were very successful in spreading white, middle-class norms to a small but influential black stratum whose economic conditions typically belied their class aspirations.

14. For a detailed discussion of Du Bois's culturalist project and its context, see Sundquist (1993).

15. Twain's interest in psychic phenomena was as serious as his cynicism toward spirit mediums; see Susan Gillman's "Mark Twain's Travels in the Racial Occult" for a recent overview. David Zimmerman discusses Frank Norris's and Hamlin Garland's relationship with psychical research in "Frank Norris, Market Panic, and the Mesmeric Sublime" (2003).

16. For another reading of Hopkins's use of the veil, see Sundquist 573–74.

17. See, for example, Hazel Carby's introduction to the magazine novels and, especially, Sundquist, who argues that "Hopkins placed in one concentrated allegorical form a virtual catalogue of Pan-African ideas" (573).

Conclusion

1. There are innumerable sources on theosophy, including many works published by the Theosophical Society. A recent popular history is Peter Washington's *Madame Blavatsky's Baboon: A History of the Mystics, Mediums and Misfits Who Brought Spiritualism to America* (1995). The most current scholarly source is by Antoine Faivre, *Theosophy, Imagination, Tradition: Studies in Western Esotericism* (2000).

2. Any attempt to discuss the New Age movement quickly confronts problems of definition. Even more so than nineteenth-century spiritualists, who at least shared common rituals and organized comprehensive conventions, most practitioners of New Age religions don't identify with the term, preferring to pick and choose from a wide menu of spiritual doctrines and practices. The movement grows particularly indistinct in its more mainstream variants. Determining whether angelmania is a highly occult New Age movement, a grassroots Christian revival, or a mass-marketing phenomenon is impossible, since it is all of these things simultaneously. Similarly, the success of a film like *Ghost* signifies the mainstreaming of spiritualist ideology, but its popularity was hardly confined to New Age audiences.

3. Michael Brown, in his excellent study of the more extreme fringe of the New Age, *The Channeling Zone* (1997), makes many of the same connections.

4. Two of the most thorough critics of New Age appropriation of native culture are Wendy Rose, "The Great Pretenders: Further Reflections on White Shamanism" (1992), and Deborah Root, *Cannibal Culture: Art Appropriation and the Commodification of Difference* (1996). Michael Brown offers a cogent summary of the issue in *The Channeling Zone,* pp. 160–67. For a more detailed, dispassionate account, see Catherine L. Albanese, *Nature Religion in America* (1990). Paula Gunn Allen gave

one of the earliest, and still one of the harshest, critiques of New Age shamanism in *The Sacred Hoop*.

5. Interestingly, the terms of cultural access are the opposite of those that prevailed in the nineteenth century. Writers from these minority positions have enjoyed critical acclaim, and sometimes gained canonical status, while New Age spiritualists, typically white, well educated, and prosperous, find little welcome in the mainstream media and intellectual institutions. Much of this has to do with the rationalist secularism of the cultural elite, who, while happy to entertain spiritualism as a metaphor, are far less likely than their nineteenth-century counterparts to entertain mediums or channelers seriously. It is important to remember, of course, that New Age literature is a highly profitable, and highly white, genre, however disparaged by America's cultural elite, and that despite the success of a few prominent writers of color, most could hardly be considered privileged.

Works Cited

Primary Periodical Sources

"Angel Eve." 1852. *Knickerbocker's* (January):47.

"The Angel Watcher." 1850. *Cherokee Advocate* [Tahlequah, Oklahoma] (30 April).

Beman, Amos Gerry. 1860. "A Visit to My Mother's Grave." *Anglo-African Magazine* (1 January):12.

Bryant, William Cullen. 1851. "The Future Life." *Copway's American Indian* [New York] (23 August):3.

"Bunkum Flat-Staff." 1854. *Knickerbocker* (August):190–93. Editor's Table.

"Editor's Table." 1852 *Harper's Monthly,* vol. 4:699–700.

Greeley, Horace. 1853. "Modern Spiritualism." *Putnam's* (January):59–64.

Hopkins, Pauline. 1901. "Sojourner Truth." *Colored American Magazine* 1 (December):124–132.

"Indian Customs." 1850. *Cherokee Advocate* [Tahlequah, Oklahoma] (23 March):1.

"The Messiah and His Prophet." 1890. *New York Times* (30 November):9.

"The Millerites." 1844. *Cherokee Advocate* [Tahlequah, Oklahoma] (21 November):4.

"The Nat Turner Insurrection." 1859. *Anglo-African Magazine* (December):386–390.

"The New Indian Messiah." 1890. *New York Times* (16 November):11.

Osgood, Frances S. 1850. "The Spirit-Harp." *Southern Literary Messenger* (January):27.

"The Phantom World" [review]. 1850. *Harper's Monthly,* vol. 1:428. Editor's Table.

"Prospectus." 1851. *Copway's American Indian* [New York] (10 July):1.

Roosevelt, Theodore. 1892. "Indian Warfare on the Frontier." *Atlantic Monthly* 69 (February):270–275.

"Spiritual Manifestations." 1853. *Southern Literary Messenger* (July):385–395.

"Spiritualism" [review]. 1853. *Putnam's* (December):680–683. Editor's Table.

"Strange Religious Possession." 1849. *Cherokee Advocate* [Tahlequah, Oklahoma] (5 February):1.

"To the Rapping Spirits." 1851. *Knickerbocker* (April):311.

"The Tranced Child of Bangor." 1849. *Cherokee Advocate* [Tahlequah, Oklahoma] (17 December):3.

"A Visit to Mt. Vernon." 1850. *Cherokee Advocate* [Tahlequah, Oklahoma](6 January):1.

Waddell, F. L. 1851. "Legend of the Mongaup, Sullivan Co., N.Y." *Copway's American Indian* [New York] (10 July):3.

"Weird Things in Dreams." 1890. *New York Times* (November 29):8.

Wigwam, C. N. 1850. "Untitled." *Cherokee Advocate* [Tahlequah, Oklahoma] (25 February):1.

"Wonders of the Telegraph." 1850. *Cherokee Advocate* [Tahlequah, Oklahoma] (6 January):3.

Other Sources

Albanese, Catherine L. 1990. *Nature Religion in America: From the Algonkian Indians to the New Age.* Chicago: University of Chicago Press.

Ahlstrom, Sydney. 1972. *A Religious History of the American People.* New Haven, Conn.: Yale University Press.

Alexie, Sherman. 1994. "Distances." In *The Lone Ranger and Tonto Fistfight in Heaven.* New York: HarperCollins.

Allen, Paula Gunn. 1986. *The Sacred Hoop: Recovering the Feminine in American Indian Literature.* Boston: Beacon Press.

———. 1995. "'Border Studies': The Intersection of Gender and Color." In *The Ethnic Canon: Histories, Institutions and Interventions,* In ed. David Palumbo-Liu. Minneapolis: University of Minnesota Press.

Ammons, Elizabeth. 1983. "Going in Circles: The Female Geography of *The Country of the Pointed Firs." Studies in the Literary Imagination* 16 (Fall):83–92.

———. 1992. *Conflicting Stories: American Women Writers at the Turn into the Twentieth Century.* New York: Oxford University Press.

———. 1994. "Material Culture, Empire and Jewett's *Country of the Pointed Firs.*" In *New Essays on The Country of the Pointed Firs,* ed. June Howard. Cambridge: Cambridge University Press.

———. 1996. "Winona, Bakhtin and Hopkins in the Twenty-first Century." In *The Unruly Voice: Rediscovering Pauline Elizabeth Hopkins,* ed. John Cullen Gruesser. Urbana: University of Illinois Press.

Ammons, Elizabeth, and Annette White-Parks, eds. 1994. *Tricksterism in Turn-of-the-Century American Literature: A Multicultural Perspective.* Hanover, N.H.: University Press of New England.

Ammons, Elizabeth, and Valery Rohy, eds. 1998. *American Local Color Writing, 1880–1920.* New York: Penguin Books.

Anderson, Benedict. 1991. *Imagined Communities: Reflections on the Origins and Spread of Nationalism*. New York: Verso.

Andrews, William L. 1986. *To Tell a Free Story: The First Century of Afro-American Autobiography*. Urbana: University of Illinois Press.

Anzaldúa, Gloria. 1987. *Borderlands / La frontera: The New Mestiza*. San Francisco: Aunt Lute Book Company.

Baetzhold, Howard G., and Joseph B. McCullough. 1995. Introduction. In *The Bible According to Mark Twain*. Mark Twain. Athens: University of Georgia Press.

Baker, Houston. 1987. *Modernism and the Harlem Renaissance*. Chicago: Chicago University Press.

Bakhtin, Mikhail. 1984. *Rabelais and His World*. Trans. Helene Iswolsky. Bloomington: Indiana University Press.

Banta, Martha. 1972. *Henry James and the Occult: The Great Extension*. Bloomington: Indiana University Press.

Barney, Garold D. 1986. *Mormons, Indians and the Ghost Dance of 1890*. Lanham, Md.: University Press of America.

Barrow, Logie. 1986. *Independent Spirits: Spiritualism and English Plebians, 1850–1910*. New York: Routledge.

Baym, Nina. 1978. *Women's Fiction: A Guide to Novels by and about Women in America, 1820–1870*. Ithaca, N.Y.: Cornell University Press.

Beers, Henry. 1969. *Nathaniel Parker Willis*. New York, 1885. Reprint; New York: AMS Books.

Bell, Millicent. 1991. *Meaning in Henry James*. Cambridge: Harvard University Press.

Bellamy, Edward. 1887. *Looking Backward: 2000–1887*. Boston: Houghton Mifflin.

Bender, Thomas. 1986. "Wholes and Parts: The Need for Synthesis in American History." *Journal of American History* 73:120–136.

Bercovitch, Sacvan. 1993. *The Rites of Assent: Transformations in the Symbolic Construction of America*. New York: Routledge.

Bergland, Renée. 2000. *The National Uncanny: Indian Ghosts and American Subjects*. Hanover, N.H.: University of New England Press.

Bibb, Henry. 1969. *Narrative of the Life and Adventures of Henry Bibb, an American Slave*. New York: Lucius Matlock, 1849. Reprint; Miami, Fl.: Mnemosyne Publishing.

Blair, Sarah. 1996. *Henry James and the Writing of Race and Nation*. Cambridge: Cambridge University Press.

———. 1998. "Realism, Culture, and the Place of the Literary: Henry James and *The Bostonians*." In *The Cambridge Companion to Henry James*, ed. Jonathan Freedman. Cambridge: Cambridge University Press.

Blanchard, Paula. 1994. *Sarah Orne Jewett: Her World and Her Work*. Reading, Mass.: Addison-Wesley.

Blassingame, John. 1972. *The Slave Community: Plantation Life in Antebellum America*. New York: Oxford University Press.

Boyer, Paul, and Stephen Nissenbaum, eds. 1977. *Salem Witchcraft Papers: Verbatim Transcripts of the Legal Documents.* 3 vols. New York: DaCapo.

———, eds. 1993. *Salem-Village Witchcraft: A Documentary Record of Local Conflict in Colonial New England.* Boston: Northeastern University Press.

Braude, Anne. 1989. *Radical Spirits: Spiritualism and Women's Rights in Nineteenth-Century America.* Boston: Beacon Press.

Breen, T. H. 1984. "Creative Adaptations: Peoples and Cultures." In *Colonial British America: Essays in the History of the Early Modern Era,* ed. Jack P. Green and J. R. Pole. Baltimore: Johns Hopkins University Press.

Breslaw, Elaine G. 1996. *Tituba, Reluctant Witch of Salem: Devilish Indians and Puritan Fantasies.* New York: New York University Press.

Brodhead, Richard. 1993. *Cultures of Letters: Scenes of Reading and Writing in Nineteenth Century America.* Chicago: University of Chicago Press.

Brogan, Kathleen. 1998. *Cultural Haunting: Ghosts in Recent Ethnic American Literature.* Charlottesville, Va.: University of Virginia Press.

Brooke, John. 1994. *The Refiner's Fire: The Making of Mormon Cosmology, 1644–1844.* Cambridge: Cambridge University Press.

Brown, Diana DeG. 1986. *Umbanda: Religion and Politics in Urban Brazil.* Ann Arbor: University of Michigan Research Press.

Brown, Michael F. 1997. *The Channeling Zone: American Spirituality in an Anxious Age.* Cambridge: Harvard University Press.

Budd, Louis J. 1962. *Mark Twain, Social Philosopher.* Bloomington: University of Indiana Press.

Burnham, Michelle. 1993. "'Loopholes of Resistance': Harriet Jacobs's Slave Narrative and the Critique of Agency in Foucault." *Arizona Quarterly* 49:2 (Summer): 52–73.

Cabron, Eliab Wilkinson. 1855. *Modern Spiritualism, Its Facts and Fanatacisms.* Boston: Bela Marsh.

Calef, Richard. 1914. *More Wonders of the Invisible World.* London, 1700. Reprint; in *Narratives of the Witchcraft Cases, 1648–1706,* ed. George L. Burr. New York: Barnes and Noble.

Calhoun, Craig, ed. 1992. *Habermas and the Public Sphere.* Cambridge: MIT Press.

Capeci, Dominic, and Jack C. Knight. 1990. "Reactions to Colonization: North American Ghost Dance and East African Mahi-Mahi Rebellions." *The Historian* 52:2 (August).

Carby, Hazel. 1988. Introduction to *The Magazine Novels of Pauline Hopkins,* by Pauline Hopkins. New York: Oxford University Press.

Carroll, Bret E. 1997. *Spiritualism in Antebellum America.* Bloomington: University of Indiana Press.

Chesnutt, Charles W. 1969. *The Conjure Woman.* Boston: Houghton Mifflin, 1899. Reprint; Ann Arbor: University of Michigan Press.

———. 1973. "Superstitions and Folklore of the South." *Modern Culture* 13 (1901):

231–35. Reprint; in *Mother Wit from the Laughing Barrel: Readings in Afro-American Folklore,* ed. Alan Dundes. Englewood Cliffs, N.J.: Prentice Hall.

———. 1993. *The Journals of Charles W. Chesnutt.* Ed. Richard Brodhead. Durham: Duke University Press.

Creel, Margaret Washington. 1990. "Gullah Attitudes Toward Life and Death." In *Africanisms in American Culture,* ed. Joseph Holloway. Bloomington: Indiana University Press.

Cross, Whitney. 1950. *The Burned Over District: The Social and Intellectual History of Enthusiastic Religion in Western New York, 1800–1850.*

Crowley, Daniel. 1977. *African Folklore in the New World.* Austin: University of Texas Press.

Davis, Andrew Jackson. 1852. *The Great Harmonia.* Boston: B. Marsh.

Dimmock, Wai Chee. 1997. "A Theory of Resonance." *PMLA* 112:5 (October): 1060–1071.

Dogma. 1999. Culver City, Calif.: Columbia Tristar. Motion picture.

Doherty, Amy. 1997. Introduction to *The Collected Stories of María Cristina Mena.* Houston: Arte Publico Press.

Donovan, Josephine. 1983. *New England Local Color Literature: A Women's Tradition.* New York: Frederick Ungar Publishing.

———. 1993. "Breaking the Sentence: Local-Color Literature and Subjugated Knowledges." In *The (Other) American Traditions,* ed. Joyce Warren. New Brunswick, N.J.: Rutgers University Press.

———. 1993. "Jewett and Swedenborg." *American Literature* 65:4 (December): 731–750.

Douglass, Ann. 1975. "Heaven Our Home." In *Death in America,* ed. David Stannard. Philadelphia: University of Pennsylvania Press.

Douglass, Frederick. 1855. *My Bondage and My Freedom.* New York: Miller, Orton and Mulligan.

Doyle, Sir Arthur Conan. 1926. *The History of Spiritualism.* London: Cassel.

Du Bois, W. E. B. 1965. *The Souls of Black Folks.* 1903. Chicago: McClurg and Co., Reprint; in *Three Negro Classics,* ed. John Hope Franklin. New York: Avon.

Dundes, Alan. 1973. *Mother Wit from the Laughing Barrel: Readings in the Interpretation of Afro-American Folklore.* Englewood Cliffs, N.J.: Prentice Hall.

Eagleton, Terry. 1991. *Ideology: An Introduction.* London: Verso.

———. 1994. *Ideology.* London: Longman.

Eastman, Charles. 1916. *From the Deep Woods to Civilization.* Boston: Little, Brown and Co.

Edel, Leon. 1984. *Henry James: A Life.* New York: Harper and Row.

Edmonds, John W., and George T. Dexter. 1853–1855. *Spiritualism.* 2 vols. New York: Partridge and Brittan.

Edmundson, Mark. 1998. *Nightmare on Main Street.* Cambridge: Harvard University Press.

Eliot, George. 1963. *Essays of George Eliot.* Ed. Thomas Pinney. London: Routledge.

Elliot, Michael. 1998. "Ethnography, Reform and the Problem of the Real: James Mooney's *Ghost-Dance Religion.*" *American Quarterly* 50:2 (June):201–33.

Emerson, Everett. 1984. *The Authentic Mark Twain: A Literary Biography of Samuel L. Clemens.* Philadelphia: University of Pennsylvania Press.

Equiano, Olaudah. 1995. *The Interesting Narrative of the Life of Olaudah Equiano, or Gustavus Vassa, the African.* New York: W. Durell, 1791. Reprint; ed. Robert J. Allison. Boston: Bedford St. Martin.

Erdrich, Louise. 1989. *Tracks.* New York: Harper and Row.

Faivre, Antoine. 2000. *Theosophy, Imagination, Tradition: Studies in Western Esotericism.* Trans. Christine Rhone. Albany: SUNY Press.

Farwell, Julie. 1994. "Goophering Around: Authority and the Trick of Storytelling in *The Conjure Woman.*" In *Tricksterism in Turn-of-the-Century American Literature,* ed. Elizabeth Ammons and Annette White-Parks.

Ferguson, J. B. 1854. *Spirit Communion: A Record of Communications from the Spirit-Spheres.* Nashville: Union and American Steam Press.

Fetterley, Judith, and Marjorie Pryse. 1992. *American Women Regionalists, 1850–1910.* New York: Norton.

Foreman, Gabrielle. 1996. "Manifest in Signs: The Politics of Sex and Representation in *Incidents.*" In *Harriet Jacobs and Incidents in the Life of a Slave Girl: New Essays,* ed. Deborah Garfield and Rafia Zafar. Cambridge: Cambridge University Press.

Foucault, Michel. 1977. *Discipline and Punish: The Birth of the Prison.* New York: Random House.

Fraser, Nancy. 1992. "Rethinking the Public Sphere: A Contribution to the Critique of Actually Existing Democracy." In *Habermas and the Public Sphere,* ed. Craig Calhoun. Cambridge: MIT University Press.

French, Stanley. 1975. "The Cemetery as Cultural Institution." In *Death in America,* ed. David Stannard. Philadelphia: University of Pennsylvania Press.

Freud, Sigmund. 1955. "The 'Uncanny.'" 1919. Reprint; in *The Standard Edition of the Complete Psychological Works of Sigmund Freud.* Vol. 17. London: The Hogarth Press.

Furtwangler, Albert. 1997. *Answering Chief Seattle.* Seattle: University of Washington Press.

Gates, Henry Louis Jr. 1988. *The Signifying Monkey: A Theory of African American Literary Criticism.* Cambridge: Harvard University Press.

———, ed. 1986. *"Race," Writing and Difference.* Chicago: University of Chicago Press.

Gillman, Susan. 1995. "Mark Twain's Travels in the Racial Occult: Following the Equator and the Dream Tales." In *The Cambridge Companion to Mark Twain,* ed. Forrest Robinson. Cambridge: Cambridge University Press.

———. 1996. "Pauline Hopkins and the Occult: African American Revisions of Nineteenth-Century Science." *American Literary History* 8:1 (Winter):57–82.

Godbeer, Richard. 1992. *The Devil's Dominion: Magic, Religion and Witchcraft in Early New England.* Cambridge: Cambridge University Press.

Goldsmith, Barbara. 1998. *Other Powers: The Age of Suffrage, Spiritualism and the Scandalous Victoria Woodhull.* New York: Knopf.

Gooder, R. D. 1984. Introduction to *The Bostonians,* by Henry James. New York: Oxford University Press.

Greene, Sandra E. 1999. "Cultural Zones in the Era of the Slave Trade: Exploring the Yoruba Connection with the Anlo-Ewe." In *The African Diaspora: African Origins in New World Identities,* ed. Isidore Okpewho. Bloomington: Indiana University Press.

Greeson, Jennifer Rae. 2001. "The Mysteries and Miseries of North Carolina: New York City, Urban Gothic Fiction and *Incidents in the Life of a Slave Girl.*" *American Literature* 73:2 (June):277–309.

Guthrie, John J., Jr., Charles Lucas, and Gary Monroe, eds. 2000. *Cassadaga: The South's Oldest Spiritualist Community.* Gainesville: University of Florida Press.

Habermas, Jürgen. 1989. *The Structural Transformation of the Public Sphere.* Cambridge: MIT Press.

Hackett, Charles, ed. 1970. *Revolt of the Pueblo Indians of New Mexico and Otermin's Attempted Reconquest, 1680–1682.* 2 vols. Trans. Charmion Shelby. Albuquerque: University of New Mexico Press.

Hall, David. 1989. *Worlds of Wonder, Days of Judgement: Popular Religious Belief in Early New England.* New York: Alfred A. Knopf.

Hansen, Chadwick. 1969. *Witchcraft at Salem.* New York: George Braziller.

Hatch, Benjamin. 1859. *Spiritualist Iniquities Unmasked.* New York: B. F. Hatch.

Hawkes, David. 1996. *Ideology.* London: Routledge.

Hemenway, Robert. 1973. "The Functions of Folklore in Charles Chesnutt's *The Conjure Woman.*" *Journal of American Folklore* 13.

Hewitt, Nancy A. 1984. "Amy Kirby Post." *University of Rochester Library Bulletin* 37 (1984):5–21.

Hittman, Michael. 1997. *Wovoka and the Ghost Dance.* Lincoln: University of Nebraska Press.

Hoffer, Peter Charles. 1996. *The Devil's Disciples: Makers of the Salem Witchcraft Trials.* Baltimore: Johns Hopkins University Press.

Homans, Margaret. 1986. *Bearing the Word: Language and Female Experience in Nineteenth Century Women's Writing.* Chicago: University of Chicago Press.

Hopkins, Pauline. 1988. *Of One Blood. Or, The Hidden Self. Colored American Magazine* 6:1–11 (November 1902–November 1903). Reprint; in *The Magazine Novels of Pauline Hopkins,* ed. Hazel Carby. New York: Oxford University Press.

Hyatt, Harry Middleton. 1970. *Hoodoo-Conjuration-Witchcraft-Rootwork.* Washington, D.C.: American University Bookstore.

Irwin, Lee. 1994. *The Dream Seekers: Native American Visionary Traditions of the Great Plains.* Norman: University of Oklahoma Press.

Jacobs, Harriet. 1987. *Incidents in the Life of a Slave Girl, Written by Herself,* intro. by Jean Fagan Yellin. Cambridge: Harvard University Press.

James, Henry. 1974. *Letters.* Ed. Leon Edel. Vol. 1. Cambridge, Mass.: Belknap Press.

———. 1984a. "The Art of Fiction." 1884. *Literary Criticism: Essays on Literature: American Writers: English Writers.* New York: Library of America.

———. *The Bostonians.* 1984b. London: Macmillan, 1886. Reprint; New York: Oxford University Press.

———. 1987. *The Complete Notebooks of Henry James.* Ed. Leon Edel and Lyall H. Powers. New York: Oxford University Press.

James, Henry Sr. 1852. "Spiritual Rappings." In *Lectures and Miscellanies.* New York: Redfield. Facsimile reprint; New York: AMS, 1983.

James, William. 1960. *William James on Psychical Research.* Ed. Gardner Murphy and Robert O. Ballou. New York: Viking.

Jameson, Frederick. 1994. *The Seeds of Time.* New York: Columbia University Press.

Jewett, Sarah Orne. 1896. *The Country of Pointed Firs and Other Stories.* Boston: Houghton Mifflin. Reprint; ed. Mary Ellen Chase. New York: W. W. Norton and Co., 1981.

Jones, Alice Eley. 1998. "Sacred Places and Holy Ground: West African Spiritualism at Stagville Plantation." In *"Keep Your Head in the Sky:" Interpreting African American Home Ground,* ed. Grey Gundaker. Charlottesville: University Press of Virginia.

Kaplan, Amy. 1991. "Race, Region and Empire." In *Columbia History of the American Novel,* ed. Emory Elliott. New York: Columbia University Press.

Karcher, Carolyn. 1994. *First Woman of the Republic: A Cultural Biography of Lydia Maria Child.* Durham: University of North Carolina Press.

Karlsen, Carol. 1987. *The Devil in the Shape of a Woman: Witchcraft in Colonial New England.* Cambridge: Cambridge University Press.

Kassanoff, Jennie. 1996. "'Fate Has Linked Us Together': Bood, Gender and the Politics of Representation in Pauline Hopkins's *Of One Blood.*" In *The Unruly Voice: Rediscovering Pauline Elizabeth Hopkins,* ed. John Cullen Gruesser. Urbana: University of Illinois Press.

Keating, Ana Louse. 1996. *Women Reading Women Writing: Self-Invention in Paula Gunn Allen, Gloria Anzaldúa and Audre Lorde.* Philadelphia: Temple University Press.

Kehoe, Alice Beck. *1989. The Ghost Dance: Ethnohistory and Revitalization.* Fort Worth, Tex.: Holt, Rhinehart and Winston.

Keller, Frances. 1978. *An American Crusade: The Life of Charles Waddell Chesnutt.* Provo: University of Utah Press.

Kenny, Michael G. 1986. *The Passion of Ansel Bourne: Multiple Personality in American Culture.* Washington, D.C.: Smithsonian Institution Press.

Kerr, Howard. 1972. *Mediums, and Spirit Rappers, and Roaring Radicals: Spiritualism in American Literature, 1850–1900.* Urbana: Illinois University Press.

Kerr, Howard, John W. Crowley, and Charles Crow, eds. 1983. *The Haunted Dusk: American Supernatural Fiction, 1820–1920*. Athens: University of Georgia Press.

Kerr, Howard, and Charles Crow, eds. 1983. *The Occult in America: New Historical Perspectives*. Urbana: University of Illinois Press.

Kessler, Carol Farley. 1983. "The Heavenly Utopia of Elizabeth Stuart Phelps." In *Women and Utopia: Critical Interpretations*, ed. Marleen Barr and Nicholas D. Smith. Latham, Md.: University Press of America.

Knaut, Andrew. *1995. The Pueblo Revolt of 1680: Conquest and Resistance in Seventeenth-Century New Mexico*. Norman: University of Oklahoma Press.

Kroeber, Karl. 1983. "The Wolf Comes: Indian Poetry and Linguistic Criticism." In *Smoothing the Ground: Essays on Native American Oral Literature*, ed. Brian Swann. Berkeley: University of California Press.

Lan, David. 1985. *Guns and Rain: Guerillas and Spirit Mediums in Zimbabwe*. London: James Curry Ltd.

Leventhal, Herbert. 1976. *In the Shadow of the Enlightenment: Occultism and Renaissance Science in Eighteenth-Century America*. New York: New York University Press.

Levine, Lawrence. 1977. *Black Culture and Black Consciousness*. New York: Oxford University Press.

Lewis, I. M. 1989. *Ecstatic Religion: A Study of Shamanism and Spirit Possession*. 2nd edition. New York: Routledge.

Long, Lisa. 1997. "'The Corporeity of Heaven': Rehabilitating the Civil War Body in *The Gates Ajar*." *American Literature* 69:4 (December):781–811.

Longfellow, Henry Wadsworth. 1858. *The Song of Hiawatha*.

Lopez, Tiffany Ann. 1994. "María Cristina Mena: Turn-of-the-Century La Malinche, and Other Tales of Cultural (Re)Construction." In *Tricksterism in Turn-of-the-Century American Literature: A Multicultural Perspective*, ed. Elizabeth Ammons and Annette White-Parks. Hanover, N.H.: University Press of New England.

Lubiano, Wahmeena. 1996. "Like Being Mugged by a Metaphor: Multiculturalism and State Narratives." In *Mapping Multiculturalism*, eds. Avery F. Gordon and Christopher Newfield. Minneapolis: University of Minnesota Press.

Luciano, Dana. 2003. "Passing Shadows: Melancholic Nationality and Black Critical Publicity in Pauline E. Hopkins's *Of One Blood*." In *Loss: The Politics of Mourning*, ed. David L. Eng and David Kazanjian. Berkeley and Los Angeles: University of California Press.

Mannheim, Karl. 1936. *Ideology and Utopia*. London: Routledge and Kegan Paul.

Marx, Karl. 1972. *Capital*. Vol. 1. London, 1867. Reprint; in *The Marx Engels Reader*, ed. Robert C. Tucker. New York: Norton.

———. 1972. *The German Ideology*. Moscow: Marx and Engels Institute, 1932. Reprint; in *The Marx Engels Reader*, ed. Robert C. Tucker. New York: Norton.

Mather, Cotton. 1862. *Wonders of the Invisible World*. Boston: Benjamin Harris, 1692. Reprint; Amherst, Wisc.: Amherst Press.

Maybee, Carleton. 1993. *Sojourner Truth: Slave, Prophet, Legend.* New York: New York University Press.

McFeely, William S. 1991. *Frederick Douglass.* New York: Norton.

McKay, Nellie. 1996. Introduction to *The Unruly Voice: Rediscovering Pauline Elizabeth Hopkins,* ed. John Cullen Gruesser. Urbana: University of Illinois Press.

McLoughlin, William G. 1984. *The Cherokee Ghost Dance.* Mercer University Press.

———. 1993. *After the Trail of Tears.* Chapel Hill: University of North Carolina Press.

Mena, María Cristina. 1997. *The Collected Stories of María Cristina Mena.* Ed. Amy Doherty. Houston: Arte Publico Press.

Michelson, Bruce. 1995. *Mark Twain on the Loose: A Comic Writer and the American Self.* Amherst: University of Massachusetts Press.

Mills, Bruce. 1994. *Cultural Reformations: Lydia Maria Child and the Literature of Reform.* Athens: University of Georgia Press.

Mohrbacher, B. C. 1997. "The Whole World is Coming: The 1890 Ghost Dance as Utopia." *Utopian Studies* 7 (winter):75.

Mooney, James. 1973. *The Ghost Dance Religion and Wounded Knee.* Washington, D.C.: Government Printing Office, 1896. Reprint; Mineola, N.Y.: Dover Publications.

Morris, Rosilind C. 2000. *In the Place of Origins: Modernity and Its Mediums in Northern Thailand.* Durham, N.C.: Duke University Press.

Moses, L. G. 1984. *The Indian Man: A Biography of James Mooney.* Urbana: University of Illinois Press.

Mott, Frank Luther. 1938. *History of American Magazines.* Cambridge: Harvard University Press.

———. 1938. *A History of American Magazines,* Vol. 2: 1850–1865. Cambridge: Harvard University Press.

Newquist, David L. 1994. "Mark Twain Among the Indians." *Midamerica* 21:59–72.

Niehardt, John G. 1961. *Black Elk Speaks: Being the Life Story of a Holy Man of the Oglala Sioux.* New York: William Morrow and Co., 1932. Reprint; Lincoln: University of Nebraska Press.

Nowatzki, Robert. 1995. "Passing in a White Genre: Charles Chesnutt's Negotiation of the Plantation Tradition." *American Literary Realism.* (Winter).

Ohman, Richard. 1996. *Selling Culture: Magazines, Markets and Class at the Turn of the Century.* New York: Verso.

Oppenheim, Janet. 1985. *The Other World: Spiritualism and Psychical Research in England, 1850–1914.* Cambridge: Cambridge University Press.

Owen, Alex. 1990. *The Darkened Room: Women, Power and Spiritualism in Late Victorian England.* Philadelphia: University of Pennsylvania Press.

Owen, Robert. 1860. *Footfalls on the Boundary of Another World.* Philadelphia: J. B. Lippencott and Co.

Palumbo-Liu, David. 1995. Introduction to *The Ethnic Canon: Histories, Institutions and Interventions,* ed. David Palumbo-Liu. Minneapolis: University of Minnesota Press.

Paredes, Raymond. 1982. "Evolution of Chicano Literature." In *Three American Literatures: Essays in Chicano, Native American and Asian American Literature*, ed. Houston Baker. New York: MLA.

Parsons, Elsie Clews. 1996. *Pueblo Indian Religion*. Vol. 1. Chicago: University of Chicago Press, 1939. Reprint; Lincoln: University of Nebraska Press.

Phelps, Elizabeth Stuart. 1885. *Beyond the Gates*. Boston: Houghton Mifflin.

———. 1887. *The Gates Between*. Boston: Houghton Mifflin.

———. 1896. *Chapters from a Life*. Boston.

———. 1964. *The Gates Ajar*. Boston: Fields, Osgood, 1868. Reprint; Cambridge: The Belknap Press.

Podmore, Frank. 1902. *Modern Spiritualism: A History and Criticism*. New York: Charles Scribner's Sons.

Porter, Dorthy B. 1982. "Pauline Hopkins." In *Dictionary of American Negro Biography*, ed. Rayford W. Logan and Micheal R. Winston. New York: Norton.

Posnock, Ross. 1998. "Affirming the Alien: The Pragmatist Pluralism of *The American Scene*." In *The Cambridge Companion to Henry James*, ed. Jonathan Freedman. Cambridge: Cambridge University Press.

Post, Isaac. 1852. *Voices from the Spirit World*. Rochester, N.Y.: C. H. McDonnell.

Post-Lauria, Sheila. 1995. "Magazine Practice and Melville's Israel Potter." In *Periodical Literature in Nineteenth-Century America*, ed. Kenneth Price and Susan Belasco Smith. Charlottesville: University of Virginia Press.

Pratt, Mary Louise. 1992. *Imperial Eyes: Travel Writing and Transculturation*. New York: Routledge.

Price, Kenneth, and Susan Belasco Smith, eds. 1995. *Periodical Literature in Nineteenth-Century America*. Charlottesville: University of Virginia Press.

Pryse, Marjorie. 1984. "Women at Sea: Feminist Realism in Sarah Orne Jewett's 'The Foreigner.'" *Critical Essays on Sarah Orne Jewett*, ed. Gwen Nagel. Boston: G. K. Hall.

———. 1993. "Sex, Class and Category Crisis: Reading Jewett's *Country of the Pointed Firs*." *American Literature* 70:3 (September):517–49.

Raboteau, Albert. 1978. *Slave Religion: The "Invisible Institution" in the Antebellum South*. New York: Oxford University Press.

Rees, Robert A. 1970. "*Captain Stormfield's Visit to Heaven* and *The Gates Ajar*." *English Language Notes* 7 (7 March):197–202.

Reynolds, David S. 1981. *Faith in Fiction: The Emergence of Religious Literature in America*. Cambridge: Harvard University Press.

Rice, Julian. 1991. *Black Elk's Story: Distinguishing Its Lakota Purpose*. Albuquerque: University of New Mexico Press.

Ripley, Peter, ed. 1985. *The Black Abolitionist Papers*. Vol. 3. Chapel Hill: University of North Carolina Press.

Root, Deborah. 1996. *Cannibal Culture: Art Appropriation and the Commodification of Difference*. Boulder, Colo.: Westview.

Rose, Wendy. 1992. "The Great Pretenders: Further Reflections on White Shamanism." In *The State of Native America: Genocide, Colonization and Resistance,* ed. M. Annette Jaimes, 403–21. Boston: South End Press.

Rosenthal, Bernard. 1993. *Salem Story: Reading the Witch Trials of 1692.* New York: Cambridge University Press.

Ryan, Mary. 1992. "Gender and Public Access: Women's Politics in Nineteenth Century America." In *Habermas and the Public Sphere,* ed. Craig Calhoun. Cambridge: MIT University Press.

Sawaya, Francesca. 1997. "Emplotting National History: Regionalism and Pauline Hopkins's *Contending Forces.*" In *Breaking Boundaries: New Perspectives in Women's Regional Writing,* ed. Sherrie A. Inness and Diana Royer. Iowa City: Iowa University Press.

Schrag, Mitzi. 1999. "Whiteness as Loss in 'The Foreigner.'" In *Jewett and Her Contemporaries: Reshaping the Canon,* ed. Karen Kilcup and Thomas S. Edwards. Gainesville: University of Florida Press.

Schrager, Cynthia. 1996. "Pauline Hopkins and William James: The New Psychology and the Politics of Race." In *The Unruly Voice: Rediscovering Pauline Elizabeth Hopkins,* ed. John Cullen Gruesser. Urbana: University of Illinois Press.

———. 1996. "Both Sides of the Veil: Race, Science and Mysticism in W. E. B. Du Bois," *American Quarterly* 48:4 (December 1996):551–86.

Segal, Ronald. 1995. *The Black Diaspora.* New York: Farrar, Strauss and Giroux.

Sherman, Sarah. 1989. *Sarah Orne Jewett: An American Persephone.* Hanover, N.H.: University Press of New England.

Slosson, Annie T. 1892. *The Heresy of Mehetabel Clark.* New York: Harper and Brothers.

Smith, Helen Hootin. 1964. Introduction to *The Gates Ajar,* by Elizabeth Stuart Phelps. Cambridge: The Belknap Press.

Smith, Sidonie. 1992. "Resisting the Gaze of Embodiment: Women's Autobiography in the Nineteenth Century." In *American Women's Autobiography: Fea(s)ts of Memory,* ed. Margo Culley. Madison: University of Wisconsin Press.

Smith-Rosenberg, Caroll. 1992. "Dis-Covering the Subject of the 'Great Constitutional Discussion.'" *The Journal of American History* (December):841–73.

Song, Min. 1998. "The Height of Presumption: Henry James and Sui Sin Far in the Age of Nation-Building." Ph.D. diss., Tufts University, Medford, Mass.

Sorioso, Caroline. 1996. "'There Is Might in Each': Agency in *Incidents.*" In *Harriet Jacobs and Incidents in the Life of a Slave Girl: New Essays,* ed. Deborah Garfield and Rafia Zafar. Cambridge: Cambridge University Press.

St. Armand Levi, Bertrand. 1984. *Emily Dickinson in Her Culture.* New York: Cambridge University Press.

Stanton, Elizabeth Cady, and Susan B. Anthony. 1981. *Elizabeth Cady Stanton, Susan B. Anthony: Correspondence, Writings, Speeches,* ed. Ellen Carol DuBois. New York: Schocken Books.

Stowe, Harriet Beecher. 1856. *Dred: A Tale of the Great Dismal Swamp.* Boston: Phillips, Samson.

————. 1994. *Uncle Tom's Cabin.* Boston: John P. Jewett, 1852. Reprint; ed. Elizabeth Ammons. New York: Norton.

Sundquist, Eric. 1993. *To Wake the Nations: Race in the Making of American Literature.* Cambridge: Harvard University Press.

Swatos, William Jr., and Loftur Reimar Gissurarson. 1997. *Modernity and Mediumship in Icelandic Spiritualism.* New Brunswick, N.J.: Transaction Publishers.

Sword, Helen. 2002. *Ghostwriting Modernism.* Ithaca, N.Y.: Cornell University Press.

Tatum, Charles. 1982. *Chicano Literature.* Boston: Twayne Publishers.

Thornton, Russell. 1986. *We Shall Live Again: The 1870 and 1890 Ghost Dance Movements as Ethnographic Revitalization.* New York: Cambridge University Press.

Turner, Victor. 1968. "Myth and Symbol." *International Encyclopedia of Social Sciences.* New York: Macmillan.

Twain, Mark. 1922. *Mark Twain in Eruption,* ed. Bernard DeVoto. New York: Harper and Brother.

————. 1985. *Roughing It.* New York: Penguin Books.

————. 1995. *Captain Stormfield's Visit to Heaven.* New York: Harper and Brothers, 1909. Reprint; in *The Bible According to Mark Twain.* Ed. Howard G. Baetzhold and Joseph B. McCullough. Athens: University of Georgia Press.

Tylor, Edward. 1889. *Primitive Culture.* London: J. Murray, 1871. Reprint; New York: Henry Holt.

Wald, Priscilla. 1995. *Constituting Americans: Cultural Anxiety and Narrative Form.* Durham: University of North Carolina Press.

Walker, James R. 1991. *Lakota Belief and Ritual.* Ed. Raymond J. Demaille and Elaine A. Jahner. Lincoln: University of Nebraska Press.

Wallace, A. F. C. 1956. "Revitalization Movements: Some Theoretical Considerations for Their Comparative Study." *American Anthropologist* 58:264–81.

Warner, Anne B. 1996. "Carnival Laughter: Resistance in *Incidents.*" In *Harriet Jacobs and Incidents in the Life of a Slave Girl: New Essays,* ed. Deborah Garfield and Rafia Zafar. Cambridge: Cambridge University Press.

Warner, Michael. 1990. *Letters of the Republic: Publication and the Public Sphere in Eighteenth-Century America.* Cambridge: Harvard University Press.

Warren, Joyce, ed. 1993. *The (Other) American Traditions.* New Brunswick, N.J.: Rutgers University Press.

Warren, Kenneth W. 1993. *Black and White Strangers: Race and American Literary Realism.* Chicago: University of Chicago Press.

Washington, Peter. 1995. *Madame Blavatsky's Baboon: A History of the Mystics, Mediums and Misfits Who Brought Spiritualism to America.* New York: Shocken Books.

White, Richard. 1991. *The Middle Ground: Indians, Empires and Republics in the Great Lakes Region, 1650–1815.* New York: Cambridge University Press.

Wigglesworth, Michael. 1666. *The Day of Doom: Or a Poetical Description of the Great and Last Judgement.* Cambridge: Michael Green. Microform.

Willis, N. P. 1850. *Poems.* New York: Charles Scribner.

————. 1855. *The Rag-Bag: A Collection of Ephemera.* New York: Charles Scribner.

———. 1859. *The Convalescent.* New York: Charles Scribner.

Yellin, Jean Fagan. 1987. Introduction. *Incidents in the Life of a Slave Girl, Written by Herself.* Harriet Jacobs. Cambridge: Harvard University Press.

Zagarell, Sandra. 1994. "*Country's* Portrayal of Community and the Exclusion of Difference." In *New Essays on The Country of the Pointed Firs,* ed. June Howard. New York: Cambridge University Press.

Zboray, Ronald. 1993. *A Fictive People: Antebellum Economic Development and the American Reading Public.* New York: Oxford University Press.

Zimmerman, David. 2003. "Frank Norris, Market Panic, and the Mesmeric Sublime." *American Literature* 75:1 (March):61–90.

Zizek, Savoj. 1989. *The Sublime Object of Ideology.* London: Verso.

———, ed. 1994. *Mapping Ideology.* London: Verso.

Zolar. 1987. *Zolar's Book of the Spirits.* New York: Prentice Hall.

Index

Kaplan, Amy, 97
Kerr, Howard, 43, 157n, 158n, 161n
King, Katie, 91, 123–124
Knickerbocker, 40, 43–44, 45

Lacan, Jacques, 28, 75–76, 110–111
Lee, Ann, 3
Levine, Lawrence, 29, 167n
Lewis, E. M., 157n
Local color writing, 91, 93, 116–117, 167–168n.
  See also Regionalism
Long, Lisa, 73–74
Lowell, James, 43, 50
Lubiano, Wahneema, xxvii
Luciano, Dana, 141, 146

Mannheim, Karl, 127–128
Marx, Karl, 168n
Marxism, xxviii–xxix, 127–128
Mather, Cotton, xxiv, 159n
Mena, María Cristina, 94–95, 109–117, 152,
  168n; "The Birth of the God of War,"
  111–112; "The Gold Vanity Set," 110–111;
  "The Sorcerer and General Bisco," 95,
  113–116
Mesmerism, 2, 169n
Mexican spirituality, 110, 111–112, 114–115,
  168n; Coatlicue, 115; The Virgin of
  Guadelupe, xv, 111–112, 114–115
Middle ground, xxii
Mooney, James, 61, 64, 65–66, 67, 164n
Morgan, Lewis Henry, 63
Mott, Lucretia, 7, 9
Mount Auburn Cemetery, 70
Multiculturalism, xxvi–xxvii

Naranjo, Pedro, xvi–xvii, 151
National literary magazines, 92–94, 151
Native American spirituality, 49–50, 67–68;
  and spiritualism, 163n; visionary episteme,
  68; wakan, 68
New Age Movement, 170n; and Native Ameri-
  can culture, 170n; and Rochester Rappings,
  149–150
New Negro, 138–139, 142
New Psychology, 92, 119, 130, 139, 141–142; and
  ideology, 130; and spiritualism, 166n
New Woman, 110, 115

Norris, Frank, 140
North American Review, 40, 45
North Star, The, 41, 47–48

Ohmann, Richard, 94
Oral literature, 79
Osborne, Sarah, xix, xx
Osgood, Frances, 54–55
Otermín, Antonio, xv

Palumbo-Liu, David, xxvii–xxviii
Phelps, Rev. Eliakim, 71
Phelps, Elizabeth, 71, 76
Phelps, Elizabeth Stuart, 60, 70–82, 95,
  96, 99, 100, 151–152, 165n; *Beyond the
  Gates*, 72, 75, 77; *Chapters in a Life*, 71;
  and feminism, 73–74; *The Gates Ajar*,
  71–72, 75, 76, 80; *The Gates Between*,
  72–73, 74, 75, 77; and liberal Christianity,
  71; and spiritualism, 71
Podmore, Frank, 157n, 158n, 159n, 166n
Poe, Edgar Allan, 154
Popé, xvi–xvii
Post, Amy, 1, 3, 4, 6–7; and Frederick
  Douglass, 16
Post, Isaac, 4, 9–10, 17
Post-colonial criticism, 80–81
Pratt, Mary Louise, xvii, xxviii, 93
Pryse, Marjorie, 95
Public sphere, 38–39, 163n
Pueblo Revolt, xii–xviii, 150–151
Putnam's Monthly, 40, 44–47

Quakers, 6–7

Realism, 127
Regionalism, 93, 165–166n, 169n. *See also*
  Local color writing
Revitalization movements, 65, 76–77
Rochester Rappings, xi, xii, 3–5, 92
Roosevelt, Theodore, 64
Ryan, Mary, 39

Salem Witchcraft Trials, xviii–xxiv, 92, 151
Santería, xii, 29
Schrager, Cynthia, 135, 138, 142
Séance, 26–27
Seneca Falls Convention, 7, 9